POLE to POLE

POLE to POLE

with *Michael Palin*

PHOTOGRAPHS BY BASIL PAO

BBC BOOKS

Maps and endpapers by David Atkinson

Transport illustrations by David Brown

All photographs taken by Basil Pao,
except pages 13 Fraser Barber, 18, 29 and 319 Nigel Meakin,
19 and 21 Patti Musicaro.

Thanks is due to A. P. Watt Ltd for their permission
on behalf of Paul O'Prey to reproduce the extract
from his Introduction to *Heart of Darkness*
by Joseph Conrad (1983 edition) on page 227,
and on behalf of Roland Huntford to reproduce
the extract taken from his book *The Last Place on Earth*
on page 312.

Published by BBC Books
a division of BBC Enterprises Ltd
Woodlands, 80 Wood Lane, London W12 0TT

First published 1992

© Michael Palin 1992

The moral right of the author has been asserted

Reprinted 1992

ISBN 0563 36283 9

Typeset in 11½ on 13 pt Garamond
by Ace Filmsetting Ltd, Frome
Printed and bound in Great Britain by
Richard Clay Ltd, St Ives plc
Colour separations by Technik Ltd, Berkhamsted
Jacket printed by Belmont Press Ltd,
Northampton

CONTENTS

INTRODUCTION

For almost a year after my return from travelling around the world in 80 days, well-intentioned ideas for sequels were generously offered. I had only to show up with a suitcase for the 10.15 to Bristol for someone to ask, 'Off round the world again, Michael?'. A chance sighting of me far from home would prompt a cry of recognition: 'What's this, Michael . . . Round Penrith in 80 Days?'. Taxi drivers would hold me personally responsible for new traffic schemes: 'You should try going round *this* lot in 80 days!'. A moment's hesitation at a road junction would not go unnoticed: 'You can get round the world in 80 days but you can't find your way across Oxford Street!'.

It was beginning to drive me up the pole and Clem Vallance, ever the opportunist, suggested that if I was going up one pole I might as well do the other. His idea was simplicity itself – on an atlas, anyway. A journey from North to South Poles along the 30 degree East line of longitude, chosen because it crossed the greatest amount of land.

I wanted to call it *Pole to Pole by Public Transport,* but owing to the absence of a bus route through the African bush or an Awayday across Antarctica, this had to be dismissed as wishful thinking. In the event, though we relied on aircraft to get us to the Poles themselves, we completed the rest of the journey overland, on a mixture of ships, trains, trucks, rafts, Ski-Doos, buses, barges, bicycles, balloons, 4-litre Landcruisers and horse-drawn carts.

The bulk of the journey was made between July and Christmas 1991. With one ten-day break at Aswan we travelled and filmed for 5 months, passing through 17 countries and making over 70 overnight stops.

We were unable to film at the North Pole in July as no plane would take the risk of landing on the summer ice, so the section from the North Pole to Tromsø in Norway was filmed, separately, in May.

1991 was an exceptional year. A quarter of the countries we visited had undergone, or were undergoing, momentous changes. Communism disappeared in the USSR and apartheid in South Africa. We arrived in Ethiopia 4 months after the conclusion of a civil war that had occupied parts of the country for 30 years and in Zambia on the day Kenneth Kaunda's 28-year reign ended.

Pole to Pole is, like *Around the World in 80 Days*, based upon diaries and tape recordings kept at the time. They describe the pain and the pleasure of the journey as it happened. I have deliberately not used the benefit of hindsight to change any of those entries. What you get is what we saw and experienced in those extraordinary months between the Poles – warts, bed-bugs and all.

Michael Palin. London 1992.

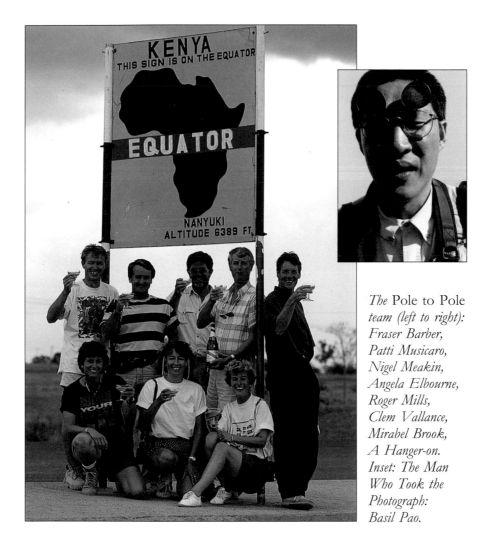

The Pole to Pole
team (left to right):
Fraser Barber,
Patti Musicaro,
Nigel Meakin,
Angela Elbourne,
Roger Mills,
Clem Vallance,
Mirabel Brook,
A Hanger-on.
Inset: The Man
Who Took the
Photograph:
Basil Pao.

ACKNOWLEDGEMENTS

Pole to Pole was in every sense, a team effort. First and foremost on the team was Clem Vallance who I must thank for the original idea, the meticulous preparation to bring it to fruition and his guidance and good company on the road.

Nigel Meakin, Patti Musicaro, Fraser Barber and Basil Pao travelled with me almost everywhere and I owe them enormous and almost inexpressible thanks for not only being the best technicians in the business but for being the very best travelling companions. Mirabel Brook shared the brunt of the preparation work and much of the travelling with patience and humour. Roger Mills, my co-director on *80 Days*, made sure the work was fun, and after work was even more fun. Angela Elbourne, another *80 Days* veteran, was, if it were possible, less flappable than ever. Mimi O'Grady in the London office was our dependable and ever-present lifeline to the outside world. At Prominent Television I must especially thank Anne James for working so hard to get the show on the road, Alison Davies for, painstakingly and encouragingly, putting my ravings and ramblings in order, Una Hoban for signing the cheques and Kath James for keeping the world at bay while I was away.

There are many more people without whose help, energy and enthusiasm *Pole to Pole* would not have happened. Besides those already mentioned in the book, I would like very much to thank Paul Marsh, who patiently and valiantly tried to teach me Russian, Roger Saunders, Chris Taylor, Sue Pugh Tasios, Gabra Gilada, David Thomas, Alex Richardson, Jonathan Rowdon, Anne Dummett and last but not least Suzanne Webber, Suzannah Zsohar, Linda Blakemore and Julian Flanders at BBC Books.

For travel information I relied heavily on the excellent *Rough Guides* and the *Lonely Planet* series, and the *Insight Guides* and Martin Walker's *Independent Travellers Guide to the Soviet Union* were invaluable.

NOTE ON THE TEXT

Not every single day is described. Rest days when nothing happened except laundry have been omitted out of consideration for the reader.

The word 'fixer' is often mentioned. Fixers are professional organizers whose job it was to ease our passage through their countries.

For Helen,
Tom, Will and Rachel

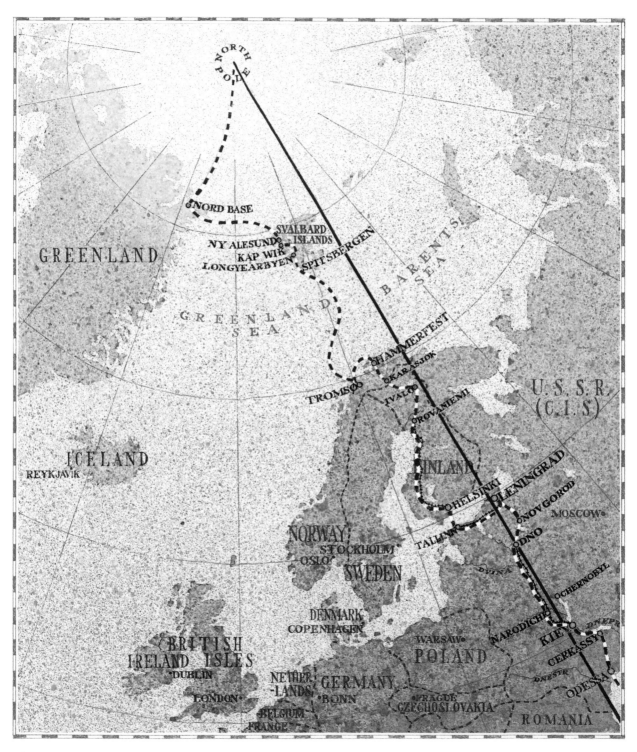

30°East, the ideal route
The actual route

NORTH POLE

NORD BASE

GREENLAND

SVALBARD
NY ALESUND ISLANDS
KAP WIK
LONGYEARBYEN
SPITSBERGEN

BARENTS SEA

GREENLAND SEA

HAMMERFEST

U.S.S.R
(C.I.S)

TROMSØ
KARASJOK
IVALO
ROVANIEMI

ICELAND
REYKJAVIK

FINLAND

HELSINKI
LENINGRAD
NOVGOROD
MOSCOW

TALLINN
ODNO

NORWAY
STOCKHOLM
OSLO
SWEDEN

DVINA

CHERNOBYL

DENMARK
COPENHAGEN

WARSAW
POLAND

NARODICHIO
KIEV
DNEPR

CERKASSY

BRITISH
IRELAND ISLES
DUBLIN
LONDON

NETHER-
LANDS
BELGIUM
FRANCE

GERMANY
BONN

DNESTR
PRAGUE
CZECHOSLOVAKIA

ODESSA

ROMANIA

DAY 1 · THE NORTH POLE

POLE *to* **POLE**

It's 3.45 on a Saturday afternoon and I'm 17 miles from the North Pole. Somewhere, a long way away, people are doing sensible things like watching cricket or digging gardens or pushing prams or visiting their mothers-in-law.

I'm squeezed tight into a small, noisy aeroplane descending through stale grey cloud towards an enormous expanse of cracked and drifting ice. With me are Nigel Meakin and his camera, Fraser Barber and his tape-recorder and Roger Mills and his pipe. Along with our two pilots, Russ Bomberry and Dan Parnham, we are the only human beings within 500 miles. Outside my window one of our two propeller-driven engines slowly eats away at a fuel supply which must last us another six hours at least. In little more than ten minutes our pilot will have to fashion a landing strip out of nothing more than a piece of ice – strong enough to withstand an impact of 12,500 lbs at 80 miles an hour. Below the ice the sea is 14,000 feet deep.

I'm sure I'm not the only one of us looking down on this desolate wilderness who hasn't wished, for an impure moment, that the North Pole, rather than being in the middle of an ocean, was solid, well-marked and even supplied with a hut and a coffee machine. But the cracked and fissured ice-pack offers no comfortable reassurance – no glimmer of any reward to the traveller who has made his way to the top of the world. The Arctic Ocean, known to the Victorians as the Sea of Ancient Ice, stares balefully back as we descend towards it, reflecting nothing but the question – Why?

It's too late to ask the producer now, too late to begin to speculate why I so eagerly agreed to come here, and completely out of order even to mention that if we survive this ice landing we have only another 12,500 miles to go.

At two minutes past four our De Havilland Twin Otter, designed in the 50s and much loved and trusted by Arctic flyers, is finally over the North Pole. One almost looks for a point, a peak, a curve offering tantalizing glimpses of those huge land masses – Alaska, Siberia, Scandinavia and Canada – which back on to the Arctic. But all there is to see is ice and the nearer we get to it the more evident it is that the ice is not in good shape. Russ, a self-contained, taciturn man about whom I know nothing other than that my life is in his hands, leans forward from the controls, scanning the conditions below and frowning.

Technology cannot help him now. The decision as to how, when and ultimately whether to drop the plane onto the ice is for his judgement alone.

He clearly doesn't like what he sees and, by my watch, we have circled the roof of the world for nearly 30 minutes before a change in engine note indicates that he is at last throttling back in preparation for a landing. We drop low, running in over a tongue of open water, Russ staring hard at the ice as ridge walls taller than I'd expected rush up to meet us. Brace myself for impact, but it never comes. At the last minute Russ thrusts the overhead throttle control forward and pulls us up banking steeply away. He checks the fuel gauge and asks Dan, the young co-pilot, to connect up one of the drums for in-flight refuelling. Dan squeezes his way from the cockpit to the back of the plane, where he begins to fiddle around with spanners and tubes until the aircraft is rich with the smell of kerosene. The Pole remains 100 feet below us, tantalizingly elusive, probably in the middle of a black pool of melted water. Russ takes advantage of some marginally increased sunlight to attempt a second landing. Once again hearts rise towards mouths as the engines slow and a blur of ice and snow and pitch-black sea rises towards us, but once again Russ snatches the plane from the ice at the last moment and we soar away, relieved and cheated.

I make a mental note never to complain about a landing ever again. Russ circles and banks the plane for another 15 minutes, patiently examining the floating ice for yet another attempt.

This time there is no pull-out. Six hours after leaving Eureka Base on Ellesmere Island, Canada, the wheels and skis of the Twin Otter find the ground, bounce, hit, bounce, hit, swerve, slide and finally grip the slithery hummocked surface. We are down and safe. I check the time on my watch, and realize that at this point it could be whatever time I wanted it to be. Japanese time, Indian time, New York time or London time – they're all the same at the Pole. It is 10 o'clock at night in London.

Home seems impossibly far away as we step out onto a rough base of ice and snow. It looks secure but water channels only a few yards away and the fact that Russ will not risk switching off the aircraft engines in case the ice should split reminds us that this is a lethal landscape. Finding the highest point in the vicinity – a pile of fractured ice-blocks, soaring to three and a half feet, I plant our 'North Pole' (kindly loaned to us by the Canadians) and we take our photos. The air is still, and a watery sun filters through grey-edged cloud giving the place a forlorn and lonely aspect. The temperature is minus 25 Centigrade. This is considered warm.

After an hour's filming, we defer to Russ's polite impatience and return to the aircraft. Concerned about fuel, he takes off quickly and unceremoniously, as if the North Pole were just another bus stop.

We have planned to follow the 30 degree East meridian all the way to the South Pole, but straight away there are problems. There is only enough fuel left to reach the nearest airstrip, a Danish base in Greenland. Even this is 480 miles away, and beyond radio range at the moment. We have no option but to fly in hope.

For some reason the only liquid we have been provided with for our journey is a litre can of tomato juice which doesn't last long between six people, and it is a thirsty, underfed, cramped and exhausted little group that puts down at Nord Base, Greenland, with only 25 minutes of fuel left. We have been away from the rest of the world for ten minutes short of twelve hours.

There is not a soul to be seen.

Russ, armed with registration documents and proof of identity, trudges off into the distance to try and raise someone.

We wait by the aircraft, in a curious state of mental and physical limbo. The only one who seems really happy is Roger who is at last able to light up his pipe.

After what feels like an eternity, Russ returns with a young Danish soldier who is in a state of considerable shock. No one had told him we were coming, and it being 3 o'clock in the morning on the north coast of Greenland, 700 miles from the nearest settlement, a knock on the door must have been like the start of a horror movie.

He bravely tries to laugh it off, 'We thought it could only be Father Christmas', before offering us what we are dying for – food and drink and a bed for the night. So day one ends in country one, which turns out, quite unexpectedly, to be Denmark.

DAY 2 · GREENLAND TO NY ALESUND

The midnight sun is shining brightly when I climb into a bunk at 3.30 a.m., and equally brightly when I wake at half-past nine. From 15 October the sun will disappear below the horizon and not rise again until the end of February, but for now, in mid-May, day merges seamlessly into day.

Greenland is a part of the kingdom of Denmark – a massive, almost uninhabited ice cap over 50 times the size of its mother country. The base at Nord is manned for the Danish government by five soldiers, but one of them is away, so Henny, Jack, Kent and Kenneth are running the place at the moment.

Two big supply planes come in each year bringing all they need – fresh videos, books, food and drink and equipment. The only thing they don't like is that it means letters . . . 'Not receiving them, *writing* them', they explain.

They're so friendly, open and hospitable that there is a great temptation to abandon the journey and stay here, drinking fresh coffee with rich Danish bread, half-listening to a rock and roll track by a Miss B. Haven entitled 'Making Love in the Snow', and gazing out to a view of icy fiords bathed in crisp bright sunshine. I ask Jack if the snow ever disappears.

'Oh yes,' he assures me, 'it melts in July. And starts snowing again in August.'

Russ is unable to make contact with our next port of call – Ny Alesund in Spitsbergen – and the Danes say they will try and raise a weather forecast from the American base at Thule. This takes some time, but at midday the news comes through that the weather is good, and after refuelling and repacking we squeeze back into the Twin Otter.

There are 325 miles between Greenland and the Svalbard Islands, of which Spitsbergen ('steep mountains' as it was named by the Dutch who discovered it 400 years ago) is the largest. Part of Norway since 1925, it is for us an important stepping stone between the North Pole and Europe, and the first place where we hope to do without aircraft and continue our journey by land and sea.

Below us, a mixture of black clear water-channels, pale blue icebergs and various shades of frozen and refrozen ice give the Greenland Sea a mottled effect, but as we cross the Greenwich Meridian and enter the Eastern Hemisphere, the effect of a warm current pushing up from the Atlantic changes the scene dramatically. The ice melts away and thick cloud hides the water for a while. When we see it again, it is only 1500 feet below the plane and a fierce easterly wind is flicking spray from the top of angry waves.

The Twin Otter is suddenly battling against a headwind and horizontally driving snow. Russ takes us down another 1000 feet but the visibility is no better, and before we hit slap-bang into the side of Spitsbergen he pulls us sharply up through the impenetrable, but mercifully low storm cloud, to calmer conditions at 2000 feet.

Judging from his expression Spitsbergen is not on Russ's regular beat and he seems as surprised as any of us to see the sweeping sides of a mountain range emerge above the clouds to the east. From the map these look to be the peaks of Albert I Land, and turning the little aircraft south we follow the coastline and descend, through the angry, drifting remains of the storm clouds into King's Fiord, where glaciers roll down to the sea and fragments of ice speckle the dark water. Dwarfed by the massive landscape two golf-ball early warning domes, a couple of tall concrete structures and a cluster of brightly painted houses mark the settlement of Ny Alesund (New Alesund). We have crossed two time zones in our two and a half-hour flight and passed south of latitude 80 degrees.

At Ny Alesund we rendezvous with David Rootes, our adviser on Arctic survival from the Scott Polar Research Institute, Engineer Geir Paulson, the organizer of our land transport and Patti, Nigel's camera assistant. Basil Pao, stills photographer and last member of our team, is to meet us in Tromsø. It's soon clear from the swirling snowstorms that sweep across the fiord and from the experiences David and Patti recount from their journey up to meet us that Greenland and the North Pole have been a picnic compared to what lies ahead.

But first the pleasure of a shower and clean clothes and a drink in the only bar in Ny Alesund. Everyone seems subdued, but this is apparently the result of multiple hangovers from a party held here last night to toast the news of our arrival at the Pole.

DAY 3 · NY ALESUND

POLE *to* **POLE** We're quartered in simple comfort in a long wooden hut comprising individual bedrooms, shared shower and lavatory, sports hall and a room for conferences and classes. It's owned, as is most of Ny Alesund, by the King's Bay Kull Company. Kull, or coal, is the main reason for a human presence on Spitsbergen but following a series of disasters in the early 1960s the Ny Alesund mines were closed down and the accommodation is now used for scientific research, intrepid vacations and the inevitable weather station. There is even a fledgling British presence here in the shape of Nick Cox and his wife Katie who are employed in setting up an Arctic research station.

Life is still run along the lines of a company town. Breakfast, at 7.30, lunch at noon and supper at five are all served in a communal canteen, a five-minute walk along a snow-covered track. The preferred mode of transport is the snowmobile, often known by one of it's trade names as the Ski-Doo. Built like a fat motorbike, it is driven by a caterpillar track with short skis on the front for steering. With flashy trims and names like *Exciter*, *Enticer* and *Phazer II* they make a lot of noise and give a great impression of speed whilst rarely hitting more than 45 m.p.h. They are to be our transport on the 155-mile journey across the mountains to the capital town of Longyearbyen.

15

Though we are crying for a day off after the polar adventure, Geir Paulsen, a round, pony-tailed adventurer with a considerable sense of humour, is of the opinion that we should try to leave before bad weather sets in. (One thing I've noticed in countries full of weather stations is that no one can give you an accurate weather forecast. They can tell you that palm trees will be growing in Iceland in 75 years, but nothing at all about the afternoon ahead.)

We load up and set off about 3 p.m. It is appropriate that our column of snowmobiles and trailers should pass, on the way out of town, a three-foot high bronze head of the explorer Roald Amundsen. It commemorates the first trans-polar flight, in his airship *Norge*, which left Ny Alesund on 11 May 1926 and landed in North America on 14 May, after a journey of over 3000 miles. Three years later Amundsen died in the Arctic, attempting to rescue his friend Nobile, whose airship, like Amundsen's, left from the 30-foot pylon which still stands on the edge of town, receding into the distance as we head for the mountains.

Determined to do all my own stunts, I send myself and my passenger David Rootes flying as I lose control of *Mach-One* (the name of the black Ski-Doo I've been allotted) round a tight bend. One handlebar is the accelerator, the other the brake, and at this stage I'm not entirely sure which is which. Fortunately the accident causes more injury to pride than to limb. The going is not easy. The sun is now lost in cloud and it's difficult to see the track. Heinrich, a young Norwegian with disconcertingly blue eyes, who can probably drive a snowmobile standing on his head, leads the procession as we climb towards the saddle of the mountain. Quite suddenly thick cloud envelops us and everything around is white. All sense of direction is lost, and when we do eventually have to pull up, David Rootes informs me drily that 300 yards to my left is a precipice, dropping sheer to a glacier. Defeated by the worsening conditions we turn back. Fresh snow is falling and a small drift has formed already on the side of Amundsen's huge and beaky nose as we re-enter Ny Alesund. Neither he, nor anyone else, seems surprised to see us back.

DAY 4 · NY ALESUND

Wake to the sound of bird-song. As I haven't yet seen a single living creature in the Arctic, I wonder for a moment if this might be one of the crew, driven mad with homesickness, playing a Percy Edwards tape. But Peter Webb, a young Englishman and one of our Ski-Doo circus, tells me at breakfast that it's a snow bunting. We're also likely to see seals, reindeer and possibly Arctic fox on our way across the island. I'm desperate to see a polar bear (having been brought up on Brumas) but might have to shoot it if I do. I glean this from a warning poster, in Norwegian and English, displayed at the door of the canteen. 'Polar bears may be very dangerous', it begins:

'The following precautions should be taken: 1 Always carry a weapon . . . 2 Do not attract bears by putting out food. Place your garbage at least 100 metres away from the camp, directly in view of your tent opening or cabin door. This may enable you to see a visiting bear in time. Report to the authorities if you have had to kill a bear, find out what sex it is, and take care of the skull and skin.'

Roger slept badly and suspects he has a sprained wrist following yesterday's excursion. This is his excuse for wearing a sinister black glove on one hand. Fraser dreamt that he gave every member of his family a Ski-Doo for Christmas. I can see why he thought of Christmas, for the snow is falling here as copiously as in any Disney cartoon, making it hard to remember that it's nearly June.

Geir is ever hopeful. The barometer is evidently rising and we should be packed and ready to leave at six this evening, after supper.

At 6 p.m. the snow is falling in great big fat lazy flakes, and we are about to settle, not unhappily, for an evening of table tennis and a good night's sleep when Geir and his colleagues suggest that the most settled conditions are often in the middle of the night and they would seriously ask us to consider a 2 a.m. departure. This is seriously considered, but not for very long. Another postponement, until tomorrow morning, is agreed upon. Back to the table tennis.

DAY 5 · NY ALESUND TO KAP WIK

POLE
to
POLE

2 a.m.: The skies duly clear and dazzling sunlight picks out mountains and glaciers obscured for 48 hours.

8 a.m. I raise my blind in expectation. The sun has gone, as if it were a dream, and the pile of snow at my window is half an inch higher. Walk through a blizzard to the canteen. I have said goodbye to the breakfast chef at least twice and he is now thoroughly confused and a little suspicious of my intentions. Am I really on my way to the South Pole or just trying out Great Mueslis of the World?

Heinrich is phlegmatic.

'Waiting . . . ,' he observes . . . 'everything about the Arctic is waiting.'

After lunch the snow begins to ease off and in the square the Norwegian flag turns abruptly to the south. This is a sign of the arrival of the settled northerly air-stream for which we have been waiting.

The journey to Longyearbyen is likely to take 12 hours at least, and it is suggested that we should break it with a stop at Kap Wik, about 5 hours away, where there is a trapper's hut with accommodation. This sounds suitably photogenic and fairytale-like and once the vehicles have been cleared of their carapace of snow, the sledge trailers lashed down and hooked up, and an anti-Polar bear rifle stashed aboard, we are once more ready for departure. Nick and Katie Cox honour us with an official British presence at the great moment, and Nick entrusts me with a bottle of whisky for Harald, the trapper. I am so embarrassed that we might have to slink back yet again that I avoid the chef's eye, and Amundsen's severe stare, as we finally pull away just after seven in the evening.

The mountains climb quite steeply to 2000 feet, and we have to stop a lot in the first hour, partly to free snowmobiles bogged down by their heavy loads, but mainly to photograph the spectacular views out across King's Fiord, fed by three glaciers and rimmed with sweeping mountain peaks. As soon as the motors are turned off and the natural silence restored, the size and scale and majesty of the landscape is indescribable. There are no trees on Spitsbergen, and therefore few birds except around the coast, and with unbroken snow shrouding the valley below us there is an atmosphere of magnificent peacefulness.

Soon we are across the pass and putting the snowmobiles down a snow-slope so steep that we are warned not to use the brake. This is to prevent the trailers from swinging round and pulling the vehicles over – and

presumably sending the driver hurtling downhill in a mass of wreckage – though they don't tell you the last bit. We twist and turn through some perilous gullies which Roger refers to with a certain relish as Walls of Death, as in, 'Michael, we'd like to do another Wall of Death sequence'. The whole adventure seems to have gone to his head since he chose the codeword 'Raving Queen' for his end of the two-way radio. Fraser, at the other end, is 'Intrepid One', and I suppose it does take away some of the terror to hear, floating across a glacier, the immortal words:

'Raving Queen to Intrepid One, Michael's on the Wall of Death . . . Now!'

On the other side of the pass another epic wintry panorama is revealed on the shores of Engelsbukta – 'English Bay', where an English whaling fleet under Henry Hudson took refuge in 1607, while in search of the north-east passage. Much of the bay is still frozen, and we see our first seals – nothing more than tiny black blobs – waiting beside their holes in the ice. A ptarmigan, in its white, winter coat, peers curiously down at us from a pinnacle of rock, and a pair of eider ducks turn low over the bay.

We head towards a wide level glacier passing ice cliffs of palest blue which are millions of years old and still moving. I ask Geir why they should be such a colour. Apparently it is caused by the presence of air inside the ice.

After the roller-coaster conditions on the pass, progress across the glacier is fast and reasonably comfortable. I am riding pillion behind David, and apart from nursing an occasional numbing cold in my thumb and fingers, I have plenty of time to sit back and take in the glories of this wide, unvisited landscape. A pair of Svalbard reindeer, not much bigger than large dogs, wander across a hillside. God knows what they find to eat.

After five hours we grind to a halt, our vehicles stuck in deep fresh-fallen snow at the top of a pass, still barely half-way to the trapper's hut. Bars of chocolate, nips of Scotch and stupendous views keep spirits up as Geir, Heinrich and the team make repeated journeys down the valley to bring up machines that couldn't make it to the top. Once all of them are up on the ridge they have to be refuelled, a slow laborious job, as is anything which involves unloading the trailers.

We are rewarded with a long exhilarating run on wide downhill slopes to our first ice-crossing – on the frozen headwaters of the Ehmanfiord. The surface is scratched and rutted, and it's only on the last stretch that the ice is smooth enough to open out, and we ride like invading Mongol hordes toward the tiny, isolated cabin on Kap Wik where, somewhat improbably, we are to spend what remains of the night.

DAY 6 · KAP WIK TO LONGYEARBYEN

It's 2.45 in the morning when we arrive at Harald Solheim's hut. A tall wooden frame hung with seal carcasses stands on a slight rise, more prominent than the cabin itself, which is set lower down, out of the wind. The first surprise is Harald himself. Instead of some grizzly bearded old-timer, a tall, pale, studious figure comes out to welcome us. He does have a beard, but attached as it is to long, aquiline features the effect is more rabbi than trapper. The second surprise is how benignly and agreeably he copes with the appearance of ten tired and hungry travellers in the middle of the night. First we fill up his minuscule hallway with our boots and bags, then we burst his sitting-room to the seams, whilst he heats up some stew on a wood-burning stove. His wood supply, neatly stacked in a workshop, is driftwood, probably from the Russian coast. His electricity supply is wind-generated.

He fetches out a leg of smoked reindeer which is quite delicious and over this and a mixture of stew, smoked salmon, Aquavit (the local spirit) and Glenmorangie whisky we thaw out and swap stories. Harald offers advice, comment and information, liberally laced with dry humour. It's like some wonderfully chaotic tutorial.

Around about 4.30 a.m. some of us start looking a little anxiously for the dormitory. Harald explains the arrangements. In a next-door room he has four bunk-beds and floor space for two. There is more space on the floor

of his workshop. Everyone else will have to sleep in the sitting-room with him. There is one sit-down loo, but as this is a bag that has to be emptied men are requested to use the Great Outdoors whenever possible, but to refrain from peeing on the side of the house from which he draws his water supply. For cleaning teeth and washing he recommends the snow.

When I wake, it's half-past eleven. The sitting-room resembles some Viking Valhalla with recumbent Norwegians scattered about and Harald sprawled on the sofa like a warrior slain in battle. Then the telephone rings. Last night my tired brain was so busy romanticizing Harald's existence that I hadn't noticed the phone, or the remote control for the matt-black hi-fi, or the visitors' book, or the collection of Rachmaninov piano concertos on CD, signed 'To Harald from Vladimir Ashkenazy'. Is it all a dream? Have we been hi-jacked in the night to some apartment in Oslo? I stumble outside clutching my toothbrush and there is the reassuring reality of empty mountains and frozen seas stretching as far as the eye can see.

I scrub snow all over my face and neck. A refreshing shock which dispels any lurking hangover. When I get back indoors Harald is off the phone and preparing coffee. This autumn, he tells me, he will be celebrating 15 years at Kap Wik. He has family in Norway, but they don't visit much. His closest neighbours are the Russians at the mining town of Pyramiden, 18 miles away. He reads a lot, 'Almost everything except religious literature' and hunts seal, reindeer, Arctic fox (a pelt will fetch around £80) and snowgeese. '"Goose Kap Wik" was served to the King and Queen of Norway,' he informs me, with quiet satisfaction.

'So it's a busy life in the middle of nowhere?'

Harald shrugs. 'Some years I don't see a living soul from autumn to July.'

I ask him if he has ever felt the need for companionship. A woman around the house perhaps.

'It's . . . er . . . ,' he smiles at his sudden inarticulacy . . . 'it's not easy to explain in Norwegian . . . but any woman mad enough to come here . . .'

He never finishes the sentence. The sound of a distant helicopter brings him to his feet.

'It's my mail', he explains, almost apologetically, as a Sea King helicopter clatters into sight across the fiord.

After a late lunch and more stories our caravan is repacked and relaunched. Harald, smiling, waves us away. I don't really understand why a man of such curiosity, fluency and culture should want to chase animals round Spitsbergen, but I feel he rather enjoys being an enigma, and though he is no hermit he is one of a rare breed of truly independent men.

The rest of the journey is less eventful. The slopes are not as fierce, and the snow is turning to slush in some of the valleys. It's becoming almost routine to turn off one glacier onto another, to roar up snowbound mountain passes and see the seals plop back into their ice-holes as we cross the fiords.

We stop for a while at the spot where Patti had an adventure on the way up to Ny Alesund. She lost her way in a 'white-out' and was not found for almost an hour. I hope this isn't an omen for the long journey ahead.

Although we make fast progress towards Longyearbyen, the weather has not finished with us. Turning into the broad valley that leads to the town we are hit full in the face by a blizzard of stinging wet snow and as Heinrich accelerates for home it makes for a hard and uncomfortable end to the ride.

After five and a half hours travelling we see through the murk the first lights of Longyearbyen, and the snowmobiles screech clumsily along the wet highway.

It's half-past ten and we have reached our first town, 812 miles from the North Pole.

DAY 7 · LONGYEARBYEN

 Everyone in Ny Alesund was rather rude about Longyearbyen, and certainly as capitals go it is no beauty. It is another coal town, largely the property of the Store-Norsk Company, but unlike Ny Alesund, coal is still mined here and there is fine black dust in the air, trucks on the road and housing blocks set out in severe grid patterns down the sides of the valley. It is ironic that

M/S NORSEL

Bunkerkapasitet	700 m³
Bunkerkapasitet, vann	17 m³
Passasjerer	8
Fart m/last	10 knop
Fart u/last	12 knop
Oljelenser	2 × 200
Fryserom	60
Tørrlasterom	500

the chief product of this treeless island should be fossil fuel. There is a theory that at one time Spitsbergen lay near the Equator and was covered by tropical forest.

In my spartan room at Hotel Number 5, the information sheet on Longyearbyen reads more like a company report than a tourist brochure. The settlement was founded in 1906 by an American, John Munroe Longyear. For 10 years it was run by men only but in 1916 the Norwegians bought him out and the first women were allowed to accompany their mining husbands here. The population today consists of 250 women, 250 children and 550 men. 'However', it adds, a little ominously, 'there are still important differences between Longyearbyen and other small towns in mainland Norway. Here there are neither pensioners, handicapped people, nor persons terminally ill'. I half expect my door to be flung open, and my birth certificate and pulse given a snap check.

There is no getting away from Ski-Doos. I dreamt about them all night and this morning I find that there is a Ski-Doo convention in town, and our hotel is at the centre of it. From 10 o'clock onwards international buyers from the world's cold countries can be heard, if not seen, attempting to scale the near-vertical slopes behind the hotel. There is something about these vehicles that bring out the Jekyll and Hyde in a driver. Once in the saddle, he will sooner or later succumb to an uncontrollable urge to do something dangerous. They are vehicles for a world without roads or policemen.

Longyearbyen has a supermarket. It doesn't actually say on the self-opening doors 'World's Most Northerly Supermarket', but, at 78.15 degrees, I can't imagine it has many competitors. Apart from an eye-catching range of canned vegetables called 'Sodd' there is not much to detain us apart from a well-stocked drinks section. As we have a long sea-journey ahead of us I fill my trolley, only to have to replace all the bottles as I don't have a valid air-ticket into or out of Longyearbyen. Alcoholic refreshment is, it appears, severely rationed. The only way we can buy even a can of beer is with a special dispensation from the Sysselmann – the Governor. We traipse round to Government House to get our chitty, feeling like naughty schoolchildren.

DAY 8 · LONGYEARBYEN TO TROMSØ

We are to continue our journey south on the supply ship *Norsel*, which leaves today for Tromsø in Norway, refuelling, or 'bunkering' as they call it, a number of fishing boats on the way. They have limited accommodation on board and it will be a slow trip (estimates vary from 5 to 7 days for the 600-mile journey), but beggars can't be choosers and there are no other ships operating out of Longyearbyen this early in the summer.

We bid farewell to all those who guided us across Spitsbergen, and I promise Geir that I will let the world know that most of our snowmobiles were made by Yamaha for whom he is the dealer, and not Ski-Doo. He in turn reveals that he's going to Tromsø anyway, but flying there in a couple of hours as any normal person would. I try to point out the delights of not being normal.

The *Norsel* is the only vessel at the dockside. Adventfiorden, on which Longyearbyen is situated, only became free of ice a week ago, and the coal ships will not start arriving for another month. She looks sturdy, if a little bruised, a slash of pillar-box red against the grey buildings of the port, and the flowing white cloaks of the mountains across the fiord. She is not a big ship, only 550 tons, and our cabins are the size of cupboards, but there is an appealingly warm and secure atmosphere below decks. Earlier in the day I had talked to a journalist from the Svalbard newspaper who raised her eyebrows when she heard I was crossing to Tromsø by ship.

'They call that sea the Devil's Dancefloor.'

I put this to the captain, Stein Biølgerud, who smiles quietly to himself in a not very encouraging way. He explains to me that the *Norsel* has an exceptional draught of 8 metres (26 feet) which means that when fully loaded most of the hull is beneath the water and much more susceptible to rolling and pitching.

'And are we fully loaded at the moment?'

His smile widens. 'Oh, yes.'

The good news is that the hull is composed of 28 millimetre-thick steel plates.

'The highest ice class . . .' he continues encouragingly. 'We can move through 60 centimetres of solid ice.'

'So we'll be safe in the ice?'

'Oh yes. Unless of course we have too much ice on the superstructure. Then the ship can topple over.'

Credit for the redoubtably solid hull of the *Norsel* must go to Hitler's shipyards, for it was constructed in Germany in 1943, but left unfinished until the Norwegians took it over in 1947. Since then it has seen service as a seal catcher, scallop trawler and expedition vessel.

There is a crew of seven. A Captain, First Mate, Chief Engineer, Cook and three deckhands. At the moment they are supervising the unloading of what seems like a year's supply of toilet rolls. This uncharismatic little ship is a lifeline up here. The captain recalls arriving late one year with a supply of beer on board.

'They only had 17 cans left on the island. There were guys waiting on the jetty.'

Shortly after 7 o'clock on an evening of piercing sunshine we pull away from Spitsbergen, round the headland, past the coal tips and out into the broad waters that lead to the Greenland Sea.

Soon a wall of grey cloud looms ahead of us and the captain says a gale is forecast. His bridge bristles with all sorts of electronic equipment, but he prefers to slide down one of the window panels, stick his head out and see what the birds are doing. He's sceptical of weather forecasts. In these waters things change so quickly.

'One thing you can be sure of, you can't be sure of anything,' he observes. Another piece of Arctic wisdom.

He has to set a course almost due west to avoid the pack ice along the coast, but it is from the west that the gale is coming. Thinking it may be the last meal we can cope with for a while we eat well – a rich stew cooked by Anthony, a small pale man dressed all in white, like an anxious dentist. We don't think he's Norwegian and Roger hazards that he is Russian.

'Are you Russian?' he asks him over another helping of stew. Anthony gives a quick, brittle smile and shakes his head, 'Polish'.

It turns out that the three deckhands are Polish as well.

Later, on the bridge, the captain (Norwegian) is worried that the wind is veering west earlier than expected.

'Not good for us,' he mutters. At the other end of the bridge the moustachioed Chief Engineer (also Norwegian) sits reading a comic book and not laughing.

DAY 9 · THE GREENLAND SEA

A night of varying degrees of instability. Occasionally some steep pitching and tossing which has clocks, books and glasses sliding onto the floor. The engine noise is a loud, persistent, constant factor we shall have to get used to. Noise insulators, like stabilizers, were never part of the *Norsel*'s specifications.

Egg and bacon breakfast. Fraser is worried that we have been given no lifeboat drill. Roger had awoken in the night to find a large sailor in his cabin. He was a messenger from the captain who had seen some ice nearby and thought that we might like to photograph it.

Wintry conditions. Snow flurries on deck and a heavy sea. Sea birds, like tern, fulmar and kittiwake, rest on the ice-covered bow before resuming their graceful gliding search of the waters.

I show Fraser the findings of an American survey, published in the shipping magazine *Trade Winds*, which asked people for whom they would give up a seat in a lifeboat. Of men, 67 per cent would give up a seat to their wives, 52 per cent to Mother Theresa, but only 8 per cent to Madonna. Of women, 41 per cent would give up a seat to their husbands, and only 3 per cent to 'men not their husbands'. I don't think Fraser's even found the lifeboat yet, so the question is academic.

I ask the captain what our maximum speed is.

'Well,' he pulls heavily on a yellowing hand-rolled cigarette, 'with a light load, good weather and the current behind us . . . ten knots.'

I reckon it will take us 30 hours just to clear the coast of Spitsbergen and another two days before we reach the fishing fleets on the Barents Sea.

Such is the pitching and tossing of the ship tonight that as I lie in my narrow bunk I experience the not unpleasant sensation of being stretched. First of all my body tries to slide out through my feet, then a moment later everything tries to escape through the top of my head. Go to sleep wondering how one could design a machine to reproduce this effect.

DAY 10 · THE BARENTS SEA

At 10 a.m. I check our position on the satellite indicator – 75.47 North and 16.25 East. We're entering the Barents Sea, named after the Dutchman who first discovered it in 1596, and the waters are shallower but cooler, fed by an Arctic rather than Atlantic current. This means that as we head east to the fishing grounds we have to push through a thickening ice field. Up to now the ice fragments have floated by rather forlornly, looking like upturned tables and chairs, or floats heading home at the end of a parade. But now, as the air gets colder, the ice-blocks are growing in size as the open water between them decreases.

Stein (pronounced Stain), as we now call the Captain, picks his way carefully. Some of these 10-foot ice-blocks have wide solid platforms below the water which could cause damage if met head on. The ideal way to deal with them, he explains, is to keep the bow riding high over the ice, which then passes along the keel and is split by the weight of the ship.

When we are in the thick of the ice, Stein cuts engines and our intrepid cameraman is winched off the deck onto a convenient floe. I personally think it's too early in the journey to get rid of him, but I'm overruled. The sight of Nigel's solitary figure drifting slowly away from us is quite disturbing and I'm sure we all take far more pictures of him than he ever does of us.

The eerie sound of ice scraping along the hull continues for much of the day, before we are through into clear but rugged seas again. Roger, puffing on his pipe, and looking increasingly like Captain Pugwash, surveys the spray flung high by waves breaking on the bow, and smiles with satisfaction.

'The devil's coming on the dancefloor, Mike.'

DAY 11 · THE BARENTS SEA

Snowstorms and high seas. I don't feel nauseous exactly, but the sight of the breakfast table replete with fried eggs, gammon, sausages, yoghurt, mayonnaise, fish paste in tubes, cheese, bacon and prawn spread and two kinds of salad in plastic tubs moves me fairly smartly up on deck. It's furiously cold and bleak but I stare at the horizon, as recommended, and take a few gulps of Arctic air until the moment of queasiness passes.

This morning everyone is slipping and sliding about, and in one 60 degree lurch all the drawers fly out of the captain's desk.

The first sign that we have reached the fishing fleets is a parade of Russian stern-trawlers, tossing about in the waves. I ask Stein if he refuels Russians. He shakes his head. 'They don't have the money.'

A week and a half from the Pole and the good news is that we are almost exactly on our target of 30 degrees East. The bad news is that we shall be around here for at least 48 hours as all the ships we are bunkering are in a 25-mile radius.

The sea is too rough for ships to be fuelled alongside, and Stein has to opt for the more tricky and time-consuming bow to stern operation. Once a ship is about 20 feet astern lines are thrown and when secured a black rubber pipe is hoisted across and the fuel is pumped through. Our first customer, the Norwegian fishing boat *Stig Magne*, has to stay connected for a hour. Great skill and seamanship is required on the part of both captains to keep their vessels the right distance apart, whilst both are soaring and plunging wildly on 30-foot waves.

In the middle of it all a sleek, battleship-grey 'Kystvakt' (coastguard) vessel prowls by, supported minutes later by a four-engined Lockheed Orion which swoops low over us before flying off to the south. Stein tells us that the coastguard plane will be looking for illegal discharges of fuel and the surface vessel checking on things like net size. The catches are constantly inspected and anyone found taking too many young fish or the wrong kind of fish is liable to be escorted out of the fishing grounds.

Around midnight, drinking a Scotch too many and being soundly whacked at Scrabble, I'm looking forward to nothing more than the womb-like, cradle-rocking security of my bunk when Stein's tall pale frame looms above us. He looks rather pleased with himself.

'There is an improvement in the weather, and I have a factory fishing ship which is happy to take you aboard and keep you there whilst they trawl.'

'What time tomorrow will that be?' asks Roger.

Stein glances at his watch. 'In about two hours.'

DAY 12 · THE BARENTS SEA

My alarm sounds at 1.30 a.m. It has to work hard to be heard above the cacophony of an engine grinding, revving, reversing and thrusting frantically. Up on the bridge Stein apologizes. The last ship he refuelled 'didn't know what he was doing'. Feeling all the better for 40 minutes sleep I scan the grey waters for whoever it is that has invited us aboard. At around 2 o'clock the *Jan Mayen*, materializes on our port side. She is two or three times the height of the *Norsel* and her stern-gate is bathed, dramatically, in a sodium orange glow. The ship to ship transfer will be by crane, and as I am to be hoisted out over the only recently unfrozen waters of the Barents Sea, I'm put into a survival suit. This is a big, clumsy rubberized affair, which looks as if it would instantly convert to a body bag once I hit the water.

'Do not be afraid' grins one of our Polish crew, with relish, as he slips a rope under my arms. He signals to some faceless figure high above me and I'm suddenly ascending, swinging like a box of toilet paper, a case of beer or any other piece of goods, over the side and across the water, then up and up into a different world. The sailors on the *Jan Mayen* are not scruffy and informal like our friends on the *Norsel*. They are smartly clad in yellow PVC with tall black boots, like policemen round a road accident. Unlike the *Norsel*, wildly bobbing below, the *Jan Mayen* is almost motionless. We are led indoors and shown an air-conditioned bridge with quietly clicking consoles and men sitting around as if they were in *Star Trek*.

The stern resembles a bowling alley along which the long green nets are wound out with a cacophonous crashing and clanging to fall 1500 feet to the sea bed. It is an impressive and exciting display, and one wonders what mighty creatures of the deep demand such terrible power. The answer is, shrimp. The *Jan Mayen*, with her million pound state of the art bridge, her 40-strong crew, her trawling Datasyncro display and her 4080 horse-power Danish-built turbine engine, is nothing but a glorified shrimping net.

They *have* been shrimping round the clock for over a month and they do have 400 tons of the little red things aboard, and they do have a factory deck with processing facilities which can transfer the catch from sea-bed to freeze-pack in 24 hours, but somehow it all seems like overkill. Who eats that many shrimps? The answer, as in so many things, is the Japanese.

At eight in the morning, in the company of two coastguard inspectors, we watch the nets drawn in. Another magnificent display of technological expertise and human organization. Another three tons of shrimp.

At 9 o'clock the *Norsel* totters alongside and we prepare once again to be swung out over the sea. Clutching our complimentary boxes we are dangled down onto the deck like children returning from a school outing.

DAY 14 · THE BARENTS SEA TO TROMSØ

Wake to calm seas and clear skies. This morning we can see the mainland of Europe for the first time. The craggy snow-capped mountains of the island of Fugløy on one side and Arnøy on the other are suitably impressive portals through which to pass into our first continent.

The cold grip of the Arctic has finally loosened. The ice on the anchor winch has melted, the sea laps lazily and placidly around the hull and the first traces of vegetation are bobbing by on the water. On the bridge all the anxiety of the last few difficult days has gone. With 12 ships successfully refuelled Stein is positively expansive, the crew are scrubbed and shaved like choirboys and the Chief Engineer is wreathed in smiles, phoning home.

For us, it's far from the end of the journey, but as we slip south of 70 degrees I can understand why everyone on the *Norsel* looks so happy. We have all survived a foray into a world where conditions are extreme and the margins of error pulled dangerously tight.

At 2 o'clock in the afternoon the First Mate spots a plane taking off from Tromsø airport. Within an hour we are moving down the Grotsundet, which I suppose is in a sense the Gateway to the Arctic, and there are all the trappings of civilization laid out – a Legoland of painted walls and roofs.

Five days and 21 hours after leaving Longyearbyen we arrive at the Tromsø dockside. Two small, attractive ladies from the Norwegian Customs come aboard and after a brief inspection we are free to step ashore.

Tromsø is the first city on my journey, and though it contains only 50,000 souls, it boasts three cathedrals, a university, a brewery and 23 night-clubs. It likes to call itself 'The Paris of the North' and, as I feel I should celebrate reaching Europe, I seek out the nearest boulevard café. I find myself sitting outside the Cormorant Bar dubiously eyeing a glass of beer whose brand name is apparently Muck.

Summer seems to have reached Tromsø early. Crowds of students enjoying the three gloom-free months of the year, when the combination of warm Gulf Stream and 24-hour sunlight give the little town an air of nervous hedonism, are today joined by football supporters from Trondheim, nearly 500 miles to the south. The Muck is flowing, though I've found out, a little to my disappointment, that 'Muck' is the local pronunciation of Mack, a brewery famous for the purity of its product and for the motto on its bottles 'First on the North Pole'.

A short walk away from the Cormorant stands a bronze statue of Roald Amundsen – first on the *South* Pole. Amundsen stands purposefully atop his granite plinth, dressed in the loose Eskimo-style outfit he favoured, gazing down the fiord. A seagull stands on top of Amundsen. I stand in silence trying to draw some comfort from those gaunt, ascetic features. After all there can't be that many of us who have left Norway for the South Pole.

In the evening we eat at a restaurant which offers an intriguing dish by the name of 'Seal Lasagna'. Ever mindful of the fury which greeted my consumption of snake in Canton, I check with the waiter.

'This isn't . . . *baby* seal, I hope?'

'Oh, no sir' he assures me, '. . . it's very old seal.'

Later, I walk back to my hotel across the main square, the Storttogret. There are queues outside the night clubs and a group of drunken boys are kicking over tables and upturning sunshades. Not violently, but with a lunging, lurching bleary desperation. They probably think they're having a good time. Nearer the hotel two quieter lads are gazing out towards the snow-capped mountains that surround the city. It's only after a while that I realize they are actually peeing into the harbour. It's midnight and in the west, over the cold hills of the island of Kvaløy, the sun is already starting to climb again.

DAY 15 · TROMSØ

Is this the same city I was in last night? This morning it seems butter wouldn't melt in its mouth. People are vertical rather than horizontal, and the chaos of the night before has been replaced by a pristine calm.

We drive across the slim long bridge that connects

Tromsø in the sunshine: MP – wishful thinking, Amundsen – Man of the Year 1911, Trondheim and Sheffield Wednesday supporters fraternize.

Day 15: Norway

Tromsø Island with mainland Norway. It's a bright, beautiful Sunday morning and bells ring out from the Arctic Cathedral, a striking modern building comprising 11 interlocking triangular sections – representing every apostle apart from Judas Iscariot. Inside is as modest, well-behaved and self-effacing a congregation as you'll find anywhere. The first few rows are completely empty and the hymns are sung softly, almost apologetically.

Who are the modern Vikings – the lusty, lurching lads overthrowing the tables in the square or these sober-suited pillars of the community?

Towards evening the sun becomes obscured by cloud and a north-west wind ruffles the waters of the bay. Locals shake their heads. The weather change reminds me how near we still are to the polar ice-cap. Basil has joined us in Tromsø, as official photographer, and already he has managed to find a Mongolian restaurant with a Japanese chef. Sushi and sashimi 200 miles above the Arctic Circle. Very odd. Not that Odd is unusual in Tromsø, in fact it's one of the most common surnames. Should you ever wish to stay unnoticed in a Tromsø hotel check in as Mr and Mrs Odd.

DAY 16 · TROMSØ TO HAMMERFEST

The weather has changed. The clouds are low and grey, and Tromsø has shed its Mediterranean glow and taken on the aspect of Northern Scotland. To cheer ourselves up we visit the Arctic Museum. This is a mistake. All it does is remind us how lucky we are to have lived this long. Polar life offers few comforts, and the faces staring back at us from seal hunts and shipwrecks are prematurely aged. Objects, on the other hand, survive well in the intense cold, and Amundsen's pipe, mug, comb, typewriter and sewing kit are all beautifully preserved, as is this menu for a special dinner to mark the safe return of Amundsen and his crew from the South Pole in 1912:

Polar Soup
Whale with fat oil
Saelhundsblod (Seal Dog Blood)
Pork from Haakon VII Plateau
Pigviner (Penguins)
Polaris mit Hvalrostuender
(Polar Ice with Sea Elephant's Teeth)

And no vegetarian alternative.

We've strayed some way off our 30 degree meridian and should be striking directly across Norway, but the desolate mountain ranges of Finnmark

provide such an impassable natural barrier that all land-routes east must first
go north.

At four in the afternoon we board the MV *Nordnorge*, a stout,
workmanlike vessel of 2600 tons which forms part of the Hurtigrute (literally
'rapid route') service from Bergen to Kirkenes on the Russian border. The
ships take 11 days to work their way there and back through the channels
and islands of this convoluted coastline. Also boarding at Tromsø are sacks
of potatoes and onions, sides of meat, televisions, wash-basins and mail. The
Hurtigrute is a delivery service, a bus service, a postal service, and for tourists
a way of experiencing the life as well as the physical spectacle of the fiords.

This is not a good day for spectacle. A line of low grey cloud has settled
a few hundred feet above the water, reducing fiord spotting to an act of
imagination. There is a restaurant, with a lady organist, playing 'Beatles songs
like you've never heard them before'. She's as good as her word.

When I repair to my windowless cabin in the bowels of the ship, we
are making a steady 15 knots and the organist is playing 'The Happy
Wanderer'.

DAY 17 · HAMMERFEST TO KARASJOK

My bunk is comfortable enough, but every time anyone in
the vicinity turns on a tap the result is a series of
sledgehammer thuds, and a short night's sleep. Up on the
bridge at a quarter to seven to film our arrival at Hammerfest,
only to be told we're running an hour late and we could have
stayed in bed and listened to the taps. There isn't much compensation in the
landscape. An unrelieved horizontal band of cloud hangs, like a pelmet, over
the treeless headlands. When Hammerfest does appear, a smudge nestling
in a bowl of tundra-covered hills, it lacks the sparkle of Tromsø. Bleak and
beleaguered, one can well believe that when the town was first settled in 1789,
early occupants had to be encouraged with the promise of a twenty-year tax
exemption.

The *Nordnorge*, which has taken 15 hours to bring us from Tromsø,
unloads and turns toward the North Cape, leaving us on a cold, damp
dockside. Norwegians grin and shake their heads wearily when I use the word
'cold'. Maybe they just take it for granted, as we might the word 'air'.

'There's no such thing as bad weather, Michael, only bad clothes.'

The town's Director of Tourism is almost lyrical about the weather. Did
I know that only three days ago the temperature in Hammerfest had reached
28 degrees Centigrade?

'Well, of course that's *too* hot,' he grimaced, rather spoiling the effect.

Did I also know that only yesterday the QE2 had been in port?

'Two thousand five hundred people . . . all shopping at once.'

I look round at the food stalls in the market place selling reindeer sausages and cod's tongues and bright hats and sealskin boots and try, without success, to visualize the scene.

Was I familiar with the Royal and Ancient Polar Bear Society? Taking my look of incomprehension for one of curiosity, the Director of Tourism ushers me, without further ado, into the presence of the Mayor of the World's Most Northerly Town who, in fluent and persuasive English, enlightens me as to the role of the Polar Bear in the history of Hammerfest. It has clearly been a submissive role, requiring the Polar Bear to do little more than lie still and not get up, but the town is proud of its part in the hunting and fishing of Arctic waters.

With brisk Scandinavian efficiency I am enrolled as member 116,747 of the Royal and Ancient Polar Bear Society and issued with card, stickers, hat, badge, certificate and a carrier bag to hold them all in. Which all goes to show that if you run a town 300 miles north of the Arctic Circle with no sight of the sun for three months of the year you have to make the best of what you've got.

One escape from the melancholy of the long dark winter months is through alcohol, and its use and abuse has forced the authorities into Draconian measures. I learn of some of them from Troels Muller, our Norwegian fixer, as I drive my hire car south towards Lapland. In Norway police in unmarked cars can stop motorists at random and breathalyze them. If they are found to have more than 0.5 millilitres of alcohol in their blood – that is the equivalent of one light beer – they can be sentenced to three weeks in prison. There is no appeal. This has led to some unusual problems.

'People are waiting one or two years to get in prison. And then when you go off to prison you don't want your friends to know obviously, so you tell them that you're going to travel.'

Troels pauses as I pull out to avoid a couple of dejected reindeer, wandering along the side of the road with all the panache of footballers sent off in a Cup Final.

'There is a prison near Oslo they call Costa del Ilseng, because, everyone . . . you know, goes to Spain . . . and, well, they're not in Spain at all . . .'

Some way further on we come to a stretch of treeless hillside from which rises a pointed tent made from tall branches covered up to three quarters of its height with canvas and skins. It's a laavu, the traditional dwelling of the Same (pronounced Sar-mi) people who are the original inhabitants of Northern Scandinavia and parts of Russia. Many of them still live by reindeer herding including the two we are going to visit, Johan Anders and his wife Anne Marie. Unfortunately their reindeer herd has disappeared.

We return in the direction of Hammerfest, but even the stragglers I'd seen earlier on the roadside have vanished. The reindeer quest turns into pure farce when we find ourselves bouncing up a rocky track to what appears to be a rubbish tip. Amid stacks of rotting cardboard, waste paper, rusting machinery and frozen food packets stands the unhappy figure of Mr Anders, arms spread in a rather unlikely 'they were here a minute ago' pose.

Somewhere between Hammerfest and the Same 'capital' of Karasjok, 130 miles to the south-west, I must have fallen asleep. When I wake the scenery has changed completely. The treeless plateau has given way to an endless vista of lake and forest. A comforting sign that we are once again heading in the right direction.

Elk for dinner. Almost impenetrable.

DAY 18 · KARASJOK

The SAS Turisthotell in Karasjok. Outside my window a flock of sparrows is breakfasting off a bed of newly sown grass. I rang home last night, then remembered that the family are all on holiday in France. Rang France. It had rained since they got there. Here, above the Arctic Circle, the sun shines and I'd be in shirt-sleeves if it weren't for the mosquitoes. From what I can gather Lapland is where mosquitoes who can afford it go for the summer. Heavy duty repellent is required, and I'm ready for them with 'Jungle Formula Repel – with added Deet'. Deet, like so many other deadly substances, was apparently developed for the US forces in Vietnam. I'm busy squirting it on any available patch of flesh, when Patti kindly offers the information that it's strong enough to strip paint off cars, and Fraser maintains that it once melted a wristwatch of his.

It's a day of *Boy's Own* adventures, starting with a ride up the Karasjoka (the Karas River) on a low, swift, wooden canoe in search of gold. My guides are two Same yuppies – Nils Christian who's visited Beverly Hills, and Leppa who carries a radio telephone in his national dress. The river is big business. Though frozen for several months of the year, it is still, according to Nils Christian, the best salmon river in Europe, yielding 133,000 kilos last year.

The tributaries of the Karasjoka are also rich, and in a bubbling stream beside a cool, damp, mosquito-infested stretch of woodland I am initiated into the recondite art of gold panning.

Required: one pair of thigh-length rubber boots, a plastic pan, a shovel and a natural sense of rhythm. The plastic pan has replaced the metal pan (as used in the movies) because the gold shows up better against the blue of the plastic. The shovel is required to ladle mud and the natural sense of rhythm helps with the sifting. Gold, being the heaviest of metals, will always sink to the bottom, and the skill lies in the delicacy required to filter out the gravel and mud without losing the grains of gold as well. Being the sort of person not noted for either rhythm or delicacy I experience a childlike sense of glee when, after a few minutes of sifting and spilling, I catch a glimpse of gold amongst the pitch-dark graphite sand. Not enough to open a Swiss bank account and probably not as much as you might find on one of Elizabeth Taylor's eyelashes, but the mere fact of having retrieved it, by my own efforts, from the mud of this remote river, gives satisfaction way beyond the value. My self-sifted fortune is estimated to be somewhere in the region of £9.50 sterling. Decide to buy the crew a beer and invest the rest.

Sven Engholm is the Martina Navratilova of dog-sled racing. He's won the *Finnmarkslopet*, Europe's longest race, nine times. Like everyone else in this inhospitable northernmost corner of the continent he has a mobile telephone and a shrewd eye for a tourist opportunity. In the laavu in his garden, a few miles from Karasjok, he and his wife Ellen serve us a traditional Same lunch. Smoked salmon, with egg and fresh-baked brown bread, is followed by reindeer bouillon and reindeer stew served from a smoke-encrusted black pot over an open fire. We sit on reindeer skins and eat off wooden platters. Just when you think the meal is getting conventional, Sven produces a large hunting knife, reaches for a charred brown lump hanging above the fire and offers each of us a slice of dried reindeer heart with our coffee.

The dogs which Sven breeds so successfully are outside in a compound. Thirty-seven adults and ten yearlings. They seem wildly hyperactive, straining at their leads, barking and lunging at Sven as he passes. I suppose the secret of being a good musher (as they call the dog-sled drivers) is to be able to translate this manic energy into forward momentum. That Sven and his team can race 1000 kilometres across the frozen Finnmark plateau in less than five days is an indication of his success. During our interview, as Sven is earnestly explaining the need for the dogs to relate socially, not just to each other, but to people as well, I notice the camera crew convulse with laughter. Seconds later I feel a warm, damp glow on the back of my trousers. I look down just in time to see that one of Sven's dogs has just finished relating socially to my right leg.

DAY 19 · KARASJOK

There isn't much to see in Karasjok. It's a transit town, straddling the E6 Arctic Highway on the tourist route to the North Cape. But if you look a little closer, if you stop for more than the statutory half-hour the coach tours allow at the gift shop, there is evidence here of a thriving culture which is not Norwegian or Swedish or Finnish. It is Same, and it is alive and well, with its own museum, radio station and since 1989, a gleaming new Same Centre, incorporating their own parliament. I meet Gunhild Sara, who has travelled all over the world and lived and worked in Canada and Tanzania.

I ask her if this is not just Lapland by another name.

'Lapland doesn't exist. We are in Sameland.'

So she isn't Norwegian then? She shakes her head dismissively.

'I am Same. I shall always be a Same. Whatever passport I hold I shall die a Same.'

I ask what took her to Tanzania, and she smiles, which is rather a relief.

'Very common thing, you meet a handsome fellow and then you just go!'

Sawo scenes. Filming on the Karasjoka River, panning for gold, waiting for the reindeer, tea in a laavu, dog eats BBC contract.

She preferred the Tanzanians to the Kenyans, 'They have more self-confidence, more self-pride. The Kenyans just want to be British,' but she didn't have much time for Julius Nyerere's social reforms.

'He made long moral speeches on the radio . . . tried to get the local Masai to wear underpants when they got on the buses.'

Later in the day I witness a truly surreal piece of Same culture – a joiking ceremony. A joik (pronounced yoik) is an improvised chant, delivered in a semi-yodelling waver. It has no beginning, middle or end. It is musical but not actually a song. It contains the essence of a feeling or a character or an emotion that is wholly personal and cannot be transferred except possibly within a family. Our presence makes the joikers self-conscious to start with. They puff heavily on cigarettes (smoking is widespread up here) until some beers arrive and then the curious wobbly chanting begins. It all feels very Irish, or perhaps Indian and later I find out that joiking is very much part of an international folk tradition. Indeed one of them had just come back from joiking in Reading.

Angela is of the opinion that we may well have been had, but I prefer to give them the benefit of the doubt. It's late when we drive back to the hotel. The light of the midnight sun combines with a gentle drifting vapour off the river to create a magical stillness and beauty around the half-harvested fields.

DAY 20 · KARASJOK TO IVALO

 South towards Finland on the Postilinjat, the post bus that is the only form of public transport available. I was beginning to feel becalmed in Northern Norway and am glad to be on the road again. A shower has passed over, Nigel is napping and Basil is worried that he's spelt reindeer 'raindear' on a card to his daughter. The bus is a 50-seater, but few of the seats are taken. A Japanese couple sit efficiently in front, a bearded Frenchman hunches over a backpack and a young Norwegian boy is off to spend the summer with his Finnish grandparents.

We cross the Norway–Finland border at a sleepy hamlet called Karigasniemi. The Japanese couple, who have been clutching documents for the last half hour, cannot believe that no one wants to see their passports. I look, in vain, for signs of Finnishness. There's a Shell garage and a café, with a Mercedes outside, serving pizza. The only locals are clustered around a Space Invaders game.

There are quite a few more Mercedes on the 90-mile run down to Ivalo. Many of them are towing hefty caravans on their way north, to the lakes and forests for summer with the mosquitoes. Finland strikes me as more obviously affluent than Norway. They even seem to have more reindeer, and the bus, when it's not stopping to deliver mail into makeshift roadside boxes, is pulling up to avoid them. I'm told that the reindeer, now that they are shedding their winter coats, are tormented by the clouds of flies and mosquitoes and find relief in the cooling wind that blows down the highway.

The switchback, single carriageway is well kept and the time passes lazily as the colour on the lakes turns in the evening light from black to deep green to silver. At Inari, a lakeside town bristling with outboard motors, the intrepid Japanese get off to be replaced by a few locals, including a teenage girl who is on her way to a disco in Ivalo. She says she will have to be back home by ten o'clock this evening. Her English is good, the result, she tells us, of a summer spent in Hastings. Feel embarrassed, as always, at the efforts foreigners make to learn English, compared with the other way round. But by any standards Finnish is a tough language, unlike any other in Europe except Hungarian. Verbs have *sixteen* cases.

Travel, at its best, is a process of continually conquering disbelief, and to be in a Finnish hotel on the Arctic Highway, with a sign outside my window reading 'Murmansk 313 kilometres', and the sound of a plaintive violin accompanying daylight that refuses to disappear is, I feel, after a beer or two, the sort of thing that makes life worth living.

DAY 21 · IVALO TO ROVANIEMI

I wasn't the only one at breakfast to have noticed that, apart from plaintive violins, our hotel in Ivalo also sported a full-blooded disco which set to work around midnight and was conveniently located beneath the bedrooms. At 7.30 we're on the way south again. A white reindeer crosses the road. These are rare, and hopefully as propitious as a black cat.

Troels left us at the border and we are now in the hands of Kari Vaatovaara, a young man from Helsinki, who, among other things, plays the lute. I ask him about reports I've read of the effects of nuclear fall-out from Chernobyl in this part of the world. His reaction is swift and dismissive:

'Everything was tested!'

The need for such tests must have been especially urgent here as the area was directly beneath the crescent cloud of contamination during a period of heavy rain. The staple grazing food of the reindeer is a rootless lichen which absorbs all its moisture from the atmosphere. Most of the forest foods – berries, fungi and the like – also absorb atmospheric pollution, and those

who live off them and the reindeer that eat them, must be at greater than average risk. So goes the theory (expanded on in the excellent *Rough Guide to Scandinavia*), but Kari would have none of it. Everything in Sameland is fine.

An unusual encounter on the bus. The crew have gone ahead to film and I am left in the company of an inebriated Finn.

He smiles blearily. I smile back. He starts to talk. I can't understand a word. He looks pained. I feel I must help. I speak slowly and deliberately, 'I am an Englishman.'

Amazingly, a look of recognition crosses his face.

'Ah . . . Eenglishman!' he cries, and before I have time to compose a smile of complacent acknowledgement, he blows a long and disgusting raspberry.

We pass summer homes in the forest and occasional clearances where grass has been cut and hung to dry on long rails, or else swathed around single sharp sticks like gravestones. We pass through Sodankyla, which announces itself as the home of the Arctic Film Festival, and 80 miles further on, at 66 degrees 32 North, we pass the most southerly point at which the sun stays above or below the horizon for more than 24 hours, commonly known as the Arctic Circle.

There is a bus stop on the Arctic Circle and a sign half-way down a ditch marking it in several languages, but these are completely overshadowed by the bizarre presence of Santa Claus Village. This roadside complex, which resembles a small airport, contains, among other things, a shopping mall, a café, and Santa's Post Office. With brisk opportunism the Finns have managed to ensure that half a million letters a year, many of them vaguely addressed to Santa somewhere in the north, are directed to this particular spot. Presiding over the enterprise is a crew-cutted ex-DJ and journalist who is so big that when he says he's Father Christmas you don't argue.

He doesn't seem particularly at ease with us, torn between being avuncular and jolly and protecting this considerable investment from smart-arsed snoopers and cynics. He talks evangelically about combining the 'commercial' and 'ideological' aspects of Christmas, but it's hard to keep a straight face when you can see behind him a line of oddly shaped women in red capes and tasselled hats emerging from a Portakabin. He catches my eye and turns.

'Ah, those are the elves coming on for the afternoon shift.'

The elves sit at desks, with red and white computers, dealing with the world's largest concentration of begging letters.

'Everyone receives a personal reply from Santa,' the Big Man tells me with fierce pride.

After Finland, most of Santa's mail comes from Japan – a hundred thousand letters last year. The Big Man spent six weeks last summer touring Japan dressed up as Santa.

As if to underline the Japanese connection we later see our couple from the Ivalo bus emerging purposefully from Santa's Grotto clutching a certificate.

A steady stream of state of the art tourist buses from Germany are pulling in off the Arctic Highway, and though it's high summer they too expect to see Santa. This has thrown the Big Man into a bit of a state, as he has agreed to give me a personal audience, whilst one of his colleagues looks after the tourists.

'It will not be good for them to see two Santas,' he mutters.

But eventually all is well, and for the first time in 41 years I get to sit on Santa's knee.

A short distance beyond the Village is the town of Rovaniemi (Finnish pronunciation accentuates the first syllable only: '*Ro*-vaniemi'). Flattened during the war, it was rebuilt by the famous Finnish architect Aalvar Aalto, who laid the roads out in the shape of a pair of reindeer horns.

'There are only 35,000 people here and they still get lost,' Kari remarks, unpatriotically.

More importantly for us, Rovaniemi marks the northern limit of the Finnish railway system, and at 7.20 in the evening, with the sun about to set for the first time since we left the North Pole, we pull out of the station on the overnight train to Helsinki, finally turning our backs on the Arctic.

DAY 22 · ROVANIEMI TO HELSINKI

 The railway line to Rovaniemi was built when Finland was a part of Tsarist Russia and the Soviet Union is still seen as a baleful presence, a lurking threat to the spectacular prosperity the Finns have experienced since their independence in 1917.

There are only five million people in Finland, and they enjoy the second highest standard of living in Europe. They also share a long border with a country that is cracking up, and one of their great fears is that Gorbachev's reforms will one day lead to a flood of Russian immigrants. I ask the daughter of a Finnish family I meet in the train's restaurant car what she knows of Russia.

She grimaces. 'I have heard there is very robbery there. One of my friends is robbery in money and clothes and a clock.'

Kari joins in enthusiastically. A friend of his had been robbed by a taxi driver in Estonia.

'Left him with no money, no luggage, no passport.'

I can't wait.

Our train pulls into Helsinki an hour early. It's a warm Sunday morning and after I've been filmed arriving we have the rest of the day off. Helsinki, with a population of half a million, is by no means a brash or daunting city, but it requires a conscious mental adjustment to be back where humans control the environment, rather than the other way round.

The station is a remarkable building, an example of what is known as the National Romantic Style, developed by Saarinen and others at the turn of the century to express, in architecture, a Finnish culture and tradition that was not dominated by either Sweden or Russia. It makes much of indigenous materials such as pink granite, brass, wood and copper, decorated with reliefs of trees and plants. Dark and mystical, redolent of mead halls and medieval castles, it contrasts strongly with early nineteenth-century Helsinki, down by the sea. This is light and graceful and neo-classical, a reflection of Leningrad, only 180 miles to the east.

I've found that the best places to aim for in a new city are stations, for the buzz and the newspapers, markets, for food and colour, botanical gardens, for peace and contemplation, and, whenever possible, harbours, for space and spectacle. The joy of Helsinki is that you can visit all of them in a couple of hours.

In the early evening I take my first run of the journey, around the Toolonlahti, a shallow lake close to the centre of the city. The temperatures are in the low 70s and it's hard work. At 11.15, as I turn in, the lights are on along the Mannerheimintie – the main road into the city from the north, where the sun will still be shining.

At a quarter to midnight the telephone rings. It's a particularly insistent Finn who wants to talk to me for his university newspaper. In vain I point out the time, the fact that I was asleep, and the work I have to do tomorrow.

'I am down here in the lobby,' he persists.

'Well it's not really a good time.'

'I am doing an article, please, on John Cleese and I think you know him . . .'

That does it.

'I am *in* bed. I have four months' travelling ahead of me, and I have *no* time to talk about John Cleese!'

Somewhat surprisingly, this seems to amuse my caller greatly, and only then do I recognize in the cackle of non-Finnish laughter, the unmistakable tones of a tall fellow Python.

'I just rang to see how you were getting on,' wheezes John cheerfully . . . and I remember how much he enjoyed doing Scandinavian accents.

DAY 23 · HELSINKI

Today I am to be initiated into the pleasures of the sauna, pronounced 'sow-na' in these parts. It is not a Finnish invention, for the Red Indians used hot stones to keep their tepees warm, and it spread to the West out of Asia. But the Finns have endorsed it with an almost religious zeal, and like any religion it has its orthodoxies and its heresies. One of the most kosher of Finnish saunas is in the grounds of a lakeside house called Hvittrask, a half-hour's drive from Helsinki. The house is remarkable in itself. Built 90 years ago by Saarinen, Gesellius and Lundgren – the architects responsible for Helsinki's idiosyncratic railway station – it embodied many of the most advanced ideas in decoration and design, such as *en suite* bathrooms, central heating and the first use of textiles as wallpaper. All these things that the middle classes eventually adopted were, at the time, deliberately unconventional and anti-bourgeois.

The sauna is traditional, with a wood fire rather than electricity and the emphasis on dark beams, tiles and log and granite walls. It's built, like a boathouse, where tall trees meet the lake, to which it is connected by a long wooden jetty.

My companions are a Finnish writer and ex-MP called Lasse, and Neil, an Englishman, who has produced comedy shows on Finnish television and hosted a controversial chat show here. But, as Lasse says, as we squeeze our fleshy white bodies onto the slatted wooden shelves of the sauna, 'no one knows who you are when you're naked.'

Well they certainly know none of us is Madonna. Lasse waxes lyrical, as Nigel tries to frame shots which will be acceptable to BBC Television.

'It's meditative, contemplative, reflective . . . not a place for angst or anxiety or argument . . . that's why you have settled so many disputes in the sauna in Finland – political ones, economic ones . . . whatever. Because who wants to argue when they are naked, you know . . .'

'What are those twigs for?' I ask, meditatively.

'They're birch twigs. They must be picked about midsummer when the leaves are soft . . .'

Lasse picks up the bundle and proceeds to whack himself about the face and upper body, before offering it to me.

I begin to apply them gently. Neil looks unimpressed.

'No, you've got to get the circulation going . . .'

He grabs the twigs and lays into me. Lasse looks on with approval.

'Try it on the face, very nice on the face . . . you get a nice sort of scent from it . . .'

The flagellation does produce a pleasantly aromatic tingling sensation and I feel it's only polite to offer to scourge someone else. Lasse accepts and I go to work.

'Say when . . .

This all seems very energetic and I'm still waiting for the contemplative and reflective bit when Neil suggests we go and jump in the lake.

The dip is very refreshing today, and apart from possibly frightening a group of schoolchildren swimming nearby, fairly harmless. In the winter they break a hole in the ice.

'You can only be there for half a minute . . . then you roll in the snow.'

Back in the intimacy of the sauna, we discuss Finland and Finnish attitudes. They're anxious to dispel the myth that Scandinavians talk about sex all the time, but Neil says that in the north of Finland the girls are very direct. At a dance or disco they will always make the first move. 'Even the old and ugly ones,' adds Lasse.

'You should have got off with someone by 11 o'clock.'

For some reason my mind went back to the elves toiling over Santa's correspondence and dreaming of the evening . . .

The Finns, it seems, are egalitarian, eschewing formality and anything that smacks of class. They have a sense of humour, but not much sense of irony. Humour is introspective and personal, there's no tradition of getting together in a theatre to laugh communally.

An example of all of this is perhaps their national AIDS campaign. The fact that they have such an extensive campaign when there is a comparatively low incidence of AIDS in the country is very Finnish. Fastidious about their health and efficient and far-sighted enough to attack the problem before it

			KE	TO	PE	LA	SU
Helsinki	10.30	10.30	10.00	—	10.30	10.30	10.30
Tallinna	14.00	14.00	14.00	—	14.00	14.00	14.00
Tallinna	18.30	18.30	—	18.30	18.30	18.30	18.30
Helsinki	22.30	22.30	—	22.30	22.30	22.30	22.30

Telakointi 15.01.—31.01.1991

becomes a problem. But it's all done very seriously. Neil tells me that public figures have gone on television to advocate the advantages of masturbation, under the slogan 'Give it a hand!'.

'These are country people,' says Lasse, 'this is not an urban society, not yet.'

DAY 24 · HELSINKI TO TALLINN

There is a swimming pool at the Hesperia Hotel in Helsinki and though it means getting up a little earlier, I feel I must take advantage of such luxuries, for today we enter the Soviet Union where things will be very different.

An hour and a half later I'm down at the dockside. The early sea mist has cleared and it looks set for another hot day. The harbour is busy with boats coming in from the surrounding islands – the Suomalinen. Some are bringing produce for the market; potatoes, carrots, onions, strawberries, cherries and plums; some are fishing boats bringing in crayfish, sea salmon, and Baltic herring, and some are ferries bringing in commuters. The ship that will be taking us to Estonia is the *Georg Ots*, a slim, trim Russian-registered vessel owned by the Baltic Shipping Company.

As we wait for clearance on our 30 pieces of film equipment, I get talking to one of the customs men. He repeats what I've heard elsewhere in Helsinki about the existence of a Russian Mafia which runs a drug and prostitute racket between penurious Estonia and prosperous Finland. It's hard to overestimate the contempt which Finns seem to have for all things Russian.

With a sonorous blast of the horn the *Georg Ots*, named after an Estonian opera singer, pulls away from Finnish soil punctually at 10.30. The copper domes and wide sloping green gables of the harbour-master's house recede into the distance as the ship picks her way along narrow channels between the jigsaw of little islands and sandbanks that lead to the Gulf of Finland, and, 50 miles away to the south, Estonia. Not a wide gulf geographically, but in many other ways, enormous.

Thinking myself somewhere exotic, I scan my fellow passengers for clues to their nationality. The first one is reading the *Daily Mail*, the next *Newsweek*. Leaning artfully against one of the bulkheads, face turned towards the sun, is a striking girl in dark glasses and a black and white cloche hat. She could be Audrey Hepburn in *Breakfast At Tiffanys*, if it wasn't for the lycra cycling shorts. I'm not surprised to learn that she is in the fashion business. She's German, and on her way to a festival in Riga, the capital of Latvia. It is, she explains, the one fashion festival held in the Soviet Union at which Russian designers are permitted to mix with their western counterparts.

The man with the *Daily Mail* is English. His father, an Estonian from the town of Tartu, left at the end of the war, to escape Stalin's ruthless purges of Estonian nationalists. In one night in 1944, he tells me, sixty thousand people from the Baltic states were rounded up and taken away.

'It may be that my grandfather was amongst the sixty thousand, or my relatives were amongst the sixty thousand . . . I'm not raising my expectations, but I do feel . . . it's an adventure out there . . .'

He looks out over the flat calm sea, and in a sense I know what he means. Three weeks in the empty untroubled wilderness of the Arctic and cossetted by the comfortable materialism of Scandinavia has done nothing to prepare me for what lies ahead in a land that has been on the receiving end of so much violence.

The *Georg Ots* has a shiny chrome and mirrored bar serving beers, vodka and coffee. American-made MTV pop videos run remorselessly on a screen. Everyone at the bar looks like a mechanic. Peter is a young Estonian who's done his two years compulsory service in the Soviet army, has a currency shop and a very smart briefcase which he bought in Singapore. He teaches me to say 'hello' in Estonian, and proffers other advice.

'Russian girls very good . . .'

'Do you have a Russian girlfriend?'

'Yes . . .' he glances around to where the crew are sitting, 'but not in front of camera, I have wife too.'

He won't elaborate on what is so good about Russian girls but tells me where to find them.

'The night bar of the Palace Hotel.'

Later I ask Clem where we're staying in Tallinn. It's the Palace Hotel.

I'm unapologetically excited by my first sight of Tallinn which appears to starboard from a low green coastline about 1 o'clock in the afternoon. I have never quite believed in the existence of Estonia. It always sounded more like a name out of fable than fact, this tiny country at the tip of a spur jutting out into the Baltic. Quite suddenly, since glasnost, the existence or non-existence of Estonia has become a crucial political issue, and as we approach I feel I am not only on the verge of satisfying a lifetime's curiosity, but of seeing some history in the making.

Rising around soft brown city walls are the spires, turrets and towers of a medieval city, but the docks present a dejected picture. In marked contrast to the bustling cosmopolitan harbour we left three hours ago, our only companions on the Tallinn waterfront are rusty-hulled colliers and cargo ships in need of a coat of paint. All bear the hammer and sickle on their funnels. The immigration forms are faint xeroxes, and as there are long queues to process them I go back to take a last picture of the *Georg Ots*. A car pulls up almost instantly and a soldier gets out and eyes me with contempt.

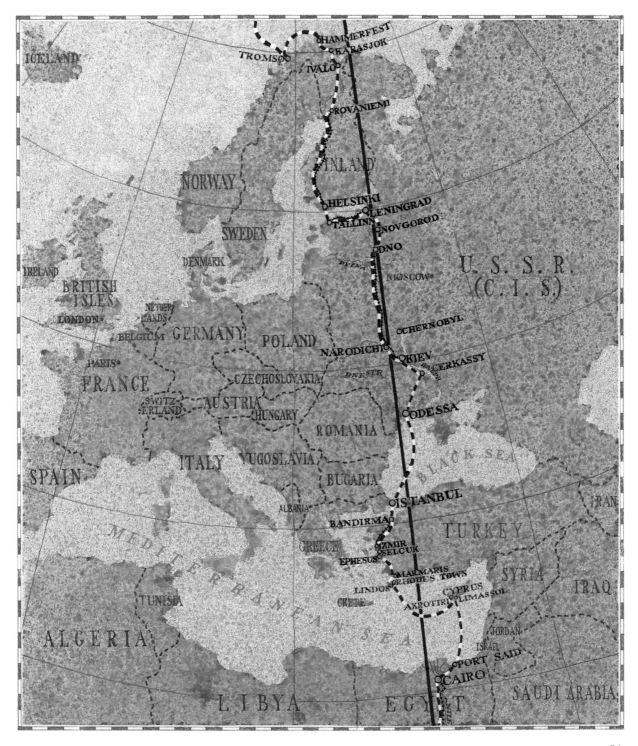

I have tried to learn some Russian but this is not how I wanted my first stab at the language to be.

'I am from London, making a television programme,' I blurt out.

I don't think he understands a word, for his expression doesn't change. He climbs back in his car and drives scornfully away.

The feeling of being watched persists later as I take my first stroll away from the hotel. Both soldiers and police are much in evidence. The soldiers are thin, scrawny conscripts, some with the dark, smooth-skinned features of far-off Asian republics. They look lost compared to the police, who, whilst being no less thin or scrawny, patrol the streets more purposefully, in groups of five or six, holding nightsticks. I feel myself being sized up on all sides. Some lads approach and offer to change my dollars into roubles at an absurdly generous rate. This is because the rouble is almost useless. When I tried to acquire some at the hotel earlier the cashier thought I was mad. She asked me how long I was staying in the Soviet Union.

'About three weeks,' I replied. She pointed to an English five-pound note.

'That will be enough.'

Next door to the hotel is a small cosy-looking bar, but as we push open the door a trio of bouncers appear, and for the second time today I feel I'm expected to explain myself.

'We just want a beer . . .'

Heads are shaken unhelpfully.

'Only vodka or champagne.' Meaning, of course, only hard currency. In the evening I visit a cabaret at one of the tourist hotels. The tourists are mainly Russian, some of them in family groups, despite the fact that the floor show features a full frontal strip-tease and a sinuous and erotic dance sequence spoilt only by the man dropping the woman at one point.

We end up in the Skybar Disco of the Palace Hotel. MTV videos pump out images of America, the lights circle and flash, but at least you can have a beer. And probably a Russian girl if you'd wanted.

DAY 25 · TALLINN TO LENINGRAD

POLE *to* **POLE** I eat a breakfast of good fresh bread, honey and coffee to the strains of Marianne Faithfull's 'This Little Bird', then walk out into the city. The newspapers are full of the news that in Moscow yesterday President Bush demanded a measure of independence for the Baltic states as the price of 'most favoured nation' trading status for the USSR.

On the way up to the Toompea Castle huge blocks of rock and concrete lie across the road, moved there only recently by the civic authority in response to the recent military repression in Lithuania. The present feels tense here and yet the past, in the shape of an extensive and beautifully preserved Old Town, seems serene and comforting. Not a modern or unharmonious building intrudes on long cobbled streets lined with merchants' houses and Guild halls. At the centre is Raekoja Square, a wide and handsome area bounded on one side by the imposing and elegant fourteenth-century Town Hall. A weather vane called Vana Toomas (Old Tom) has topped the building since 1530.

The unpretentious beauty of the old town bears out Colin Thubron's observation that there's nowhere like a modern socialist state for preserving the past it replaced so vociferously.

On a side road a passer-by offers Patti something in a bag for fifteen dollars. It turns out to be a gun. Patti shakes her head categorically, at which, unfazed, he drops the price to ten dollars.

Pick up a copy of the *Tallinn City Paper*. It's in English; well-produced, anti-Russian and easily available. It pronounces on politics – hoping that talks with Moscow may reduce the 180,000 Soviet troops stationed in the country but holding out little expectation, seafood – 'In this seaside city, the best fish . . . goes to Leningrad, Moscow . . . and not to Estonia' and national differences – 'Estonians complain that the Russians here are hot tempered, uneducated and haven't bothered to learn about the culture to which they've migrated. Russians . . . complain that Estonians are cold tempered, arrogant and dull'.

Back in Raekoja Square a group called the Johanson Brothers are entertaining a small crowd. Jakov Johanson maintains that: '. . . singing has been for the Estonians . . . the most effective way to use the language . . . to sing out loudly . . . that we are Estonians.'

He sees similarities with the Irish, whose songs they perform as well, and draws a parallel between the Russian occupation of Estonia and the British occupation of northern Ireland.

For our last meal in Tallinn we take the advice of the *City Paper* and eat in a restaurant irresistibly described as 'about the best you will find

anywhere in the Soviet Empire'. It's called The Maharajah and to be eating fine and delicate Indian curry in a fourteenth-century Estonian town house seals an intense, if confused, memory of this extraordinary city.

I would very gladly have lingered here a day or two more but we have another Pole to get to and having run due south from Arctic Norway to the southern shores of the Gulf of Finland it's time to turn eastward once again to pick up the 30 degree meridian, which will be our guideline down through Russia and Africa. To this end we assemble beneath a dominating bas-relief of Lenin on the wall of Tallinn station to make the eight-hour journey to the city to which he gave his name.

Every coach of the train bears the emblem of a wreath intertwined with banners on which is written, in the languages of the 15 republics, 'Proletariats of all Countries Unite!', and beneath this a crossed hammer and wrench. Bold design which makes British Rail's spectral swallow look pathetic. Prices, too, are competitive. My fare for the equivalent of a journey from London to Newcastle is eight roubles and forty kopecks – about thirty-five pence. The train is very hot and slow. Everyone seems helpful and friendly, none more so than the beleaguered proprietor of the buffet. He has two problems. One is having nothing to sell and the other is having to explain this to an Englishman who wants to try out his Russian conversation.

'Have you tea?'

'No . . .'

'Have you coffee?'

'No . . .'

'What do you have?'

His reply, being more elaborate than in previous exchanges, is quite incomprehensible, and I end up with a cherryade and a piece of cake.

We cross the Estonian–Russian border at Narva – from the smallest of the Soviet republics (27 thousand square miles) to the largest (11 *million* square miles). Within two hours we have reached Leningrad. A hot and sticky night as we hit our 30 degree meridian for the first time since the fishing grounds of the Barents Sea.

DAY 26 · LENINGRAD

The Okhintskya Hotel has only been open for two months. It's a tall, anonymous, modern block, about 20 minutes from the centre of the city and my room has, apart from a fine view of the River Neva, a fitted carpet, bidet, hot water and a massive throbbing Cheshinka 304 refrigerator, which I have to unplug in the night after dreaming of a tank coming through the wall.

There is a huge party of Italian tourists here which explodes into the lobby every now and then, but apart from them and us the place seems empty.

Our Russian hosts give us an introductory tour of the city. The roads are in terrible condition, holed and pitted, and the ubiquitous tramlines have often completely parted company with the road surface, sticking out of their sockets like ribs on a corpse.

We're taken in the evening to a gypsy restaurant. Our regular drivers have the day off and Volodya, one of our Russian fixers, is at the wheel. He always looks harassed, but tonight as the vehicle jerks erratically forward, he seems more than usually unhappy. Reaching for the indicator as he swerves to avoid a pothole he succeeds only in activating the windscreen wiper. Unfortunately there is no wiper in the fitting and there is a horrid screech as the metal claw scrapes blindly at the windscreen, which is already broken anyway. Almost everything to do with the vehicles is a headache for Volodya and his team. The chronic shortage of petrol means that to be sure of supplies our regular drivers have to fill up at three in the morning, and the chronic shortage of glass is why every other windscreen in the city is cracked. At the restaurant we have zakuski – an hors d'oeuvre comprising slices of tomato, cucumber, pickle, tinned ham, beef and pork on a bed of lettuce, hard boiled eggs in mayonnaise, fish paste and caviar. Vodka and wine are liberally supplied, and because the wine is so rough and beer seems impossible to come by most of us attend to the vodka. This leg of the journey is going to be quite a test of survival.

DAY 27 · LENINGRAD

Alexander 'Sasha' Godkov is my guide to Leningrad today. He is a professional Lenin impersonator and the very fact that he can walk the streets masquerading as the father of the Revolution without being removed to the nearest branch of the KGB shows how lukewarm traditional communism is becoming. He takes me to the Finland Station at which his factual predecessor turned up twice in 1917, once courtesy of the Germans, who encouraged the growth of communism to help win the war, and the next time disguised as a railway fireman. The locomotive he fired is preserved in a perspex case, which, considering it contains one of the icons of the Revolution, is remarkably grubby and uncared for. Outside the station a single withered rose lies at the base of the full-length bronze likeness of the great man.

From the melancholy of a past no one seems to want any more, to the liveliness of a tram ride down the Nevsky Prospekt. Our driver is a stout

blonde lady in a flowery print dress. Tickets are bought in carnets and then stamped in a knob and spring device mounted on the side of the tram into which you insert your ticket and give the knob a sharp bang. Some burly men on the seat opposite are watching me cope with this and smiling broadly. Sasha gets into conversation with them. They are from Armenia and having heard me speak English wish to shake my hand and tell me that English and Armenians worked closely together after the earthquake (of 1988) and how much that had been appreciated. More big smiles and handshakes and at the next stop they disappear. We reach Winter Palace Square, a massive and belittling open space surrounded by classical and Baroque façades that places Leningrad firmly as a European city. The Alexander Column in the centre of the square was designed by a Frenchman, Montferrant, even though it was to commemorate the victory over the French in 1812. The Tsar's specifications insisted it should be taller than the obelisk in the Place Vendôme and taller than Trajan's Column in Rome. It weighs 610 tons and is carved from one single piece of granite.

A few minutes walk away is the equestrian statue of Peter the Great. Set on a huge granite rock, garlanded Peter, his bronze horse rearing into the air, looks as if he is about to leap the Neva River. It is a powerful and stirring embodiment of controlled strength and so much loved by the people of Leningrad that there is nearly always a line of newlyweds waiting to be photographed beside it. This set me to thinking of Lenin's statue at the Finland Station and its solitary faded rose. It's clear that Peter, old despot that he was, retains a much stronger place in the affections of the inhabitants.

The city was built by him and may well go back to him. In a recent poll 52 per cent voted to change the city's name to St Petersburg.

We eat at a Georgian restaurant tonight. Set in an anonymous block in a side street it has a striking avant-garde interior, which I think is meant to recreate the centre of an Egyptian pyramid. It looks to be full of fashion models. Very tasty Georgian meatballs and a fresh bread called lavash. Fraser has ordered real French champagne for us to toast the third birthday of his son Jack. The only problem is that Volodya has to drive the van again. As we swerve and shudder our way home I ask Volodya where he spent his two-year national service.

'In tanks,' he shouts, and we end the day on a laugh.

DAY 28 · LENINGRAD

A rough night's sleep. Had to dig out the paracetamol for the first time on the journey so far. At breakfast found that two others in the crew had suffered as well. We reluctantly agree that the champagne must have been too good for us.

I take a launch from the front of the hotel and am swept upstream to the Monastery of Alexander Nevsky. Nevsky is a great Russian hero who defeated the Swedes by the River Neva in 1240. The monastery, the third biggest in Russia, was built as a tribute to him by Peter the Great in 1710. Today it's a very busy place, an indication that religion is alive and well despite 75 years of official atheism. Spastics and other disabled people are lined up inside the grounds. They are brought here to beg because families receive only a pittance from the State to look after them.

Inside the main church, beneath domes and columns decorated with epic, brightly coloured Biblical scenes, priests who seem to have been chosen for their likeness to the prophets are moving around, conducting services, swinging censers, and in one case receiving a line of penitents who approach, kiss the icons, wait for a few words of comfort, receive a blessing and move on. I cannot take my eyes off one encounter. A woman, young and headscarved, is talking urgently to the priest, but softly too, so he has to bend and listen intently. He asks her something, she pauses and looks ahead for a while, then nods slowly. It's an incongruous moment of intimacy in the middle of this crowded, bustling place. She wipes away tears and bows her head. The priest lays a cloth over her head and makes the sign of the cross. She kisses the icons, crosses herself and moves away. She has an expression of inconsolable sadness as she passes by me.

In the crypt they are preparing for the first public baptism of the day. Christenings were not approved of in the hard-line days and had to be conducted secretly, but now things have changed. There are two ceremonies a day and four on each Saturday and Sunday. I take my place among the families of the 30 or 40 babies who have been brought along. Everyone but me seems to be in their best clothes. The priest is an imposing, charismatic figure, though not above sneaking a small comb from beneath his robes and attending to his thick black hair every now and then.

Impervious to a constant barracking of coughs, gurgles and whines, he gives a long opening address, before making his way round the gathering anointing those present on the forehead, base of the neck and ears in the sign of a cross. As he approaches I notice men are rolling up their trouser legs. Nigel, tracking back at a crouch, whispers urgently,

'Better roll up your trousers. They're all doing it.'

I don't imagine the priest will notice me anyway, curled as I am into the curve of the vault. But I'm wrong. Not only does he notice me but brings the entire service to a halt as he looks at my knees with considerable suspicion.

'What is your belief?'

Church of England sounds rather insipid in the middle of all this, so I opt for the more general . . .

'I believe in God.'

His anointing brush remains poised in mid-air. He turns to his assistant. They confer. He looks back at me. The Russian congregation look on, quite baffled.

'I have been baptized!' I add, helpfully.

More consultation. The priest regards me sternly, but with faint alarm.

'Do you want to change your religion?' he asks.

Life is complicated enough at the moment without becoming a member of the Russian Orthodox church, so I politely decline.

'Now is the time . . .'

I'm desperately trying to become one with the wall.

'No . . . er . . . it's all right . . . thank you.'

The camera edges closer, and the priest breaks into a smile.

'I can act, if you like . . .'

He's already acting me off the screen so we don't pursue this offer. He moves on to the font. By this time the first baby is ready. Her clothes have been removed, and the chubby naked figure is lifted in the priest's massive hands, so high that for a moment the scene resembles one of those paintings of the Massacre of the Innocents. Then Tatiana (he has announced her name) is plunged down and through the water, not once but three times. The force of this triple immersion reduces Tatiana to stunned silence and before she knows what's hit her, she is passed on to the assistant priest who dabs oil on her eyes, nose, ears and chin and places a cross round her neck.

Soon the whole crypt is filled with the sound of wailing babies, and cooing parents. Later there is chanting, singing and a candlelight procession which is still going on when I leave.

In the grounds of the monastery is the Tikhvin Cemetery, which has a section reserved for the remains of 'Masters Of Art'. The quality is impressive. In a 10-minute stroll I visit Dostoeovsky, Rimsky-Korsakov, Mussorgsky, Borodin and Tchaikovsky. Tchaikovsky's memorial is particularly sad. The great man's bust, marooned in a bed of begonias and flanked by a gross pair of overacting angels, is like something on the top shelf of a junk shop.

Leningrad '91: Two faces of the Hermitage, two faces of food supply — publicly owned, privately owned.

Later in the afternoon a visit to two contrasting food sources. One is the private market, to which people can bring their home-grown produce to sell. It looks much like any big covered market, though the standard of hygiene is low, especially on the butchery counters where stallholders are constantly swatting flies away from pig's heads. But there is an air of bustle and good humour – one man is a brilliant mimic of bird noises, and whenever Fraser raises his microphone to do a wild track of market atmosphere, the place is suddenly full of exotic birdsong. According to Irena, our interpreter, the average Russian would not be able to afford to shop here. Even her parents, who are quite well off, could only come maybe two or three times a month, for a treat. A bag of seven pears costs me 15 roubles. The average wage in Leningrad is 70 roubles a week.

The alternative, the State food shop, is across the road. It is clean, well-lit, hygienic and almost entirely devoid of food. Assistants in starched white hats and overalls stand behind large mounds of margarine and unsold tins of pilchards. With desperate irony it's called Gastronomia. I try to buy a bottle of genuine Russian vodka here. The bottles look unusual and I check I'm asking for the right thing. Yes, it is vodka, but there is such a shortage of glass in the Soviet Union, that they're having to put vodka in bottles that once contained children's orange juice. As it turns out, I can't buy vodka anyway, as it's all strictly rationed and I don't have coupons. I ask for wine instead but there is no wine on the shelves as Gorbachev's anti-drinking reforms have resulted in enormous cuts in production. Apparently 60 per cent of the Georgian wine crop was deliberately destroyed.

DAY 29 · LENINGRAD

POLE *to* **POLE** A rare honour has been accorded me today, and I wish it hadn't. I am to be permitted to fire the noonday gun from the roof of the barracks of the Peter-Paul Fortress. This is a tradition stretching back 250 years to the days when the sound of the gun was the only way of giving the city a daily time check. It's still taken very seriously and today everything depends on my ability to fire a 152-millimetre Howitzer cannon, built in 1941 and with a range of 8 miles, at precisely 12 o'clock. For obvious reasons practice is out of the question, so an elderly gunnery officer prepares me by describing everything that could go wrong, ending up by offering me earplugs. As the moment grows closer crowds of Russian tourists begin to assemble. I have never felt more like a condemned man. The crew adjust their earplugs, the officer orders everyone, except me, to stand well away, and I'm left looking out, beyond the barrel of my Howitzer, towards the glinting towers and domes of this imposing city. My last thought is that there are over 5 million people out there and it'll have to be a hell of a loud bang, when down goes the officer's hand and before I know it, I've pulled the rope and ignited the cannon. There is a city shattering boom and I am turned instantly from a jelly to an artilleryman, and can't wait to do it again.

The afternoon is almost as bizarre. I spend it in the company of Edward Bersudsky, who works in a small studio making what he calls his Kinematic Sculptures. These are intricate machines, assembled in Heath Robinson style which turn, whir and animate in a one-hour long performance.

One is called 'The Great Idea' and features a wooden Karl Marx in a loin cloth, turning an old-fashioned handle to set in motion a manic scrapheap of cogs and pulleys, springs, levers and flywheels. Another construction, called, somewhat forbiddingly, 'An Autumn Walk During the Epoch of Perestroika' brings to life a suitcase from which appears a skeletal hand, a pair of automatically walking army boots on a red bentwood chair, an accordion which plays itself, a German helmet complete with lavatory chain and a rocket which springs erect and with a loud pop discharges a tiny ball, very slowly. Edward sees his machines as a symbol of order rather than disorder. He wants to show that we are all at the mercy of the circle of life and death and paradise and hell. Everything is moving but remaining in place. The Hindus call it *Sansara*. He calls it 'Soviet Absurd'.

We end up drinking tea in a friendly, cluttered kitchen behind the studio. The tablecloth is a Soviet map of the world, but Edward has never been out of the country. He's Jewish, one of the 'nationalities' for whom travel is difficult. He is about to go abroad for the first time, to show his work at the Glasgow Festival, but his passport will still make specific mention of the fact that he is Jewish. As a soft sunlight warms the room I feel for a moment as if I'm back at home on one of those Sunday afternoons when time slows down and people drop in and the talk goes round like one of Edward's machines. I find Edward and his helpers very sympathetic. Kindred souls I suppose. He laughs a lot. He says the Russians all do. They couldn't survive without laughter.

'And politics?' I ask. He makes a face.

'We're sick of politics! . . . We've had politics for the last 70 years!'

DAY 30 · LENINGRAD TO NOVGOROD

Wake up to my 13th-floor view of Leningrad for the last time. I shall miss the comforting presence of the broad river, with its embankment pathway along which I ran in the early evening, past boys fishing and men walking dogs and lovers arguing. One evening I discovered a dream house along there, number 40, Sverdlovskaya. It must have dated from the eighteenth century – the golden age of Tsarist Leningrad – for it had an elegant three-storey classical façade from which extended curving crescents, each one culminating in a perfectly proportioned pavilion. The front of the house was guarded by a heavy chain running through the mouths of 15 stone lions. It was deserted, a relic of another time, of Leningrad's aristocratic past, now almost lost among the factories, warehouses and apartment blocks of the proletarian present.

At the bus station in Leningrad is one of the small ads boards which offer details of neighbourhood services, things for sale and lost and found. The preoccupations of Leningraders look pretty similar to our own – 'Back massage, manual therapy', 'Rotweilers Club', though there was one which surprised me: 'Seal . . . intelligent, lovable, tender'. Required for Lasagne?

The bus is comfortable. There is even air-conditioning, though when I adjust it the ventilator falls apart in my hand, so I have to content myself with opening the window, which is what everyone else has done anyway. Pass a sign reading 'M20. Kiev 1120 kilometres'. Kiev is another city on the 30 degree meridian but on the way is Novgorod, 117 miles from Leningrad down the main road to Moscow. One of Novgorod's eternal claims to fame is that it is twinned with Watford and I have been charged with helping to cement the relationship by taking Novgorod a gift from Watford. (How do these twinnings work? Is there an agency? Maybe they advertised: 'Handsome walled town, icons, gilded onion domes, seeks English town/city with railway connections, pref. handy for Gatwick/Heathrow'.) Most of the traffic on the single-carriageway south consists of noisy, smoke-belching trucks, and the scenery consists of flat fields, interspersed with birch and poplar trees and occasional small settlements, some of which boast brightly painted wooden houses, surrounded by allotments and beds of sun flowers. We've been travelling south for over a month, and I'm tempted to think we must soon be in Mediterranean climes, but in fact we are still at the same latitude as the Shetland Islands.

The weather feels continental, hot and humid, still and muggy. Combined with the unevenness of the road and the miasma of truck exhaust fumes, it doesn't make for a good introduction to Novgorod. I'm just jotting in my notebook that everything, as far as the eye can see, is filthy, when a mirage appears in the distance. Rising between a screen of blackened roofs and smokestacks, are four shining domes, one gold, the others silver. It's my first sight of the historic heart of Novgorod, squeezed and surrounded by unrestricted industrial expansion, a jewel on a rubbish tip.

We are staying at the Party Committee Hotel, which looks like a 70s police station on an Essex housing estate. I have been allotted a suite, very grand and shining with freshly varnished wood. It comprises of a hallway, reception room complete with glass cabinet full of crockery, a small sitting-room with a television and a sideboard, a bedroom and a bathroom with two lavatories, but no soap and only 12 sheets of toilet paper, which I think might not be toilet paper at all, but a notepad. In the lobby of the hotel are bound copies of *Pravda* and *Isvestia* – the two party newspapers. Both are very thin – eight closely printed pages each. I'm told that *Pravda*'s readership has fallen from 10 million to 3 million in the five years of Perestroika.

A local photographer drives me and Basil out a little way from the city onto the flood plain of the River Volkhov. The flat countryside is dotted about with churches, and once again I'm struck by the paradox of an atheist state going to such lengths to keep them standing. I think perhaps the key lies in the other monuments amongst these low watery fields – war memorials. The impact of the war on this part of Russia was so savage that the restoration of the churches, like the memorials of tanks and aeroplanes, is an act of defiance and pride – to show that the soul and spirit of Mother Russia can never be defeated.

DAY 31 · NOVGOROD

POLE *to* POLE Woken by the sound of mowing machines. Not one or two, but a squadron of them, unleashed on the grass surrounding the hotel in a rare and impressive display of formation lawnmowing.

In the morning I make the acquaintance of a film-maker and vodka-maker by the name of Edward Ranenko. I find him at the Correspondent Film Centre, situated in a long, low, whitewashed building on a leafy avenue. He is tall and thin and stands as straight as a Guards officer. Long silver-grey hair is swept back from a high, domed forehead and he sports a moustache. A charismatic figure for whom people will clearly do anything. How else can I explain the fact that we all solemnly follow him to a muddy pond surrounded by housing blocks, a main road and a building site, to shoot a film about crayfish?

Edward is about to offer me a part in the proceedings, possibly as second crayfish, when word comes that I must return at once to the Party Committee Hotel and vacate my room. A VIP is arriving from Moscow. This must explain the onslaught of the lawnmowers. It's no use protesting. The receptionist is firm but apologetic. The Deputy Prime Minister of the Soviet Union needs my room.

'The Deputy Prime Minister of *Russia*?' I ask.

'No.' She spreads her arms wide. 'Of the whole Soviet Union.'

As I go through the hotel every shiny floor is being made even more treacherous by an army of cleaners, and there is an elderly, bald and very sweaty plumber in my bathroom trying to fix the heated towelrail. He finishes his work and shuffles off. I complete my packing and take a last look at my bed, soon to be occupied by the second most powerful man in the Soviet Union. Toy with leaving him a note – 'Keep up the good work . . . we know everyone in Russia hates Gorbachev but we think he's doing a good job' . . . that sort of thing – but, as I've discovered, the notepad is actually toilet paper. I'm about to close the door when I become aware of a widening pool of liquid creeping out from the bathroom. A jet of water is gushing merrily from the end of the heated towelrail.

Edward Ranenko has offered me traditional Russian hospitality at the Correspondents Club tonight. He wants to treat me to crayfish and samogon – homemade vodka that he brews up in his garage.

He assures me: 'Mine is only the best. With samogon you have no headache in the morning.'

Dinner is laid out on the most remarkable table I've ever seen. It's 10 foot long, carved in an irregular outline, varnished and stained the colour of raw meat. The surface is engraved and from the centre of the table rears a horse's head with a brass harness of bells attached. It is, Edward tells me, the work of Vladimir Grebenikov, a father of five and a great and unappreciated genius. His fantastical designs are evident in the rest of the decoration – intricately worked chairs and elaborate lampshades the size of Roman breastplates. The whole effect is as if someone had gone berserk with a Black and Decker.

So begins the Night of a Thousand Toasts. Edward has assembled a party of family and good friends, none of whom speaks much English. There is Valery, quiet and uncomfortable, but a great crane operator, Igor the cook, jolly and companionable, with a son in the army, Edward's son Michael, whose names, in the Russian way of using a patronym, come out the same as mine – Michael Edvardovitch, and Sasha, a journalist from Moscow radio. Edward's illegal vodka is served with slivers of garlic in it from a litre Coca-Cola bottle. To get the best effect he adds another refinement – two fresh-picked cherries to be placed in the mouth before each glass.

The toasts start early and follow rapidly. Almost anything will do . . . 'To the guests!', 'To Michael!', 'To the crayfish' . . .

After each toast the glass must be drained. Pretty soon I can hardly stand up and am laughing insanely at everything, including a toast to the Romanov dynasty, rightful rulers of Russia, which is not a joke at all but taken very seriously by Edward. By the end of the meal I have put away at least a bottle of vodka, and sung 'The Lumberjack Song' from Monty Python to a rapturous reception. Mindful of the fact that I have to do my stuff as an ambassador for Watford in the morning, and that my hosts are beginning to sing long, maudlin Russian songs, I make my farewells. Never was there such a kissing and a hugging and an embracing. It was as if the world had ceased to exist outside the Correspondents Club. All the warmth and the

Ranenko directs the crayfish. Ranenko, and friends,
eat the crayfish.

Days 31 and 32: USSR

sadness and the madness of the Russians, poured out in a waterfall of emotion as we clung to each other.

I just about remember ending the evening sitting on a seat outside the Party Committee Hotel, impervious to the clouds of mosquitoes, enjoying the hot, humid night, and waiting for the Deputy Prime Minister of the Soviet Union to arrive. The hotel staff were still in a high state of excitement and at one point the receptionist rushed out into the night holding a cardboard box at arm's length.

'What is this?' she cried. 'I think it is a bomb!'

Everyone recoiled except those of us who knew exactly what it was – Basil's box of exotic sauces for improving local cuisine. To be known from now on as 'The Bomb'.

DAY 32 · NOVGOROD TO DNO

POLE to POLE

Edward Ranenko was right about one thing, considering the prodigious amount of samogon I consumed I have a remarkably clear head. But my stomach is not happy and I've been bitten to pieces by vodka-loving mosquitoes. Reduced to a room the size of a samovar I suffer further indignity when the basin I lean heavily on in the bathroom proves not to be attached to any other part of the bathroom. It turns a half somersault into my arms which gives me such a shock that I quite forget what I wanted it for. After yesterday's jollity and exuberance, this morning is a let down. Even the Deputy Foreign Minister has come and gone by the time I get up.

With its history, its handsome buildings and 200 small churches one might expect Novgorod to be rather proud of itself. But there seems to be not even a postcard in sight. I'm directed to the souvenir shop which bears a hopeful sign 'Open, 9 till 6'. The door's locked and barred though it's 10.15 in the morning. I give up and prepare myself for the twinning ceremony. This involves taking a couple of Arret capsules to make sure my bowels behave, and giving a little thought to the virtues of civic togetherness.

It appears that Novgorod has not been altogether faithful to Watford, for when I go to inspect the silver birch tree planted on 9 September 1983 to symbolize the accord between the two great cities, I find the place positively littered with tokens of friendship. There are trees from Nanterre and Bielefeld, Uusikau Punki in Finland and Rochester in New York.

The ceremony is to be held, outdoors, in the most prominent part of old Novgorod, with the domes of Saint Sofia rising behind. A folk group has turned out and a bulky but impressive sound system has been erected and tested. I am wearing a jacket and tie, for the first time on the journey, and clutching the Watford glass decanter inscribed 'Presented to the People of Novgorod, August 1991'. The only element missing is the Mayor of Novgorod. A couple of lads with hands in their pockets observe our discomfiture with polite interest. It turns out that one of these lads *is* the Mayor of Novgorod.

He delivers a shirt-sleeved speech in fluent English, extols the benefits of free enterprise in Novgorod and hands over a beautiful but delicate ceramic dish, which will be lucky to reach Kiev in one piece let alone Watford. He then goes back to running his city, leaving me with the athletic folk group, who are anxious to involve me in a Russian Kissing Dance. This is a particularly frenetic activity for which a jacket and tie and a set of loose bowels are not helpful.

If only I had been able to spend more time with the Mayor, and less in the dances, I could have asked him why, in a city of 250,000 people, there are only five restaurants. And why the one we end up in is described as a restaurant at all. It's part of the Palace of Culture, a huge, desolate, shabby, modern building in the suburbs of Novgorod, which must once have been the face of a golden proletarian future, and is now, literally, rotting. In the middle of its drab and dusty halls is a canteen serving the worst pizzas I've ever eaten. This is only a minor cloud over a grim day. Earlier this afternoon one of our drivers collapsed in great pain and is now in hospital with a perforated ulcer.

It's a subdued team that sets off from the Palace of Culture to drive 60 miles south-west to pick up the Leningrad–Kiev express at the town of Dno. Dno, in Russian, means literally the bottom, the pits. Three hours later we are completely lost. Total darkness and the lack of anything resembling

a road sign have completely floored our drivers, who are all Muscovite, and know nothing of these marshy flatlands.

Eventually, negotiating country roads by a process of elimination, we bump into and over what miraculously turns out to be a railway track.

DAY 33 · DNO TO KIEV

It's 1 o'clock in the morning at Dno station. The main lines from Tallinn to Moscow and Leningrad to Kiev cross here, and it has enjoyed its moment of history, too. On this station, in April 1917, Nicholas II was persuaded by his generals to abdicate, ending 450 years of Tsarist rule.

I know it's not fair to judge somewhere after a one-hour wait for a train in the middle of the night, but it does seem a place of desperation. A group of teenagers emerge from beneath a goods train and running across the line jump up onto the platform. They are wild-eyed and grubby and very drunk. One boy looks heavily beaten around the face and there is mud and blood in equal parts on his clothes. They push close to the little circle of light where

71

we are set up to film the train, demanding we give them beer. We're used to people wanting to join in the filming but this time there is an ugly air of aggression and potential violence. There is no help from the railway staff and the other travellers are completely uninterested. We're all relieved when the mournful boom of a diesel horn heralds the approach of the Kiev express. All its compartments are dark except for a silver light in the buffet car where a few staff are watching a soft porn video. Console myself with the thought that though Dno may be the pits, it is the start of a 620-mile run, due south, in less than 24 hours. Compared to our recent progress, this constitutes a sprint.

To bed at two, wake at six and stumble to the uncongenial toilet and washroom which serves the entire coach. There is a wooden frame for a washbasin in my compartment but the basin has gone, as have most of the light fittings.

At breakfast time we are passing Orsa, 100 kilometres west of Smolensk. We are now in Belorussia, our third Soviet republic, after Estonia and Russia. From here on down to Odessa and the Black Sea, we shall be following the Dnieper, Europe's third longest river, and a significant part of one of the great trade routes of history, linking Russia and Scandinavia with Asia and the Mediterranean. There is a real sense of putting the north behind us and heading toward the centre of things.

I walk along the train. Windows are lowered as the temperature rises. The open mixed-sleeper coaches are crowded, but oddly peaceful and intimate. Everyone makes the most of their own space, people sprawl asleep, unembarrassed by public exposure. I squeeze past bare feet, stockinged feet, recumbent grandmothers, chess-playing old men, children clustered at the window. The click of wheel on rail is the loudest sound, and even that is lulling and hypnotic.

At the town of Zlobin, some 200 miles from Kiev, we cross to the left bank of the Dnieper, and into the Ukraine. I'm sitting with a Ukrainian writer and film-maker, Vadim Castelli, and we drink a toast to his country in pomegranate juice. He is vehemently proud of his homeland.

'Ukraine is potentially such a rich land . . . we produce about one-third of all industrial output of the USSR, we produce more than one-third of all agriculture of the USSR. About 80 to 85 per cent of all these riches just go . . . to this bottomless pit which is the Soviet economy . . .'

I ask Vadim if he thinks there will ever be an independent Ukraine.

'It's not going to be very fast. We are still conservative . . . we've seen what's happening in the Baltics, we've seen what's happening in Lithuania – we wouldn't want this . . . but the process of secession is inevitable . . . I hear people on the streets of Kiev . . . speaking Ukrainian . . . , the culture which many people thought is gone for ever. If one feels Ukrainian, if one feels it's one's roots, this is a very exciting period to live through.' It's moving to hear feelings like this expressed with such eloquence, the more so when I hear Vadim's personal experience at the hand of Soviet institutions. His father, a writer and film director, was arrested by the KGB in 1977, after works of his, critical of the regime, were published in the West. A healthy 49-year-old, he was sent to a KGB prison in Kiev, from which he emerged six months later, paralysed and confused. He was taken to hospital but died six months afterwards. Two months later, his father's prison diaries appeared in the West. The KGB were furious and yet could find no way in which these writings had leaked out of his high security confinement. For 12 years Vadim was subject to harassment, until the extraordinary effects of glasnost enabled him to publish both his father's original work and the diaries in the Ukraine. But all is not over for him. The authorities still have his father's papers, and as Vadim warns again,

'The KGB is still very strong, the military are very strong . . . we have to be very cautious . . .'

Somewhere between Gomel and Cernikov our steady southward progress comes to a halt. We go to see the train 'chief'. In his cabin there are two pictures, one a scantily-clad dancer with high-sided boots and tasselled nipples, the other a Madonna and child. He says there is a broken rail ahead and we will be held up for two and a half hours.

The passengers accept this news quite philosophically and most of them leave the train, some crossing the rails to a house where ducks, goats and scrawny chickens run round a well in the garden. From this well, and for no apparent payment, the locals are drawing buckets of water to fill a collection of jugs, tins and plastic bottles produced by the passengers. Other passengers have slipped on bathing costumes and made off, through the woods, to a large flooded gravel pit. This turns into an impromptu holiday beach. Some men build a diving board from tree trunks, others hoist each other onto their shoulders. There's terrific crashing and splashing and laughter. Others, less extrovert, watch from the edge of the forest, or walk through the bushes picking blueberries and redcurrants. The wind half-heartedly rustles a tall willow, but can do little more than waft around the heavy heat of the afternoon.

After a swim I return to the train, to find our coach supervisor and two colleagues tucking into a smoked fish and vegetable stew which she has cooked up on a small primus. She smiles as I look in, and offers me some. The effects of Ranenko's vodka and crayfish orgy are still upon me and I mime a stomach ache. Much laughter.

At half-past five the engine's whistle reverberates through the trees, and the bathers and sunbathers and lovers and loners and berry pickers and water gatherers make their way slowly back to the train, and I feel quite a pang of

The train to Kiev: With Vadim (nearest window) and friend in the restaurant car, two-hour delay — Russian style.

regret as we jerk into motion. I search the map and locate this spot in case I should not believe all this ever happened. As I do so, I notice, less than 100 miles to the south-west, the name of the small, almost insignificant town of Chernobyl.

At 9.45 in the evening we are at Nezin, two hours late already and still no sign of Kiev. Even with the windows and doors open there is no relief from the clammy heat. The train chief has pulled off his shirt altogether and his huge white gut hangs out of the window. As happens on train journeys that have gone on long beyond their appointed time, no one seems to care anymore. The layered dirt and dust gradually attaches itself to the passengers who only a few hours ago looked scrubbed and glowing. Try to read. Vadim and Roger are deep in discussion as to whether or not Lenin died of syphilis.

At a quarter to midnight we pull into Kiev, capital of the Ukraine, third largest city of the Soviet Union. The station is packed solid. I've seen nothing like it since India. Our admirable fixers find trolleys and somehow we're out of this madhouse within an hour and driven to a tall new hotel overlooking Dynamo Kiev's football ground. No porters to be seen but the room is fine. Until I draw the curtains, when first one then the other slides slowly up to the end of the rail and off onto the floor.

DAY 34 · KIEV

 I celebrate the end of my 24-hour, post-crayfish fast with a slap-up breakfast at the Warsaw Hotel. This consists of a thin sliver of cheese, some equally thin slivers of bread, a jam smear and a cup of coffee.

Soviet restaurants exist for one purpose, and that is to keep the customer out, and if by any chance he or she should get in to make life so uncomfortable that they wish they hadn't. Even to get as far as the sliver of cheese involves a considerable amount of bureaucratic negotiation. A card, which can only be issued at reception, must be produced and exchanged for a voucher, which is thoroughly scrutinized by the restaurant gauleiter, who will then turn you over to the waitresses who will ignore you.

It's all very depressing and is, I suppose, just the Soviet system in microcosm – unwieldy, paranoid and impersonal.

This morning I witness evidence of encouraging change, when I accompany Vadim to see the Deputy Procurator of the Ukraine, who has been examining the case for returning Vadim's father's papers, held by the KGB. For whatever reason, this senior Soviet law officer is welcoming and affable, even happy for the meeting to be filmed. Short, square-shouldered, with a wide, strong face and a well-cut suit he personifies Gorbachev Man, assiduous in attention to the smallest public relations details.

He reassures Vadim that the rehabilitation committee set up by Gorbachev last year to investigate the cases of political prisoners in the USSR had cleared 1200 people in less than five months, and that he himself will personally try to expedite matters in the case of Vadim's father. Then he offered us all green tea from Uzbekhistan complete with a special herb which, he tells us proudly, he has grown himself. It was altogether a smooth performance, but Vadim, who has grown very cynical about Soviet justice, felt that there was substance there as well.

We take a quick tour of Kiev, which looks a green and handsome city with broad boulevards and trees everywhere. It's hard to imagine that, in my lifetime, these green and pleasant hills were the scene of unspeakable suffering. During the time the Nazis occupied Kiev – from October 1941 to October 1943 – 400,000 people were killed, either in the city or in extermination camps, 300,000 were deported to forced labour camps in Germany, and 80 per cent of all residential houses were destroyed. The reconstruction of the city, especially the fine old buildings, like the Monastery of the Caves, must be one of the more tangible achievements of the Soviet regime. There has been a price to pay, such as the erection of an enormous stainless steel statue of a female warrior, 320 feet high, dominating the heights above the Dnieper. Huge, gross and unavoidable, it dates from the 70s and is known locally as 'Brezhnev's Mother'.

Kiev has been very close to modern tragedy as well. If the prevailing wind had not been blowing from the south on 26 April 1986 – the day the reactor blew up at Chernobyl – Kiev, only 55 miles away, would have been a dead city. No one knows how serious the effects might still be. The wind started blowing towards Kiev five days after the explosion, but the reactor wasn't sealed for a month. Looking down from the old city walls I can see people splashing about in the Dnieper. I ask Vadim if it's safe. He tells me a friend of his, a nuclear physicist, told him that it was fine to swim as long as he didn't touch the bottom, for radioactive material always sinks. But, he shrugs, on a day as hot as today there will always be people who will take risks.

Back at the hotel, Volodya has defused a potentially embarrassing situation. Two months ago a local girl was made pregnant by an Englishman staying in this hotel, whose name was Michael. Since then her mother has scoured the guest lists for an Englishman called Michael, and this morning she turned up trumps. With her wronged and freshly impregnated daughter in tow she spent all day camped in the lobby, waiting for Michael Palin to return. I'm just relieved not to have been first through that door.

DAY 35 · KIEV TO NARODICHI TO KIEV

Today we are going close to Chernobyl to visit towns and villages that have been, or are about to be, evacuated as a result of the disaster. We shall not be entering the 30-mile exclusion zone but will be in contaminated areas and Volodya, Irena and the rest of our Russian team will not be coming with us. Mirabel too has decided not to risk it. Roger has been in contact with the National Radiological Protection Board at Harwell, whose advice offered mixed comfort. They said radiation levels would be the same, if not less, than at the Poles, with their concentration of magnetic forces. However, the knowledge that there is still confusion and debate over the effects of the disaster, and the advice from scientists that we wear shoes and clothing we could throw away afterwards adds a frisson of danger to the journey, and there is some nervous joking over the slivers of cheese at breakfast.

We head north and west from Kiev, making for the town of Narodichi. It's 42 miles due west of Chernobyl, two of whose reactors, Vadim reminds us, are still operational. The Ukrainian Parliament has voted unanimously to close them down. The Soviet government has refused. The Ukrainians claim 8000 died as a result of the accident. The official Soviet figure is 32.

We are passing through woodlands of pine and oak scrub interspersed with harvested fields and cherry and almond orchards. An army convoy of

40 trucks passes, heading south. After a while the woodland gives way to a wide and fertile agricultural plain. The first indication that this abundance is tainted comes as quite a shock. It's a sign, set in brambles and long grass, which reads, 'Warning: It is forbidden for cattle to graze, and to gather mushrooms, strawberries and medicinal herbs'.

We stop here and put on our yellow TLD badges, which register radiation levels, and which will be sent back to Harwell for analysis after our three-hour visit. Armed with these and a radiation detector, we enter Narodichi where people have lived with radiation for over five years. It's a neat, proud little town with a chestnut-lined main street and a silver-painted Lenin in front of the party headquarters. In a year's time there will be no one here.

In the municipal gardens the grass is uncut but a fountain still plays. There are several memorials. One is a scorched tree with a cross on it – local people think that the forest protected them from the worst of the blast. Beside the tree are three large boulders, one of which commemorates four villages and 548 people evacuated in 1986, another 15 villages and 3264 people evacuated in 1990. Twenty-two more villages and a further 11,000 people will be going in 1991. An inscription reads: 'In memory of the villages and human destinies of the Narodichi region burnt down by radiation.'

One of the most polluted areas is the children's playground, with 13 to 17 times normal gamma radiation levels. The red metal chairs hang down from the roundabout and blue steel boats swing gently in the breeze, but no one is allowed to play here anymore.

Michael, the local schoolmaster, is short and podgy and his face is an unhealthy grey. There were 10,000 children in the region, he tells me, now there are 3000. Two of his pupils pass by on bicycles and he grabs them and introduces us. The boys, just back from a Pioneer camp in Poland, look bored, and reply in monosyllables, which Michael translates thus: 'The children send fraternal greetings to children throughout the United Kingdom'. He smiles proudly and a little desperately. I ask if the children's work has been affected by their proximity to Chernobyl. He sighs and nods.

'There is not a single healthy child here.'

As we drive out of Narodichi, Michael talks proudly of the history of his town, interspersing this with casually chilling present-day observations.

'This is the bridge over the Oush river. It is area of highest pollution.'

We come to the village of Nozdrishche, which was evacuated last year. There are no ruins, there is no devastation or destruction. Wooden cottages with painted window-frames stand in their orderly rows. Flowers are in bloom and grasshoppers dart around in lush overgrown gardens. It is a hot, soft, gentle summer's day. Yet scientists who have visited the area say it could be 700 years before this place comes back to life. It is hard to know what

to believe, for whatever curse lies over these villages is the more frightening for being invisible. It is how one has heard the countryside would be after a nuclear war – benign, smiling, deadly.

A year's exposure to the weather has not yet dissipated a faint smell of disinfectant in a small, deserted maternity hospital. A poster on the wall depicts the American space shuttle spinning round the earth, with the single word 'Nyet!' beneath. There is a book on breastfeeding, its leaves nibbled by mice, an examination chair, medical records still in files, and a portrait of Lenin which has fallen out of its frame and lies in a corner beneath a scattering of glass slides and syringes. Conscious of the limited time we have been advised to spend here we move on through the village. I catch sight of two figures down a lane to one side of the main street. One is a very old lady, whose name is Heema, and the other her nephew. Heema is 90 years old and has refused to be moved from the village. She says she has been moved five times since the disaster and now she is too old and ill. Her one wish is to die in the house in which she was born, but that is now cordoned off with barbed wire, so she will remain here with her daughter. They are the only inhabitants of Nozdrishche.

Further along the road, at the village of Novoye Sharno, the radiation detector bleeps for the first time.

'Pay attention, please,' says Michael, 'the radiation is very high here.'

This is one of the villages evacuated in 1986, immediately after the explosion and fire, and the village shop is now almost submerged in the undergrowth. Inside it is a mess of broken shelves, abandoned goods, smashed bottles.

'There was a panic here,' Vadim explains, unnecessarily.

We drive back through Narodichi, where, as in Novoye Sharno and Nozdrishche and over 40 villages in this region alone, the grass will soon grow around doors that will never be opened again, and anyone who comes here will be informed of the dangers and the risks which those who lived here were not told about until it was too late.

Back in Kiev, two and a half hours later, I'm struck once again by the spruceness of the city compared to Leningrad or Novgorod. A Russian, writing in the *Insight Guide*, relates even this to Chernobyl: 'The terrible effects of the tragedy made many people, in Kiev and other towns, take another look at themselves. Kiev is cleaner, and not merely because the streets are watered twice a day now; once the people were shown the frailty of human existence, they changed.'

We end up the day in a brick-vaulted cellar in the Andreevsky Spusk, a Montmartre-like street full of cafés and shops and predominantly student meeting places. The food is the best we've had in the Soviet Union – Armenian-Georgian cooking – kebabs, rabbit stew, aubergine and onion salad. An excellent jazz trio of bass, fiddle and piano plays local music and well-served-up classics like 'Take the A-Train'. Vodka flows freely. It is one of the best evenings, and in a sense, the only way of dealing with what we have seen today.

DAY 36 · KIEV TO CERKASSY

Alarm wakes me at six. It's a Sunday, but no day of rest as we continue southwards. We are travelling as far as Cerkassy by river, on the *Katun*, a 215-foot barge with a canary-coloured hull, carrying a mixed cargo of bottles, fabrics, sports equipment, clothes, children's push-chairs and electrical appliances down the Dnieper to the port of Cherson on the Black Sea.

The *Katun* is a barge of character. She's 40 years old next year, and her interior features wood rather than plastic or the ubiquitous formica. Two small cabins below the bridge have been set aside for our use. One has a writing desk and chair, an old oak wardrobe and an enamel washbasin, with an alcove containing what looks like the world's most comfortable bed. Sitting at the desk, looking through a porthole, I imagine I could be Joseph Conrad, though the football team photo above my head, featuring the chunky lads of Metalworkers Zaporozje doesn't quite fit the romantic illusion.

On the bridge there is a big and handsome ship's wheel and a book of river charts painted in water-colours. So much of the image of the Soviet Union is of vast institutional spaces and faceless buildings that it comes as a constant surprise to find warm, intimate, friendly corners of life like the *Katun*. We progress at an unhurried 10 knots beneath the bridges of Kiev leaving behind the remarkable prospect of Baroque church towers, white-washed walls, malachite-green roofs, and spires crowned always with gold. Roger is leaning over the side, examining the water.

'Have you ever been to a sewage treatment plant?', he asks me after close study of the Dnieper. 'Well this is what it looks like before it goes in.'

It's a pleasantly lazy day, which I think is what we all need. Basil sleeps, Irena sits at the desk with a copy of Longman's *Dictionary Of Common Errors*. Her English is fluent but she's desperately keen to polish up her Cockney rhyming slang.

We pass through a network of small islands and beaches busy with holidaymakers. Hydrofoils, scuttling along the surface like great white cockroaches, drone past at frequent intervals. Barges pass, mostly carrying coal. The captain says that the Dnieper is navigable as far north as Mogilov, about 300 miles from Moscow. Since the Chernobyl catastrophe (as he describes it) he doesn't go north of Kiev. There's nothing to bring down any more.

The mighty Dneiper: Foolhardy bathers and 'Brezhnev's Mother', south on the Katun.

He's a slim, weatherbeaten, good-looking man but roundly refuses to be interviewed. 'I'm not an actor,' he says. Even filming on the bridge causes some consternation. There is a flurry of activity as the first mate hides something the captain doesn't want us to see. It turns out to be his brown jacket which he says is 'very old'. Later I notice that they only have one pair of sunglasses between them.

The Dnieper has been dammed at a place called Kanev where a lake two miles wide is squeezed into one lock, with a 14-metre drop. The smell inside the dank and slimy walls of the lock is appalling, and as it takes a good 15 minutes to fill up, there's very little escape from the odour of decay and dead fish.

All this is made up for by a Sunday lunch of stew and mashed potato, a lazy afternoon reading and a drop of Scotch as we sit on the top of the hold taking in a glorious sunset that dazzles and fades over a landscape of low, wooded sandbanks. I realize that what I missed in the Arctic was not so much darkness as the sunrises and sunsets that go with it.

At eleven at night we reach Cerkassy, threading our way toward a container-stacked dockside with the help of a sharp, stabbing searchlight.

Our drivers have followed us down from Novgorod, and the ill-luck which has already put one of them in hospital has persisted. One of the vehicles, a Volga limo, has been written off in an accident, and the other, the 'Latvia' minibus, survived two blow-outs, one at full speed.

DAY 37 · CERKASSY TO ODESSA

Breakfast at the Hotel Dnieper, Cerkassy offers some odd fare. There's very sweet yoghurt, served in a glass, cottage cheese with sugar, and a choice of either dry hard white bread or dry hard brown bread with slices of sausage. There is no coffee, but tea from the samovar.

As I'm upstairs packing, for what I estimate to be the 17th time on the journey so far, I look down at my bed and experience a most unusual feeling of foreboding. I'm not normally given to precognition but something warns me against proceeding to Odessa by road. Two out of three vehicles are damaged, one beyond repair, and I've experienced enough of the haphazard inefficiency of Soviet life, to make me fear for the safety of the third.

Our problems in the end aren't mechanical, as much as navigational. Somewhere between Cerkassy and Uman we get horribly lost on unmarked maps and unsigned roads, finding ourselves stranded in sprawling landscapes of weed-ridden wheat fields. Eventually we find ourselves on the Kiev–Odessa main road, which is narrow and fortunately not busy. We cross the fast-flowing River Bug, and 12 miles north of Odessa, pass the first vineyards I've seen in the Soviet Union. The people down here are darker, almost Turkish in looks, and the blonde hair of the north gives way to the lustrous jet black of the south.

By six, after a drive of 300 miles, we reach Odessa safely. From the top of the Potemkin Steps, a few hundred yards from the hotel, I give thanks beside the Black Sea.

DAY 38 · ODESSA

In the middle of the night I'm woken by the sound of voices from the street below my window. A man and a woman are talking. The woman's voice is deep, rich and smooth. The talk turns into an argument. I lie for a while contemplating, rather enviously, the exotic, Mediterranean feel of Odessan street life, when the argument turns into a violent shouting match. Suddenly the woman screams repeatedly and with such primal intensity that I'm up and rushing to the window. There is a sound of car doors slamming, engine revving, tyres squealing but by the time I've pushed the curtains back nothing there but the disturbing echo of her cries.

We're staying at the Londonskya Hotel, situated on a tree-lined esplanade overlooking the port. It has a heavy neo-classical façade, was built in 1910 and had its name changed to the Odessa Hotel in 1948, as part of a policy called 'anti-cosmopolitanisation'. Thanks to glasnost, it has, from last week, returned to being the Londoner. The lobby is a reasonably accurate representation of a London club, dark and rather grand with columns, stained glass windows and a wide and self-important marble staircase.

Equally decorative, but much more seedy, is the Kuyalnik Sanatorium, one of the most famous institutions in Odessa, to which people from all over the Soviet Union repair for mud treatment. The mud is drawn from a nearby lagoon which was once open sea, and which retains mineral deposits believed to be good for arthritic and respiratory complaints, as well as for the nervous system, slipped discs, thromboses and kidney trouble. Built in 1892 as a series of rococco pavilions, it has never quite recovered from being submerged in 1941, when a nearby dam was blown to try and halt the advance of the German armies. It stayed underwater until 1948.

After the rigours of our journey from the North I'm ready to try anything with soothing properties and so find myself following the holiday-makers up the steps of the sanatorium. Ahead of me are three women, dressed for the sun and chewing corn on the cob. Once inside the building I am led along corridors past waiting patients and through small atria whose damp and grubby walls are decorated with peeling stucco. A sulphurous, bad egg smell becomes more intense the closer I get to the treatment room, and I am beginning to regret the whole thing.

The beds, or treatment tables, are laid out in two rows on either side of a tiled sluiced floor. There is no privacy at all and gentlemen in various intimate stages of treatment are on full view. One man is heaving his blackened and naked body off the bed like someone escaping from a swamp. Another is being administered a mud enema with the aid of a white plastic plunger. The whole grotesque scene resembles a cross between a hospital and an abattoir.

My time has come, and I'm led by the supervisor, a benign, motherly sort with pink earrings the size of ships' lifebelts, to a changing cubicle, from which I emerge, uncovered, to find a lady with a white coat, red hair, pink spectacles and a rubber pipe squeezing a layer of evil black slime onto a stained brown undersheet. She beckons to me to get into the middle of all this. My first surprise is how warm the mud is, the second how soothing it is to have it rubbed all over me, and the third how deeply tranquillizing it is to lie wrapped in the stuff like a piece of *boeuf en croûte*. Everything, the dreadful smell, the cattle-shed conditions, the slurping of distant enemas, is forgotten in the sheer tactile pleasure of lying in warm mud.

Glowing with health and smelling very gently of marine deposits I take a walk on the beach from which the therapeutic mud is gathered. Because the mud is best applied only to those parts which need it, and because most of the applicants are very white, the shoreline offers the bizarre sight of what appear to be human crossword puzzles. A local lady doctor strides into the sea with her daubed legs looking like thigh-length black boots. 'I bathe and then I don't wash it off for five days,' she enthuses.

At lunch I meet a local historian. Discussing the recent past it's clear that sunny, seaside Odessa has not escaped the tragedies that have befallen most of the western USSR. Romanians occupied Odessa in the war – Hitler had promised their leader Antonescu large stretches of the Black Sea coast-line. They burnt 20,000 locals in an arsenal and hanged 5000 from trees around the city to frighten the populace. Today the major problem is severe industrial pollution. The sea of Azov, a huge area east of the Crimea, is so badly affected that its beaches have been totally evacuated.

Later I go down to the Arkady Beach, one of Odessa's most famous, and find that there is not a space to be found, and, as in the waters of the

ODESSA: August 14th —

These are the famous Odessa S...
known in Russia + outside becau...
film Battleship Potemkin when t...
and there are some classic moments —
the length of the steps. —

Odessa: The Potemkin Steps, the miracle of mud —
as recommended by doctors, Arkady Beach (mud-free).

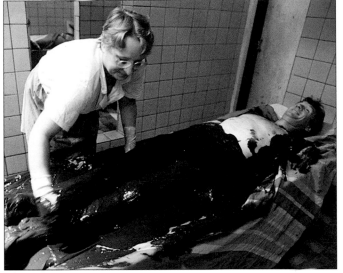

Dnieper at Kiev, there are still plenty of people for whom cooling off on a sunny day is more important than any health risk.

We have dinner at the Krasnaya Hotel. Huge bare-breasted ladies support the balustraded balcony above the door, and the whole pale green and white façade is like a richly adorned cake. Inside there is a mirrored and chandeliered barn of a dining-room, the inevitable zakuski, and a very incompetent band fronted by a fat lady in a gold dress. She probably gives mud enemas in the daytime but at night she murders Beatles songs.

We have a party on the balcony of my room to celebrate having made it this far. It's late when I get to bed, and when I get up there is a faintly detectable trace of black sediment on the bottom sheet.

DAY 40 · ODESSA TO ISTANBUL

It's 12.48 by the digital clock in the main passenger terminal of the port of Odessa. As far as I can remember it's the only public clock I've seen in the Soviet Union that is still going. After a day of rest, the crew and myself are in transit again, bound for Istanbul. At the moment we are in the limbo land of customs and immigration, waiting for something to happen. They have tried to brighten up the arid bureaucratic wasteland in which we are confined by sticking travel posters to the walls – rugged mountains, ski slopes, folk dances and children gambolling on beaches. The pleasures of these places may be beyond the range of most of the Soviet people and yet they do represent one of the more acceptable aspects of this country, an ability to relish, whenever the opportunity arises, an escape from the surrounding gloom. We have seen the petrol queues and the empty shops, the shabbiness of the surroundings and the hard face of privilege, but we've also seen spontaneous delight in the countryside (as on the train to Kiev), happily packed beaches and just this morning, holidaymakers on the Potemkin Steps asking me if I would mind taking a family snap for them. All you can say is the Soviet Union is never quite what it seems. We have eaten old tasteless bread in hotels, but found, here in Odessa, a shop around the corner baking fresh baguettes. We have seen one bag of fruit costing over 20 per cent of a weekly wage and country gardens groaning with produce, we have looked into stony faces but never been hugged as hard.

Once cleared by customs we are free to have a last lunch in the USSR. The good news is that the terminal has an outdoor restaurant, something we've been looking for for the last two weeks, the bad news is that it is on a crumbling concrete terrace, which looks as if it has been reprieved half-way through demolition. The catering is standard to bad – our twenty-fourth zakuski, a gristly hamburger topped with fried egg, and coffee from chipped cups with broken handles. It's the sort of experience that makes you want to get to Istanbul as fast as possible, but we have a 36-hour journey ahead of us, and to all intents and purposes it will be another day and a half in the Soviet Union. Our vessel is Odessa-registered and built in Bulgaria. She is a 30-year-old, 280-foot-long, 1000-ton, training ship. Her name *Junost*, means 'Youth'. She has only recently been converted to take passengers and runs a ferry service to Turkey every five days. There is no alternative.

In the late afternoon the time comes to say our goodbyes to the team of Russian drivers, interpreters and fixers who have become our friends. They have guided us through the labyrinth of official obstruction with great skill and the fact that we have been able to film all we wanted and travel as and when we wanted is down to them. Volodya looks exhausted, and though there must be relief in their farewell waves, I think there is also regret, not just that we are going but the fact that we can go, so easily. For all the fatigue I feel after crossing the Soviet Union, the sight of their faces as the *Junost* pulls slowly away makes me aware of how fortunate I am.

Our bow swings round, pointing for a moment straight up the 192 stone steps, called the Potemkin Steps after a dramatic sequence shot on them in Eisenstein's film *Battleship Potemkin*, which rise grandly from the port to the tree-lined esplanade. A staircase into the USSR. Then we are turning away from this warm, unassuming city and slowly out of the immense dock area past the hydrofoils they call Comets and Meteors which race about the harbour, the grey battlecruisers and a vast Soviet freighter improbably called *Mister Michael*. As we run slowly south-westwards along the low shadowy hills of the Black Sea Coast, I enjoy one of the great pleasures of travel – exploring a new ship. The *Junost* is a rag-bag. The cabin space, which is shared, is cramped and basic. The lavatories are indescribably filthy, and I pray I don't have to use them for anything but the most cursory visits, but the main deck is a very congenial space, with a strip wood floor and a number of spacious and superior deckchairs, complete with foot rests. Slung over the stern of the ship is what looks like a hastily erected shed, fashioned from corrugated plastic and painted brown. Inside is a small bar and a job lot of swivel chairs upholstered in red nylon. As well as serving nothing useful like beer and wine, but only the dreaded hard currency tariff of champagne, vodka and brandy, it embodies every fire risk known to man.

Roger has decided that the toilet facilities are so bad that we should film them. The purser, a trim, hairless man called Felix, walks past as we are emerging with all our lights and equipment and gives us a very odd look. Unfortunately we have to re-shoot. Once again we bump into Felix on the way out. This time he looks positively alarmed, but by the time we go down to dinner the lavatories have been thoroughly cleaned.

Felix is quite a character. Crisply dressed in white shirt and trousers, he not only announces dinner, but physically assists potential diners towards the restaurant. The longer you dally the more urgent are his attentions. The last arrivals are practically frog-marched to their table. I notice on the wall of the dining room, the only photo of Gorbachev I have seen publicly displayed. Is it just that he's unpopular or did he specifically discourage any personality cult? We all notice that his birthmark has been masked out.

End up the day on deck with a scotch and water and a sky full of stars, unobscured by city lights.

DAY 41 · ODESSA TO ISTANBUL

Up on deck at 7.45. To my horror, Felix is there and appears to be having a fit. He's standing half naked with eyes rolling and hands flapping wildly out in front of him. Only after a while do I realize he's doing his exercises. He smiles in my direction, a grotesque rictus of a smile which virtually slices his head in two. Fortunately this turns out to be another exercise.

I'm beginning to wonder if this is a Soviet ship at all. There is Peter Gabriel on the PA and porridge on the breakfast menu. Among the passengers is an 18-year-old girl from Ilkley, travelling with her brother who has been studying in Moscow for a year. They have just returned from a trip to Lake Baikal in Siberia, the deepest lake in the world, so far miraculously unpolluted. Their descriptions of its beauty, purity and tranquillity I found very tantalizing.

There are 54 crew on the *Junost*, 10 more than there are passengers. The first officer who told us this is engagingly frank. If he had his way he wouldn't stay in the Soviet Union. He worked once with Norwegians and they asked him how much he was paid in the USSR.

'130 dollars, I said.'

'Per day? they asked.'

'No! Per month.' He smiles wryly at this. I suggest that 130 dollars buys you a lot more in the Soviet Union than in Norway. He doesn't fall for that old one.

'I would rather live in expensive Norway.'

I'm growing fond of the *Junost*. Life on board has an innocent, anarchic quality. It's rather like being in a Monsieur Hulot film. A man in swimming trunks claiming to be the chief electrical officer bumps into me on the main staircase. He's dripping wet from a shower but anxious to know if we're happy with everything. I ask him why we were only going at 9 knots. He drips a little and considers the question.

'Well, who wants to go any faster?'

Up on deck, the girl from Ilkley has a fierce nose bleed, and all sorts of previously unseen crew members appear to help her. Felix, clutching an ice-bag, orders them all around, having her blood pressure checked and her brow wiped. But the strangest encounter is with the lovely Lyuba, proprietress of the bar. I had discovered that, up in the bows, the *Junost* sported a swimming pool. All of 6 foot long and 5 foot wide, it is in fact nothing more than a large packing case with a tarpaulin draped inside to hold the water. Deep end and shallow end change places with each roll of the ship. It's hardly large enough for one fully formed adult, so when I see Lyuba's neat but ample figure clambering down towards me I adopt an air of nonchalant British lounging, as if there's nothing more normal in the world than sharing a waterlogged packing case with a Russian barmaid. But Lyuba is in the box for some fun, and having told me that her name means 'Amore . . . love' she splashes me with water and asks if I have a woman.

'A wife . . . yes,' I reply, as if the two things are quite incompatible.

'Is she engineer . . . technician?'

An image of Helen with the Black and Decker comes to mind, and as we splash around in our boxed fragment of the Black Sea, Lyuba and I fall into intimate conversation about schools, children and how we miss our families.

DAY 42 · ODESSA TO ISTANBUL

Sleep almost 10 hours, and wake with a sense that our engines have slowed, if that's possible. Push aside the curtain to see that we are only a few hundred yards from land. We have left the Black Sea and are half-way down the Bosporus, the winding 18-mile channel that leads to the Sea of Marmara, the Aegean and eventually the Mediterranean. On deck Roger is contemplating a couple of weeks recovery time before rejoining us in Egypt. He's in professorial mood. Did I know that Bosporus and Oxford mean the same thing? In Greek legend, a priestess called Io was seeing Zeus, after work as it were, and Zeus, in order to prevent Hera, his wife, from finding out, turned Io into a cow. Hera, not fooled, sent a gadfly after her, causing the tormented Io to seek relief by jumping into the nearest stretch of water. This happened to be just about where we are now and became known as the Bous (Ox) Poros (Ford).

Everything is so different from what we have just left. Minarets and cypress trees stand out from the green hillsides, houses are being built, and many are crowned with satellite dishes. Lines of private cars are weaving their way along crowded coast roads flanked by balconied apartment blocks on one side and white-hulled yachts on the other.

The *Junost* looks what it is, a poorly maintained, overmanned country cousin of a ship, a bit of an embarrassment in the midst of this burgeoning capitalist neophilia. The *Junost* is like the Soviet Union itself, inefficient and ill-equipped but full of character. Its shortcomings create an atmosphere of closeness and warmth in the face of shared adversity. I can't wait to get off and enjoy a few creature comforts but I know I shall miss Lyuba and Felix and the dripping chief electrical officer.

As we move slowly past the 540-year-old Ottoman fortress of Rumeli Hasari, entirely built in four months, all of us on the deck-rail are excited and uncertain. The girl from Ilkley will be hearing her A-level results today. Two Afghans who have come through Russia to set up business in the West will face commercial reality for the first time. The first officer will look longingly at the glitter of capitalism, before turning his ship back to a country that's falling apart. Only Felix seems unaffected, flicking his head round in a series of neck-wrenching turns, as if desperate to achieve a full 360-degree rotation.

The sweeping graceful span of the first bridge ever to link two continents soars above us as the incomparable skyline of Istanbul comes into view. Set on headlands and curving around the inlet known as the Golden Horn, it is one of the great cityscapes of the world. Modern buildings are there, but the overall impression of grace and harmony is set by the mosques, with their clusters of domes and their attendant minarets pointing heaven-wards like defending rockets, and the sprawling beauty of the Topkapi Palace, leading the eye downhill to the ramparts of the old city walls, and the harbour, teeming with overloaded ferries.

The stealthy, tentative, introverted public face of the USSR is replaced here by shouts, waves, imprecations, noise, bustle and urgency.

We dock at ten past nine, at a quayside that seems to be run by a very proprietorial black and white cat, which, surrounded by a mangy harem, watches us tie up and sniffs each passenger as they disembark.

The formalities of customs and immigration are all conducted in a congenial and good-humoured way. Our new fixer Sevim, a formidable and energetic middle-aged lady, is organizing everyone. When there is trouble with the porters who object to being filmed because they are not in their best overalls she dismisses it briskly:

'These complexes . . . it is a problem in a third world country . . .'

As we leave the customs hall the two Afghans are the only two passengers left. The contents of their suitcases, mainly cheap gift accessories, samples of local cloth and rugs, are strewn out on the inspection table. Maybe Turkey will not be their promised land after all.

For me, things taken for granted like waterfront cafés and fresh orange juice, even a traffic jam, are new and wonderful. The young man from Ilkley, returning from a year in Russia, shakes his head in disbelief.

DAY 43 · ISTANBUL

Woken by the distorted sound of a pre-recorded muezzin calling the faithful to prayer. It's 5.30. Breakfast of orange juice, cereal and honeycomb – things I have not seen since Helsinki, three weeks ago. Fraser has had a nightmare in which he had to wire every minaret in Istanbul for sound.

Istanbul is a very noisy city, much of the noise from a huge construction programme. A companion to the famously crowded Galata Bridge across the Golden Horn is almost complete. A last massive section of its six-lane highway, waiting to be lowered into position, rears up at a right angle, a huge phallic symbol of regeneration. Sevim says the reconstruction is going on at such a pace that her husband, given a month's notice of redevelopment, went in to work one Monday morning to find his shop had gone. There are those with reservations about the pace of change. One is Altemur Kilic, a Turkish writer, diplomat and friend of Turgut Ozal, the President. He remembers

Istanbul – from Süleyman's mosque: Bosporus to the right,
the Golden Horn to the left, the new Galata Bridge points skywards.
At the dockside: Modern bridge – traditional catering.

Istanbul only 30 years ago as a city of 750,000 people, home to a flourishing number of foreign communities – Greek, Jewish, Armenian and what was known as the Levantine, comprising Italians, English and French who had lived in Turkey all their lives. He himself went to the English-run Istanbul High School for Boys whose headmaster, Mr Peach, he knew affectionately as Baba, 'Father'. The teachers caned him regularly. He smiles happily at the memory. 'My father authorized them to do so. It helped my character.' In between canings Altemur played cricket, read the *Boy's Own Paper* and grew up in an Istanbul which was small enough to give him 'a sense of rather being somebody in a big city'. Now the city population has swelled to 8 million and the real Istanbuliots, as he calls them, are very few.

As I step out of his elegant, unostentatious house on a small sloping street in Emirgan, I could be in the South of France, with the blue waters of the Bosporus catching the sunlight, people taking a drink or a coffee beneath the shade of ash and mimosa trees and the almost unbroken line of passing traffic.

Down by the Galata Bridge, close by the old spice markets, the pace of Istanbul life is at its most frenetic. Ferries are constantly loading and unloading providing a regular and copious passing trade for the street food sellers. Fishermen dart in, light up charcoal braziers and rocking crazily in the wash of the ferries sell their grilled catch then and there. You could have a street dinner every night of the week here and never eat the same menu twice. Apart from the fish, served in luscious sandwiches of hot fresh bread, tomato and onion, there are kebabs, pretzels, walnuts, pancakes and stuffed mussels, corn on the cob, succulent slices of melon and as much sweet tea as you can drink.

Back in England, it's the first day of the football season and in my hotel the new BBC World Service Television is showing Episode 5 of *Around the World in 80 Days*.

DAY 44 · ISTANBUL

The crew are up early to shoot the sunrise from the top of the 600-year-old Galata Tower, where in May 1453, the Genoese Christians handed over control of the city to the Ottoman Muslims, a key moment in European history. It is at breakfast at the Pera Palas Hotel that I hear the first news of modern history in the making. Those with short-wave radios have heard word from the Soviet Union that Gorbachev has been overthrown in a right-wing coup. Nothing more is known at the moment. I think of all the friends we made – Irena and Volodya and Edward and Sasha the Lenin impersonator, and I know that if the news is true things can only be worse for them.

Selfishly, we can only be thankful for our extraordinarily lucky escape. If this had happened three days earlier, the *Junost* may never have left Odessa, and we would have been stranded. If it had happened three *weeks* earlier we would never have been allowed into the Soviet Union.

The shadow of this great event hangs over the day, giving everything else we do a certain air of unreality. Some of the unreality is there already, especially in Room 411 of the Pera Palas Hotel. This is the room in which Agatha Christie wrote *Murder on the Orient Express.* It's small and rather cramped and you wouldn't get much writing done nowadays as they've just built an eight-lane highway below the window. After Agatha Christie died in 1976, Warner Brothers wanted to make a film about the mystery of 11 lost days of her life. An American medium, one Tamara Rand, said that in a trance she had seen an hotel in Istanbul and in Room 411 of this hotel she had seen Agatha Christie hiding the key to her diary under the floorboards. On 7 March 1979, the room was searched and a rusty key was found. The president of the hotel company, sensing Warner Brothers' interest but miscalculating their generosity, put the key in a safe demanding 2 million dollars, plus 15 per cent of the film's profits. Here the key remains. Its age has been authenticated and as Agatha Christie was highly secretive about travel arrangements it's considered unlikely that the medium can have known about the Pera Palas before she saw it in her trance.

It all makes Room 411 rather a creepy place and I'm glad to get out and into the bustle of Pera Street – the mile-long main thoroughfare of Istanbul. The best way to see it is from one of the venerable red and cream trams that run its length, though I must confess I do catch breath when I notice the number of the tram we're on – 411.

I buy a Panama hat for under £6 off an elderly French-speaking Turk at a shop by the tram stop. I'm not keen on hats but with the weather getting hotter by the day, I can see the advantages.

As a result of climate, history and geographical position, Istanbul is the quintessential trading city. Russia and the Mediterranean and Europe and Asia meet here, and though a walk through the endless arcades of the old covered market gives an overwhelming sense of richness and variety, there is no better place to see trade in its rawest, purest form than the square outside the gates of the Beyazit II Mosque and the impressive Islamic-arched entrance of Istanbul University. Here an extraordinary dance of commerce goes on. Groups are constantly gathering, splitting and reforming. Eyes are always on the move. These are furtive people on the very edge of the law, buying and selling in the spirit, if not the currency, of this great commercial city. There are Azerbaijanis, Iranians, Poles, Romanians, Ukrainians and Afghans. Most of them sell out of black plastic bags. I see Marlboro cigarettes traded for dollars and plastic train sets, cheap Eastern European trainers, an

Agatha Christie, the well-known author of the book 'Murder on the Orient Express', has stayed at Pera Palas several times.

The mysterious key, which will enlighten the lost period of 11 days in the life of the author, has been found in Room 411 of Pera Palas with the cooperation of Mrs. Tamara Rand, a psychist, and Warner Bros Film Company on 07 March 1979.

anorak, some metal ornaments — all attracting the crowds.

By the end of this hot, hard day the ministrations of a proper Turkish bath, a hammam, are irresistible.

The Cagaloglu Hammam, a splendid emporium of cleanliness, is this year celebrating 300 years in business, during which time it has cleaned, amongst others, King Edward VII, Kaiser Wilhelm, Florence Nightingale and Tony Curtis. I can choose from a 'self-service bath', — the cheapest option, a 'scrubbed assisted bath', a 'Massage à la Turk — you'll feel years younger after this vigorous revitalizing treatment' or the 'Sultan Service', which promises, modestly, that 'you will feel reborn'. At 120,000 Turkish lira, about £17, rebirth seems a snip and after signing up, I'm given a red and white check towel and shown to a small changing cubicle. Through the glass I can see a group of masseurs with long droopy moustaches, hairy chests, bulbous stomachs and an occasional tattoo. At that moment a Turkish father and son emerge from a cubicle and the little boy, who looks to be only eight or nine, is ushered toward the steam room by one of these desperadoes with a reassuring gentleness and good humour.

The steam room, the hararet, is set to one side of an enormous central chamber with walls and floor of silver-grey marble, and a dome supported by elegant columns and arches. Whilst I work up a good dripping sweat from the underfloor heating I get talking to a fellow bather, an Italian. He has driven to Istanbul from Bologna, and had come quite unscathed through Yugoslavia, where there is a state of civil war, but had found newly-liberated Romania a dark and dangerous place. Gasoline was almost unavailable. He bought a can which he found later to be water. I asked him if there was any more news from the USSR. He said he had heard that Leningrad had been sealed off and tanks had moved into the Kremlin.

Then it's my turn on the broad inlaid marble massage slab called the Gobek Tasi. I'm rubbed, stretched and at one point mounted and pulled up by my arms before being taken off and soaped all over by a masseur who keeps saying 'Good?', in a tone which brooks no disagreement. He dons a sinister black glove the size of a baseball mitt. (The brochure describes it as 'a handknitted Oriental washing cloth', but it feels like a Brillo pad.) Never have I been so thoroughly scoured. The dirt and skin roll off me like the deposits from a school rubber. How can I have been so filthy and not known about it?

There is a small bar giving on to an open courtyard at the back of the Hammam. Sitting here with a glass of raki and a bowl of grapes luxuriating in the afterglow of the bath at the end of a long day, I feel as content as I ever could.

The last news of the day is that the port of Tallinn which we entered three weeks ago has been closed by a blockade.

DAY 45 · ISTANBUL TO SELCUK

Up at 6 a.m. to get down to Sirkeci station to buy a rail ticket for Izmir. Fraser is becoming more Cassandra-like each day. This morning he's heard news that a British businessman has been killed in Istanbul and British travellers are advised to be on their guard. Unfortunately no one's told us what to be on our guard against.

On the concourse of this station at the very end of Europe, where the Orient Express used to terminate, there is a large half-relief of the head of Kemal Ataturk, founder of modern Turkey. His presence is as ubiquitous as Lenin's was in the Soviet Union but, unlike Lenin, he is still widely revered and respected, 50 years after his death. Even the cheerfully cynical Sevim, whilst telling us that he died of cirrhosis of the liver and had a prodigious sexual appetite, declares 'this was a *great* man'.

We leave Istanbul at 9 o'clock on the ferry MV *Bandirma* which takes four and a half hours to cross to the town of Bandirma on the north coast of what my school atlas used to refer to as Asia Minor. She is carrying nearly a thousand passengers - a mixture of Turkish students, businessmen clutching laptops, veiled Muslim women and foreign backpackers. The bars and cafés are already open and salesmen with drinks and sandwiches are working their way through the crowds.

Sevim looks scornfully round at some of the passengers. Turks are nomads, she feels the need to remind us, they've never settled anywhere, they use things, destroy them and throw them away. Fall into conversation with a Turkish actor, heading south to play a series of one night productions. He misses the 60s when there was a wealth of good writers. I ask him if there is a National Theatre in Turkey. 'Oh yes, they do the classics,' he smiles wryly, 'in a very classical way.' I wish him well and he gives me his newspaper which is full of the news of Gorbachev's fall. He is evidently under arrest in the Crimea, but information, like everything else in the Soviet Union, is in short supply.

At half-past one we land on the continent of Asia, and fighting past the sunglass salesmen, the pretzel pushers and the shoe-shiners – 'white shoes, very bad sir,' they cry, pointing at my trainers – we find the station and board the four-coach, diesel-hauled Marmora Express for Izmir and the south.

The train passes through brown, dry fields and open treeless country. At a military air base jets are taking off at regular intervals, an ominous sight remembering the news this morning and Turkey's border with the USSR.

In one of the fields a group of white-veiled women are tossing turnips, or possibly watermelons into a tall trailer. Behind them rises the first substantial patch of high ground since we left Hammerfest 28 days ago. As

we near Balikesir the flat plain disappears altogether and we are winding our way through tall, wooded limestone hills that give way eventually to rocky gorges.

By nightfall we are in the land of legend and ancient history. Troy is nearby, Smyrna (now Izmir) sprawls by the sea and it's quite late by the time we pull into Selcuk, a couple of miles from the ancient city of Ephesus, where legend has it that the Virgin Mary died at the age of 64.

At the guest house I have a small white-washed room with a plain pine table and a kilim that provides the only touch of colour. Outside my window at midnight the sound of street-talk merges with the incessant swish and slap of sandals on the roadway.

DAY 46 · SELCUK TO EPHESUS AND MARMARIS

At the entrance to the ruins of Ephesus by 9 o'clock, to avoid the crowds. There is a gauntlet of stalls to be run before reaching the gates. Alongside the usual stacks of guide-books, fezzes, sun hats, pipes and dresses is a small army of little figures with enormous phalluses. They are reproductions of images which date from the earliest, pre-Christian history of Ephesus when it was the centre of the fertility cult of the goddess Cybele. They're now available as car key-rings. Basil buys a few as Christmas gifts.

I'm not a great one for ruins. Generally it requires an enormous outlay of imagination and patience for relatively scant reward, but the site at Ephesus is so rich that I can walk on 2000-year-old flagstones with recognizable buildings on either side – fountains, libraries and temples donated by the rich of Ephesus to extend their influence and generally impress people. The decorated columns and friezes are often still standing, whilst others lie broken and scattered on the ground. I stumble over history, down the hill, past the remains of a pre-Christian brothel and public latrine to the graceful façade of the Library of Celsus, built around AD 135 to house 12,000 scrolls – all destroyed when the Goths sacked the city in 262.

The latest invasion of Ephesus is well underway by mid-morning, as the crowds flock to the largest classical ruin in existence after Pompeii, reducing it to yet another sight, robbing it of magic and atmosphere. The sun, reflected off the stones, burns from above and below and I'm glad when our filming's over and we can move on down to Marmaris and the sea.

This is the first unequivocally hot day of our journey. The bus passes through dry and buzzing hillsides covered with scattered bushes, low pine trees, and the occasional cypress-ringed graveyard. A heat haze rises from roadsides where peppers are laid out to dry in the blistering sun.

My thermometer registers 94 degrees at Cine where we eat an excellent lunch at an otherwise empty roadhouse. Above our heads a dim TV picture shows army vehicles and flashing lights in Moscow. The waiter looks up and shakes his head. It's serious. People have been crushed to death by tanks. But this heat wraps everything in a blanket beneath which time and the outside world cease to exist.

Then, 60 miles further on, an extraordinary moment. We have stopped in the pine forest above Marmaris to film my bus descending into town. A car with a couple of drowsy picnickers is parked, doors wide open, in the shade of a tree. A Turkish voice chunters on from its radio. Sevim stops suddenly and listens, with a frown of concentration which gradually relaxes into a look of disbelief. She talks to us as she listens:

'The news from Moscow is that the coup is over . . . some generals are dead . . .' She listens again, 'Gorbachev is coming back to Moscow'.

On this languid, lazy afternoon in southern Turkey, it seems unbelievable. History shouldn't happen as fast as this.

A few minutes later we have reached the shores of the Aegean, though the town of Marmaris is almost separated from the open sea by two tall headlands curving like crab claws to enclose a handsome blue-green bay. They call this the Turquoise Coast. The view from the harbour is wonderful, but the harbour itself is fringed by restaurants with tourist menus and expensive yachts, the fattest of which sports the red ensign and is rumoured to have Princess Margaret aboard.

Ancient civilizations – Ephesus: Twentieth-century road-sweeper, second-century library, the Great Theatre. Rhodes' skyline from the Marmaris ferry.

Day 46: Turkey

DAY 47 · MARMARIS TO RHODES

When we leave our hotel some guests are already staking out sunbeds, and frankly, I wish I could join them. Our journey across the Mediterranean now looks a lot of effort. There is no direct maritime connection between Turkey and Egypt, but if we can reach Limassol in Cyprus there is a connection from there to Port Said. However, the Greek Cypriots, still bitter about the Turkish invasion of Cyprus in 1974, will not allow Turkish-registered vessels into their ports. Our only chance is to travel to Greece first and hope to pick up a boat to Limassol from there. This will add to our schedule and our workload which, with the whole of Africa still to go, is the last thing we need.

We join the queue for tickets on the ferry to Rhodes, the nearest of the Greek islands, 50 miles to the south. The fact that we are carrying equipment and luggage for a world trip does not make things easier. These small boats are hard pushed to squeeze 200 people aboard. But persuasive and persistent work by Clem and Angela secure us the places, and we join the backpackers and the Italian bikers. My last memory of Marmaris is a quayside shop sign advertising the services of 'Doctor Satan, Gynaecologist'.

The crossing to Rhodes starts idyllically as we push through the narrow gap of the bay and run out alongside the Bozburun peninsula in what is inarguably a turquoise sea. But a stiff westerly wind lurks round the end of the peninsula and whacks us hard on the starboard side. The Italians rush to the stern to lash down their BMWs, and it only takes one substantial wave across the upper deck to cause an exodus of distressed sunbathers clutching soggy paperbacks.

Around lunchtime we land below the well-preserved mediaeval fortifications of Rhodes town. The Knights of St John built them when they took over the island in 1309. The Turks then ruled for nearly 400 years until they were evicted by the Italians in 1912. Rhodes has only been a part of Greece since 1945. Book into a tiny, characterful guest-house called the Cava d'Oro built into the city walls and bearing the date 1281. Accommodation is simple and cramped and seems to attract backpackers with huge loads who get wedged in the doorway.

A fellow Yorkshireman – the astrologer Patric Walker – has invited us for tea at his house in Lindos, some 15 miles away. Lindos is a compact little town with the neat, clean, sharp lines of its white-washed buildings gleaming in the sunlight, which, this afternoon, is hot and hard and destructive. The thistles by the road side are bleached yellow, and the wild flowers which apparently enjoy only two and a half weeks glory have long since shrivelled. In the pebble-floored courtyard of an attractive corner house beside orange and lemon and tangerine trees, Patric Walker serves us a grand English tea (he's even had a cake decorated with a map of our journey) and warns us about Mercury being in retrograde. 'It's when the planet Mercury appears to be travelling backwards in the heavens – it isn't, but it appears to be . . . and it's a time when all forms of communication and travel plans tend to be disrupted'. Apparently it happens about three times a year, and it doesn't surprise me that it's in retrograde at the moment, and will be for the next week. As the last days of any period 'tend to be the trickiest', we should expect mounting problems between here and Egypt. He consults his book of planetary movements and offers us the cheerful news that it will happen again at the end of November – when we hope to be setting off from South Africa for the South Pole.

I don't think Patric likes to be the harbinger of bad news and seeing our glum faces he seeks to reassure us. Astrology, as he says, is an art not a science.

'. . . Everybody expects the astrologer to be infallible – you're not, you know. I can be as wrong as anybody else, particularly about . . . you know, my own life.'

His own life looks very nice to me. Especially over the top of the glass of champagne he offers us, looking out to sea beyond the rooftops of houses built by the Crusaders, as the sun begins to set. For the second time today I feel the insidious pull of the sedentary life.

DAY 48 · RHODES

Wake at 2 a.m. from a recurring dream of tanks in Moscow to a far worse cacophony from the road outside. Motorbikes skidding round corners, music and loud arguments. I should have realized, the day is for TV crews and the night is for the locals. Shut my balcony doors and wake an hour later pouring sweat. Open the doors and lie there rigid with sleeplessness as dogs take over the streets. Try to prop the doors half-open and nearly break the window but at least fall asleep from the effort. Not for long. An agonizingly slow street-cleaning truck finally lumbers by at half-past six. Half an hour later Clem and the crew are ready to go.

'Why so early?'

'Best time. Before the streets get busy.'

Vangelis Pavlides, a political cartoonist and local historian has agreed to be my host to Rhodes. He appears on his vintage BMW motorbike and we grab some fresh bread from a local bakery before taking a walk round the Old Town. Vangelis is a good companion. He loves the city, though not uncritically. In his opinion it had a better sewage system 400 years before

Christ than it does now. It also had a population of 300,000, now shrunk to 80,000.

One of the most handsome thoroughfares in Rhodes is the Street of The Knights. It's said to be the oldest street in Greece, following a line originally laid out in the fifth century BC. A collection of fine medieval stone façades rises up the hill, testimony to the great wealth accrued by the mysterious order of The Knights of St John, despite being sworn to poverty and chastity. The story, which Vangelis relishes, is that they infiltrated the island disguised as sheep. Though there were never more than 400 knights (if they wanted soldiers they employed mercenaries) they held the island until 1522. The Order, which took refuge in Malta, remains in existence to this day. It has close links with the Vatican and still owns properties on the oldest street in Greece.

Back in his apartment, paved with slate slabs from Northern Greece, Vangelis kicks off his shoes and shows me some of the drawings for his history of medieval Rhodes. There is a lot of humour in the work – one Knight encased in heavy armour is relieving himself through a large household tap. The apartment has many other delights, including a very old box camera which Vangelis inherited from his uncle's father, who used to

say the Lord's Prayer to determine the length of the exposure. For lunch we eat pizza on his balcony which looks out towards a beach solid with holidaymakers. A thousand pink bodies propel a thousand red pedaloes slowly across the bay. Vangelis says many of his old neighbourhood friends have been driven away by the remorselessly increasing crowds of visitors, and he himself is away to Crete tomorrow for two weeks peace on a sailing boat.

We are off even sooner. I just have time to ring my daughter and hear her GCSE results (I think this may be the real reason I didn't sleep last night). They're good and I'd like to celebrate, but we only have time to get down to the dockside and check ourselves on board the *Silver Paloma* – a cruise liner bound for Limassol. Her final destination is Haifa, and the majority of the passengers are Israeli families returning from holidays on the Greek mainland. The security implications are explained to us at some length, and we are told to take all precautions and report any unauthorized objects. Most of our gear has been stowed securely below, which produces a gem from Basil at dinner. When asked by Clem if he has one of his sauces to enliven a dull carrot soup he says loudly and with some exasperation, 'Oh no! The Bomb's in the hold'. (Readers who've just come in, see Novgorod.)

DAY 49 · RHODES TO LIMASSOL

 Everything about the *Silver Paloma* is depressing. Breakfast is the first meal I've turned down on the whole journey. The smell of stale cigarette smoke hangs around the passageways and clings to the walls. The decks are empty but the slot machines are busy. Families bicker and argue. There seems little joy in it all.

Arrival at Limassol is protracted. We sit in one of the ship's reception areas which is fitted out in a barren blend of vinyl, chrome and plastic and wait over an hour for the disembarking queue to clear. This is followed by another half-hour's wait on the quayside in airless, muggy heat until we are allowed to begin unloading our equipment.

Times such as these are the low points of the journey. None of us is much refreshed after a night on the boat, and after 32 days of filming in the last five weeks and four national frontiers crossed in the last seven days alone all of us are expending energy much faster than we can replace it.

We drive west from Limassol beside plantations where oranges, lemons, avocadoes and kiwi fruit are grown in long orderly lines, protected by avenues of eucalyptus and fir, then out onto higher ground where there is no shelter and the grapes on the vines are burnt brown by the sun. A fine Corinthian arch standing forlornly among thorn bushes, an amphitheatre which is still used for plays, and the remains of the Roman city of Curium lie next door to the 99 square miles of the British Sovereign Area with its bobbies and post-boxes. (They were allowed only 99 square miles because 100 would have constituted an occupation.) For five miles, the road from Limassol to the west is effectively part of Britain and I suppose we could call this the eighth country we've passed through.

We are heading for a village near Paphos where Ariadne Kyriacu is today marrying Polycarpus Polycarpu. We have been invited to join the guests, which is not quite the honour it sounds, as there are likely to be over 3000 of them. A Cypriot wedding involves not only relatives but also the local community. It is not uncommon for a couple to advertise for guests in the newspaper. It's all seen as good for business.

The wedding is quite an affair, especially if it is, like the one today, traditional. About 3 o'clock the show gets on the road with a public shaving of the groom. Polycarpus is a modern Cypriot, a student in Germany, who looks very different from his beaming, ruddy-cheeked father who is the current head man of the village. He sits in the half-finished shell of the house that is being built for him and his wife, and with a brave smile submits to the attentions of an elderly barber, who has a disconcerting habit of swatting flies away with his cut-throat razor.

After what is certainly the longest shave I've ever witnessed we all walk through the village to the church. I fall into conversation with the best man's wife, who turns out to be from Kent. She married her Cypriot husband after a holiday romance. They had a thousand guests, '. . . but then I didn't want a big wedding,' she explains.

At the church Polycarpus' bride arrives, dramatically attired in white with her pitch-black hair swept up through a band of flowers and spilling out in a mass of carefully disordered curls. She looks wondrous, like some Edwardian actress, tall, very slim, with a strong face and a long, straight nose. Then three priests, in no particular hurry, begin a long recitation of the liturgy. A professional video recording is being made and the director, a man in a yellow jacket which clashes with everything, rushes about amongst the priests moving sacred objects and generally getting in everyone's way. The church is far too small for all the guests and people come and go as they please. Only the old widows – the 'blackbirds' as they call them – follow the service intently, their lips moving in time with the priests' words. Polycarpus and Ariadne remain standing heroically throughout this curious mixture of the spiritual and the secular until the moment comes for them to be linked with white ribbon, take communion and then process in a circle around a Bible.

But their work has hardly begun. At the wedding feast, held in the huge courtyard of what was once a monastery, they sit for three hours receiving guests. I am told that it is the custom on being received to slip the happy couple a small financial gift, and by the time I get there Polycarpus' pockets are stuffed with notes, of which he is occasionally relieved by one of the family.

We sit at long tables and tuck into lamb kleftiko, moussaka and To Rezi, a thick but tasty oatmeal mix which takes two days to cook, and almost as long to eat. There is music and dancing, including one dance in which the marital bed is blessed, and four men in suits have to perform a particularly tricky soft-shoe shuffle whilst holding a mattress on their shoulders. There is still no respite for Polycarpus and Ariadne. They are dragged up on stage to cut the cake, which all goes well until the best man opens the champagne over-zealously and a stream of foam deluges the bridal pair. As champagne drips down his forehead I see Polycarpus' smile wither for a split-second before he's back to being man of the moment and leading the hastily mopped-up Ariadne into a slow rather inelegant dance which could be called the Lumbago. The reason it is so slow is that during the dance relatives and friends come up and pin money to the couple. Polycarpus is no Fred Astaire at the best of times and having to trip the light fantastic festooned with currency doesn't help. By midnight they must both be carrying close on a thousand pounds each, and I now understand those who say that these

The Polycarpu wedding: The Groom, the Bridesmaid, the Best Man and a 'Blackbird'.

weddings, besides being good for public relations, can be run at a considerable profit. Not that that can be much consolation for Polycarpus, who is now quite seriously wilting, and the night still young. But his wife is beautiful and 3000 guests are having a great time and there's a near full moon in the cloudless sky.

DAY 50 · LIMASSOL AND AKROTIRI

POLE to POLE Seeing families around the swimming-pool of our hotel reminds me of the summer holidays our family have enjoyed and the one I'm missing at the moment. Basil, detecting a sniff of homesickness, cheers me up with an account of a local festival he dropped in to see last night at which he witnessed the crowning of Miss Grape 1992. Her prize was 15 pounds worth of chicken and a large fish.

QUEEN STREET

A Walk through Lynton

20p

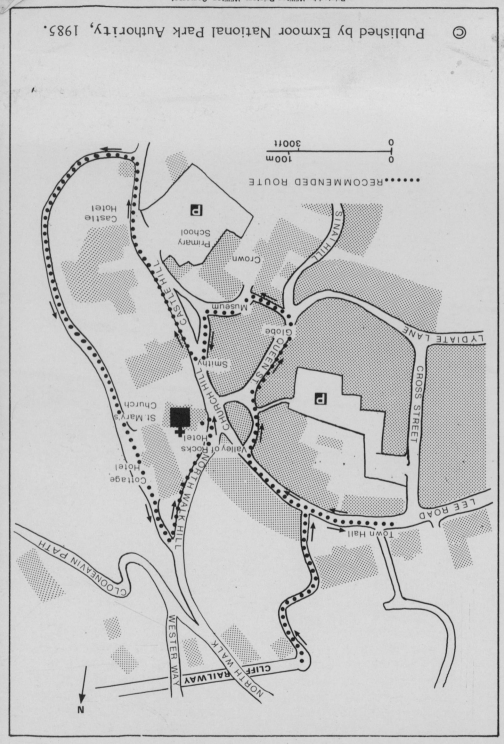

Printed by Williton Printers, Williton, Somerset.

© Published by Exmoor National Park Authority, 1985.

•••••• RECOMMENDED ROUTE

0 100m
0 300ft

Castle Hotel

P Primary School

Crown

Museum

Globe

Smithy

CASTLE HILL

QUEEN ST

St. Mary's Church

CHURCH HILL

Cottage Hotel

Valley of Rocks Hotel

NORTH WALK HILL

CLOONEAVIN PATH

WESTER WAY

CLIFF RAILWAY

NORTH WALK

Town Hall

P

LYDIATE LANE

CROSS STREET

LEE ROAD

SINAI HILL

N

There is a copy of the *Sunday Times* in the hotel – the first up-to-date English newspaper I've seen for two months. Gorbachev is to disband the Communist Party. The Ukraine and Estonia have declared independence. I have to read it again to believe it. Only 10 days ago we were in the Ukraine, which even optimists thought would not see independence for 30 or 40 years, and in a Soviet Union whose existence was inseparable from communism. Only five days ago the country was led by a group of hard-line generals. The USSR has blown up in spectacular fashion.

We are to spend this afternoon with the British forces at the RAF base in Akrotiri. Here very little has changed, or that's how it seems. There is a water shortage, which means that pitches have to be watered with 'treated effluent' i.e. sewage, but there is still polo and cricket and cream teas and brass bands.

In reality things have changed quite a bit. The garrison at Akrotiri has been reduced to 1500 from a peak of 5000. There is concern that the Turks and the Greek Cypriots may patch up their quarrel and the three bases the British still have on the island could be the first casualties of rapprochement.

Our papers checked, we are escorted onto the base past a weather bulletin board on which is scribbled the chalk message 'Cyprus will have a public holiday on the first day of rain'. A cricket match is in progress between a Youth XI and a Veterans XI, though how they can play in this heat, and on grass watered with recycled sewage, is beyond me. There is no alleviating breeze here, just air so thick with humidity it practically bubbles. But being British means not letting that sort of thing worry you and during the interval the teams are tucking into cream buns and cups of hot tea as though it were a spring day in Hove. I ask one of the Veterans if he felt he'd lost much weight out there.

'Oh, about seven bottles of Carlsberg.'

The talk is mostly of sport rather than fighting, though the base had been on full alert during the Gulf War five months previously, when an extra 400 medical staff were drafted in to deal with expected casualties. The men I speak to regard Cyprus as a good 'tour' but some of the women are less keen. Because many of the civilian jobs on the base are open to local Cypriots, the forces wives find it very hard to get work, and life, after the initial euphoria over the sun, sea and sand, can become very routine. As one of them said with feeling:

'All you can do here is have babies.'

The band of the third battalion the Queen's Regiment brings 'Sussex by the Sea' to a stirring climax, the teams come out onto the pitch again, and I'm hoisted aloft in a Wessex helicopter to have a snifter with the commander of the British forces in Cyprus, Air Vice-Marshal Sandy Hunter and his wife Wilma. They live in a long, comfortable house on top of a fortified ridge,

complete with their own helicopter pad. Our drinks are served by a Sudanese butler called Ahmed, a man of great presence and gravity who has worked for the British for 35 years. He has family north of Khartoum, 'near railway station Number 6'. Hearing that it is on our route he urges me to visit their riverside village.

'We got island sir and we got home sir. Island very nice, we give you one very good day sir.'

We drive away from Sandy and Wilma's house along a ridge from which we have a fine view of the most beautiful sunset. On one side a long, wide, pale crimson sky stretches across hazy hills, whilst on the other a full moon is rising.

At midnight I walk along the beach by the hotel. A mile or two further on is Aphrodite's Rock. Legend has it that if you swim three times round it on the night of a full moon you'll live for ever. Well, to paraphrase the chief electrical officer on the *Junost*, 'Who wants to live for ever anyway'.

I turn and head back to the hotel.

DAY 51 · LIMASSOL TO PORT SAID

Today we embark on the last stage of our zig-zag progress across the Mediterranean, aboard the *Princesa Marissa*, a Cyprus-registered, 9500-ton vessel built in Finland in 1966, which now operates a two-day 'fun-filled' cruise from 'the Island of Aphrodite' to the 'Land of the Pharaohs'. As the fun-filled cruise costs a mere £100 all-in it's well subscribed, mainly by the British, who make up around 600 of the 750 passengers on board.

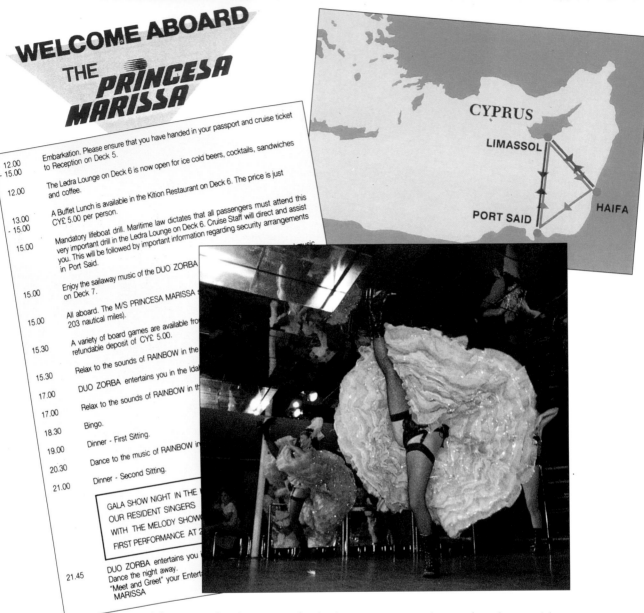

WELCOME ABOARD THE PRINCESA MARISSA

CYPRUS

LIMASSOL

PORT SAID

HAIFA

12.00 - 15.00	Embarkation. Please ensure that you have handed in your passport and cruise ticket to Reception on Deck 5.
12.00	The Ledra Lounge on Deck 6 is now open for ice cold beers, cocktails, sandwiches and coffee.
13.00 - 15.00	A Buffet Lunch is available in the Kition Restaurant on Deck 6. The price is just CY£ 5.00 per person.
15.00	Mandatory lifeboat drill. Maritime law dictates that all passengers must attend this very important drill in the Ledra Lounge on Deck 6. Cruise Staff will direct and assist you. This will be followed by important information regarding security arrangements in Port Said.
15.00	Enjoy the sailaway music of the DUO ZORBA on Deck 7.
15.00	All aboard. The M/S PRINCESA MARISSA 203 nautical miles).
15.30	A variety of board games are available fro refundable deposit of CY£ 5.00.
15.30	Relax to the sounds of RAINBOW in the
17.00	DUO ZORBA entertains you in the Ida
17.00	Relax to the sounds of RAINBOW in th
18.30	Bingo.
19.00	Dinner - First Sitting.
20.30	Dance to the music of RAINBOW i
21.00	Dinner - Second Sitting.
	GALA SHOW NIGHT IN THE OUR RESIDENT SINGERS WITH THE MELODY SHOW FIRST PERFORMANCE AT 2
21.45	DUO ZORBA entertains you Dance the night away. "Meet and Greet" your Entert MARISSA

The party begins on embarkation as we are given a brochure with a programme of events . . . 'Enjoy the sailaway music of the Duo Zorba on Deck 7' . . . 'Relax to the sounds of Rainbow in the Ledra Lounge'.

The constant pounding of disco music above and below decks is broken only by loudspeaker announcements which all seem to feature the phrase 'Deck Sexy'. It turns out to be the Greek for Deck 6. A voluble Filipino steward shows me to my spacious cabin, complete with bath. 'Anything you want, you ask for Johnny', he keeps repeating. I never see him again.

The journey due south to Port Said is a distance of 203 nautical miles, and will take fifteen and a half hours. Somewhere at sea we shall cross the 30 degree meridian, curling round to come in at Port Said at 31.17 East. Kill some of this time at the Gala Show, which features the impressively hard working Melody Dancers, a group of showgirls who, backed by a Polish band, climax their act with a Can-Can of extraordinary athleticism and energy.

DAY 52 · PORT SAID

My alarm sounds at 4.30. By 5 o'clock I'm packed, shaved, showered and off to the bridge for a first sight of Africa. My watchstrap breaks and I pray it isn't going to be that sort of day. The moon is still the only light in the sky, but way ahead on our starboard side is a tall flashing beacon and a long row of orange and white lights which must be Port Said. Below us a line of red and green flashing marker buoys indicates the mouth of the Suez Canal. As we pass another cruise ship – the *Romantica*, also from Limassol – one of her tugs breaks away and comes to manoeuvre us into position a little way out from the palm-fringed waterfront.

The first light of day breaks in the sky behind us. It's as if a veil has been lifted from the city and the dark, unfamiliar outlines resolve into handsome old colonial houses, with tall louvred doorways opening onto wrought-iron balconies, an elegant, arcaded Canal House, with its mosaic-covered dome and a fine lighthouse of yellow brick.

Port Said is not a major port of entry for passenger ships, most of which use Alexandria. This may partly explain why Louis Lines, who operate the *Princesa Marissa*, can keep their costs down, and why there appears to be no means of getting from the boat to the shore.

Then, slowly, a brown and rusty pontoon is uncoiled from the waterfront by men in boats all shouting at each other. When at last this steel snake reaches the ship, a crowd of salesmen rush along it and stand at the doors, making it almost impossible for anyone to disembark without tripping over a brass tray, a bubble pipe, a copper gong or a pile of cut-price Lacoste T-shirts.

Once the Cairo-bound day-trippers have left, we go with some relief for breakfast, but there isn't any. Even worse is to come. As the porters unload our gear the camera tripod rolls unnoticed into the Mediterranean. Could this be Mercury in retrograde? Should we have made other plans? I think it's just Egypt, where confusion seems an essential part of everyday life. There is no feeling here that life is a series of problems to be solved, rather that there is a human state, which is chaos, and that peace, calm and order is a heavenly state to which, Inshallah, we wretched mortals may one day aspire. Meanwhile six men are staring into the murky depths of the Mediterranean as if some Egyptian Lady of the Lake might suddenly hoist the tripod aloft, whilst six others are improvizing something with a fish-hook on the end of a piece of string.

Romany Helmy, our good friend who looked after us on *Around the World in 80 Days*, suggests that we should go to customs and get the formalities over with, whilst he supervises the raising of the tripod.

The tripod is retrieved half an hour later by a diver whom Romany got out of bed, but it is another seven hours before Nigel, Fraser, Patti and Basil are cleared to leave customs. Every single item on their lists is checked and double-checked, and in some cases triple-checked, during which time they are not allowed beyond the gates of the port. There are several problems. The customs officials have never had to deal with a foreign film crew before. Port Said is a duty-free zone, and they cannot believe that we are not here to take advantage of this. But what seems to throw them completely, what they simply cannot comprehend, is that we are leaving the country, by land, through the Sudan. It appears to be quite beyond belief that anyone would want to do such a thing.

Those of us not directly responsible for the equipment can only wait, guiltily, at the Helnan Port Said Hotel, which is run, ironically, by a Scandinavian company.

In its grounds and along the Mediterranean shoreline Egyptian holidaymakers are engaged in frantic physical activity – running, judo, soccer, tennis and what appear to be aerobic classes. The screams of children playing in the pool mingles oddly with the wailing chant of the call to prayer.

The day's filming is wrecked by the long wait in customs and for the crew the last straw is that all the restaurants in Port Said are dry, the work of a zealously Islamic mayor.

There are also mixed opinions over what it is safe to eat. Should we eat the salad, which looks appetizing but which my medical bible – Richard Dawood's *How to Stay Healthy Abroad* – does not recommend in Africa? Or the crayfish from the Med? In the end I eat both, because I'm terribly hungry.

DAY 53 · PORT SAID TO CAIRO

 Refreshed after eight and a half hours sleep, and tempted by the cool of early morning, I go for a run with Patti along the beach. Fishermen are examining their catch which they have hauled up in long nets. A man with a child calls out to me as I pass. My Western reflex says beware, but it turns out that he only wants to ask where I am from and to wish me welcome.

Port Said doesn't figure on Western tour itineraries, and, happily, the seafront remains typically Egyptian, complete with a ladies' beach where Arab women bathe fully clothed. Bathe is perhaps too strong a description for what consists essentially of wading into the waves and standing there.

The customs nightmare of yesterday may well be repeated for we have to go through another check today when we leave the free port and enter the rest of Egypt, so we decide not to delay our departure for Cairo. We drive down Palestine Street, where we came ashore yesterday and through squares with duty-free shops at ground level and rows of washing and occasional mattresses hung out to dry above. At cafés men, never women I notice, play backgammon, and every now and then there is a reminder of the proximity of the Suez Canal, with a dramatic glimpse of a 50,000-ton tanker gliding across the end of a side street.

At the outskirts of the city there is a cheerful sign above the road: 'Have Nice Trip'. It is here that our troubles begin.

We are turned back at the customs barrier and sent along a dusty carriageway to an address in the suburbs of Port Said. This turns out to be another customs area, for buses only. As soon as our minibus pulls up outside salesmen cluster round brandishing chocolate, sunglasses, coffee cups, razor blades, make-up, watches and even plastic rattles. We sit and wait. The temperature is climbing up towards 100 Fahrenheit. Eventually we are let through into a courtyard and after some deliberation asked to unload all our equipment for examination. Romany is doing his best to prevail upon the officer in charge telling him we have been through all this for seven hours yesterday and he has the paperwork to prove it. After an hour we are allowed to repack our bus and leave. As the imperious senior officer barks orders at the soldiers lounging by the gate, I notice his right hand is playing with a string of beads. We pull out into the road. A man supporting himself on a crutch toils by. He has a child on his back.

Egypt offers no gradual assimilation into Africa, no comfortable cultural transition. The strangeness of everything begins at the coast and doesn't let up.

For a while we avoid the busy Ismailia highway, and take a side road that runs alongside the Canal. It's quiet and restful down here. There is a station through which no train seems to pass, and a narrow side canal called the Sweetwater where kingfishers swoop, butterflies flicker in the reeds and there is not much noise until the wind sets the bullrushes hissing and whispering. Even when the northbound convoy comes up the Canal these massive vessels, hundreds of thousands of tons in combined weight, pass by almost soundlessly.

As the day fades we drive south, passing through canalside villages, past small children guiding donkeys at tearaway speeds, makeshift ferries caked in Nile mud plying the waterways, orange sellers at the side of the road. At Ismailia we turn west to run for 75 miles across the Eastern Desert to Cairo. Having extricated ourselves from Port Said morale is improved, and there is a further bonus in the shape of a breathtaking desert sunset. After the sun sets a rich peach afterglow remains which as it dies seems to intensify to a raw golden red, like the embers of a dying fire.

'C' is where the tripod
fell into the
Mediterranean

9 August
Cairo:
Well, couldn't find a card
Port Said in Port Said, but did
find one in Cairo, so just to
keep up the colour, sending
it on now.
Suez Canal,
(A) and our h
move along
da
sh
at
Se
t
d

POST CARD
EGYPT

جمهورية مصر العربية

1 9 91 3 12

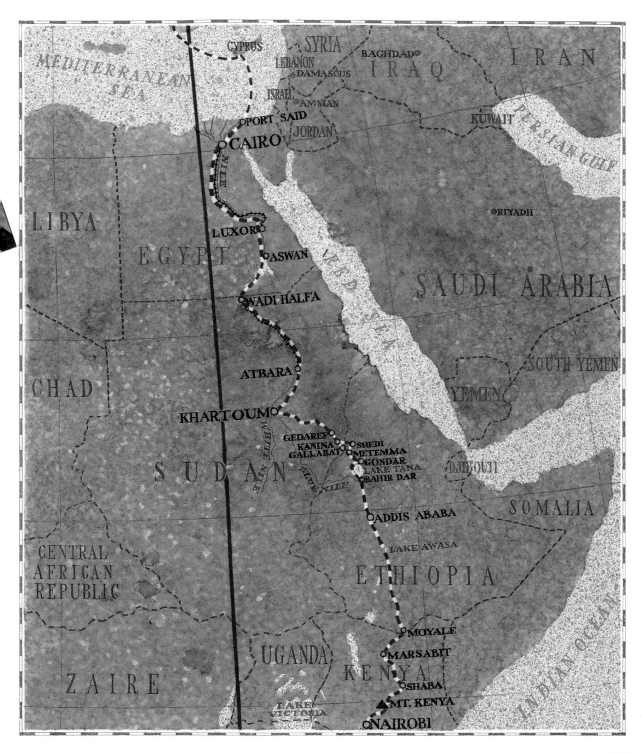

Cairo seems more enormous and manic than I ever remember it. It's 9.30 in the evening but every road and side street teems with traffic, often blocked solid. The Egyptian theory of driving is simple – everyone else on the road is in your way. There is nothing else to do but call on whichever God you feel closest to and hold on tight.

DAY 55 · CAIRO TO LUXOR

Cairo, hard up against 31 degrees East, is the only point at which our Pole to Pole course coincides with my *80 Days* route. This time we stay only long enough for a day and a half of rest and recuperation. Not that anywhere beyond the confines of my hotel room can be described as restful, but if you can endure the demanding pace Cairo is a city of all sorts of hidden delights. Before we leave for the station I take a walk out onto the Nile Bridge and a long look at the river with which our destinies are to be linked for days and weeks ahead.

Late afternoon, stuck in traffic on the way to Rameses Station. At busy intersections, everyone drives through red lights until they have to stop, which is usually when the light turns green. Nobody can then move until it becomes red again.

At the station, all the destination boards are in Arabic, and I have to ask a porter the platform for Luxor.

'Nine . . . ,' he assures me with confidence.

'No, no!' another man shakes his head with equal confidence, 'eight.'

I appeal to a sensible-looking man with glasses, 'Is it eight or nine for Luxor?'

'Luxor? . . . Eleven.'

By now it's beginning to sound like a bingo session, as passers-by helpfully shout numbers in my general direction. Fortunately a passageway is marked '8, 9, 10, 11', so I take that and am met at the other end by an extremely helpful and courteous railway official: 'Yes . . . it is Number Eight, sir.'

The train for Luxor leaves at half-past seven, from Platform Ten.

The sleeping cars on the train are run by the Wagons-Lit company and are modern and well-equipped, with air-conditioning, carpets, towels, coat hangers and Venetian blinds. I'm served an airline meal on a tray and whilst Joseph, the coach steward, makes up my bed, I wander down to the bar. I had heard how badly the Gulf War had affected tourism in Egypt, and the sight of the barman, quite alone, seems to suggest things have not recovered. Andy and Bridget, an English couple on honeymoon, are the only others who come in. They couldn't take any more of Cairo. Apart from finding 'a

120

cockroach as big as a cat' on her bed, Bridget professed herself disillusioned with the way friendship never seemed innocent, 'It always led to a shop'.

After a drink together I wish them *bon voyage* and they ask me if I'm going anywhere beyond Luxor.

I nod and try to reply as nonchalantly as possible, 'The South Pole'. Not for the first time do I notice what a conversation killer this is.

DAY 56 · LUXOR

My sleeping-car berth is comfortable but the ride is ferocious. For the last two hours to Luxor the train seems possessed by devils, and Joseph has no need to knock so hard at my door. I'm awake and hanging on for dear life.

'It's 4.45 . . . ,' he announces, and he lays a tray of unidentifiable cling-wrapped things beside me, '. . . nice breakfast sir.'

At 5.35 in the morning the train pulls into Luxor, known by the Greeks as Thebes, 420 miles south of Cairo, in Upper Egypt. I cannot conceal my excitement at being here for the first time in my life. Basil, never even in Africa before, is finding the whole journey beyond description: 'This is a great picnic . . . ,' he raves, '. . . This is the Mother of Picnics.'

Luxor Station is tastefully monumental in decoration, with tall columns, gilded details on the doors, eagle heads and a hieroglyphic design somehow incorporating power stations, railways and ancient history.

Opposite this grand façade there is a bicycle leaning against a wall and lying in the dust between the bike and the wall is it's owner, who hasn't had to get up as early as we have. Figures materialize from the pre-dawn gloom to offer us taxi rides. You will never stand on your own for long in Egypt.

We shall be joining a Nile cruise for the next leg of our journey, and as we drive along the river to find our boat – the *Isis* – I can see serried ranks of chunky four-storeyed vessels, maybe 100 in all, lined up along the riverbank, awaiting the day the tourists come back.

My guide to Luxor is a tall, straight matchstick-thin aristocrat of the business whose name is Tadorus but who asks me to call him Peter . . . 'It's easier'. I would rather call him Tadorus, but he doesn't look the sort you argue with. He wears a white djellabah and cap and carries with him a Chaplinesque walking stick which he often rests across his shoulders. An enormous pair of Esprit sunglasses almost obscures his striking but emaciated face, and when he removes them they reveal a pair of moist, sad eyes. He is 83 years old, and as a boy of 14 was present when the archaeologist Howard Carter first pushed open the door of Tutankhamun's tomb.

Peter takes me across on the Nile ferry to a cluster of mud buildings on the West Bank opposite the city. We are driven past fields of sugar cane

Day 56: Egypt

Luxor: Ferry to the Valley of the Kings, felucca at sunset.
Karnak: History at the Hypostyle Hall – Tadorus 83 years;
Palin 48 years; the column 3500 years.

and alongside an irrigation canal financed by the Russians in 1960. The greenery ends abruptly as we climb a winding road up into barren, rubble-strewn desert. We pass an ostentatious modern cafeteria. 'The Temple of Coca-Cola,' Peter announces, permitting himself a shade of a smile. Then we are into the Valley of the Kings, which resembles a gigantic quarry, littered with rock debris, bleached white by the sun. We leave the bus and walk up towards the tombs in dry and scorching heat. Peter estimates the temperature at 40 Celsius, 104 Fahrenheit. I ask him if it's usually like this.

'No . . . no . . . ,' he shakes his head dismissively, 'last month was hot!'

This vast necropolis contains the remains of 62 Pharaohs of the New Kingdom, established in Thebes 3000 to 3500 years ago. It was discovered – 'rediscovered', as Peter corrects me – in 1892. Only 40 of the tombs have been found, and all, bar one, had been emptied by robbers. That's why Howard Carter's discovery of Tutankhamun's burial chamber was of such significance. Because it had been built beneath another tomb (that of Rameses VI) the rubble left by the robbers had helped to hide the entrance and what Peter saw with Carter that day in 1922, was Tutankhamun's treasure exactly as it had been sealed in the tomb 3300 years earlier. I asked him what he could remember of the moment of discovery.

'We find all the beds and the chairs and the statues . . . stacked one on top of the other up to the ceiling.'

'What was Howard Carter's reaction?'

'He became crazy . . . when he have a look to the state coffin, which it is made of solid gold, that thick gold, not like our gold, 24 carat gold, he became crazy, you know . . . hitting like that.' Here Peter slapped at the sides of his face with his long bony hands in a passable imitation of a Pools winner, 'Unbelievable, unbelievable.'

I asked him about the curse that was supposed to have been visited on anyone who opened the tomb.

'No curse . . . no curse at all.'

'It was said that a mosquito flew from the tomb as it was opened.'

'No mosquito. They say there is a mosquito came out of the tomb and bite him and he died . . . he discovered the tomb in 1922, he's still inside the tomb up to 1927 . . . he died in 1939, he died a very very old man.' And not from a mosquito bite apparently.

We walk down into the tomb of Rameses III. The walls are covered in rich paintings and complex inscriptions illustrating the progress of the Pharaoh on his journey through the underworld, filled with wicked serpents, crocodiles and other creatures waiting to devour him. Because of the dry desert air, they are well preserved, an extraordinary historical document.

The sun is setting behind the Valley of the Kings when we return on the ferry. At this indescribably beautiful time of day, when the rich golden

brown of the lower sky spills onto the surface of the Nile, turning it an intense amber, and the palm trees along the bank glow for a few precious minutes in the reflection, it is not difficult to imagine the power and spectacle of a funeral procession bearing the God-King's body across this same river, three and a half thousand years ago, at the beginning of his last and most important journey.

DAY 57 · LUXOR

An early start to catch the sunrise over the ruins of the Temple of Karnak. The name is taken from the town of Carnac in Brittany and is a reminder that it was the French who, in 1798, rediscovered this temple under 30 feet of sand. We have a local Egyptologist with us who has obtained permission for us to climb up onto one of the pylons – the massive 150-foot high towers that flank the entrance to the temple. This involves a scramble up a narrow passageway enclosed between the tomb of Seti II and the pylon wall. We must have disturbed a colony of bats, for the dark tunnel is suddenly filled with flapping creatures trying to find a way out. My hat is knocked off as they brush my face. At the top, the view is splendid but the sunrise isn't and the crew return to our boat for breakfast. I decide to stay in the temple and enjoy some pre-tourist solitude.

The buildings and the monuments here are as impressive as any man-made thing I have seen in the world. They were created to extol the power and strength of the Pharaohs and the Gods whose likenesses they were, and it is impossible to walk amongst the columns and beside the obelisks and not feel the presence of this power. In the Hypostyle Hall, where 134 columns rise in a symbolic forest, 60 feet high, from bases whose circumference could be contained within a ring of 12 people with outstretched arms, I feel a sense of awe and wonder unlike any I've experienced before, compounded by the awareness that similar feelings must have been experienced here over thousands of years.

I'm brought back down to earth as the first wave of tourists appears, adjusting cameras, complaining about meals the night before and arguing over who has the air tickets. Then I catch sight of Tadorus, who I must remember to call Peter, like a white wraith among the massive pillars, stick at the back of his head. If you need a lost sense of wonder restored then Peter is the man. Despite his 80-odd years spent in and around these buildings with scholars and archaeologists, he still finds some things unexplainable. A statue of Rameses II, 97 feet high and made from a single piece of granite, weighs 1000 tons. Cranes nowadays can only lift 200 tons, yet this massive statue was brought to Luxor from Aswan overland, 3000 years ago. Peter strikes a theatrical pose, 'How, Tadorus, they say?'. He pauses and his big round, sad eyes blink slowly, 'My answer, magic.'

The temple of Abu Simbel, further south, was, he tells me, aligned by the ancient Egyptians so that the sun shone onto the face of Rameses twice a year – once on his birthday and once on his coronation day. When Abu Simbel was re-sited in a 40-million-dollar operation to save it from the rising waters of Lake Nasser, all the calculations of the world's experts could not enable the sun to shine on Rameses' face more than once a year.

Peter shakes his head sorrowfully, 'Nothing better,' he sighs, 'Nothing better.'

Here is surely a man born 3000 years too late. I'm sad to say goodbye to him.

It is September now and there are little things a traveller tends to forget, such as haircuts. I repair to a barber's shop in the back streets of Luxor. My barber is called Allah Gmal Idil, and he is very proud of his establishment, and of his two sons who stand and watch the whole procedure. I fear the worst and get the best from Allah, a good haircut, a cut-throat shave, a rub with pomagne scent, a trim of the eyebrows and even an assault on the nostril hairs.

In the evening, back on the *Isis*, I'm on deck looking out over another Nile sunset and dreaming off into the past when the present rudely reasserts itself.

'You don't know how Sheffield Wednesday went on last night?'

Pat and Gerald Flinders, two of our fellow passengers on the cruise down to Aswan, are from the town of my birth. Gerald has been studying Egyptology at night school.

'He can write National Westminster Bank in hieroglyphics,' says Pat proudly.

'Why would he want to do that?' Roger asks.

Pat seems surprised at the question. 'Because he works there.'

They join about 20 others whom we meet this evening, including a family from Watford, one of whom by extraordinary coincidence works in the council department responsible for twinning arrangements with Novgorod. There are three middle-aged Danish ladies on a girls-only holiday, a French couple, two handsome Italians, two Montreal Canadians, and assorted English and Americans. There is a resident archaeologist called Abdul – a big man with a shaved head. We shall set sail in the early hours of tomorrow morning for Aswan, which is a little over 120 miles upstream. It will take us a leisurely three days.

DAY 58 · LUXOR TO ASWAN

I'm up on deck at 7 a.m. The light is soft and gentle, and the air dry and warm. *Isis* glides along the lightly rippled surface of the Nile with solid ease. On either bank smoke rises from huts of mud and straw. A line of people who have just landed from a felucca – the traditional single-masted sailing boat of the Nile – winds up the short, steep, hard-baked mud bank in the shade of locust and palm trees. Two boys in a rowing boat, painted the green of Islam, moor up by a fishing net. One of the boys smacks at the water with a long pole, whilst the other bangs a drum to attract the fish. A buffalo grazes, donkeys wait in the fields. There are no roads or cars or railways, there is no concrete or neon. It is a timeless scene, containing, almost unchanged, all the elements of nature that cover the walls of tombs and temples.

By 9 o'clock the surroundings have changed considerably. We have reached the lock at Esna, 30 miles from Luxor, a bottleneck of quite serious proportions which they don't mention in the brochures. The lock was built, by the British, in 1908, and it has room for only one ship at a time. It takes 35 minutes to get each one through and, as they alternate between those going north and south, it can mean a 70-minute wait; if you're lucky. But the lock also incorporates a swing road-bridge so it is closed every alternate hour. There are four ships ahead of us, and Wahid, our cruise director, estimates we will not be through until late afternoon. 'And this is not the busy time,' he adds gloomily, 'from late September it will start to be the busy time . . . during . . . let's say, New Year's Eve, sometimes it reaches up to 24 ships each side.'

He remembers once being held up for 48 hours.

So we drop anchor beside the noisy construction site of the new two-berth lock which will not be ready until 1993. It's easily the least beautiful stretch of the Nile, and we have seven hours to enjoy it.

As we watch one of the cruise ships negotiating the lock, like a fat woman trying to get through a turnstile, our Egyptian pilot – Mohammed Ali Abu el Makeran by name – sits by the wheel, one leg hooked up under a striped djellabah. He has been with Hilton Cruises since they began in 1963, and has the quiet smile of one to whom patience is not a virtue but a way of life. He has 14 children, he says, and they all live in his house. He tells me their names but apologizes for not being able to remember the last five.

To pass the time, Wahid and Abdul the archaeologist decide to mount an expedition to the temple at Edfu, and to this end the *Isis* draws up alongside the river wall, where we are immediately besieged by traders. They obviously know what Nile cruise tourists like to buy and it's revealing that most of their wares are for women and consist largely of flashy sequined dresses – probably good for a night on the Nile but a bit of an embarrassment back in Widnes. If anyone on board shows the faintest glimmer of interest they throw the item up in a plastic bag, shouting 'One pound to look! One pound to look!'. One bag lands with a soft plop in the swimming-pool. No one pays the pound but persistence pays off. One of the Danish ladies has bought a slinky black number with 'Egypt' picked out in gold and Pat from Sheffield has just caught something in blue.

'We women can't resist shopping,' she says and leaning over the side, shouts down a price. She looks pleased at the aggrieved response.

'I love to haggle!'

The sound of Yorkshire and Arabic haggling drifts across the Nile. Pat's husband is more interested in our mutual connection with Sheffield than shopping. Did I know that the British Open Barber's Shop Quartet Champions hail from Sheffield?

I'm more worried about tonight's fancy dress party at which everyone is required to 'do a turn', and I use the quiet time after the others have gone off to Edfu to learn the Percy Bysshe Shelley poem *Ozymandias*:

> *I met a traveller from an antique land,*
> *Who said two vast and trunkless legs of stone*
> *Stand in the desert . . .*

Two curly-headed local boys approach the lock wall making signs on their palms for baksheesh. Instead I give them *Ozymandias*, at full volume and with attendant mime. As I reach the end, they applaud as enthusiastically as only a couple of natural actors can.

After an Oriental buffet the evening's fancy dress party gets underway, presided over with enthusiasm by Abdul. I have secured a makeshift Roman centurion outfit which is not quite long enough to cover an expanse of Marks and Spencer underpants, and Mirabel and Patti have sportingly agreed to be a pair of concubines and lead the audience participation by holding up the words of *Ozymandias*. At the last minute I think it might be a bit sexist to call them concubines and suggest that Abdul announce them as handmaidens.

'Oh no . . .' he says briskly '. . . concubines is *much* better.'

The glamorous Italians come along as Pinocchio, and Pat and Gerald as a pair of music hall artists. Roger bravely dons drag as Mrs Mills and sings 'The Mighty Dnieper', and the people from Watford as the Mayor of Edfu and his family, despite being mercilessly rude about the Egyptians, win first prize, largely as a result of some virtuoso belly dancing from their daughter. But for me the unquestioned highlight of the evening was seeing Nigel operating the camera dressed as a Pharaoh. This was surely the period of history his body was intended for.

DAY 59 · LUXOR TO ASWAN

Up on deck to watch the sunrise. It's Nigel's birthday, but he's already out and about trying to find somewhere to set up the camera, and muttering darkly about the vibration of the ship's engines. It's cold enough for a sweater as I settle down to watch the show. By 6 o'clock the first reflections of pre-dawn light can be glimpsed in the water. The concentration of light grows slowly, expands and then widens into an expanse of pale pink, extinguishing the stars. A half-hour later the crest of the sun edges into a whitening, cloudless sky and within a matter of seconds it is riding free of the mountains, growing in power and brilliance until it is a ball of molten gold. At this point, as if sunlight-activated, the on-board muzak tinkles into life . . . 'Raindrops keep falling on my 'ead'. I'm not sure they'd know what a raindrop is round here.

After breakfast we put in at Kom Ombo, 25 miles from Aswan, to visit the Temple of Sobek, the sacred crocodile. Pat is persuaded to come along despite claiming she has 'temple fatigue', and despite a brisk wind which is continually blowing her straw hat off.

'This hat's a mixed blessing,' I hear her muttering, as she chases it across the Hypostyle Hall.

Abdul, his hairless skull protected by a knitted white cap, is a proficient but intimidating guide. He reels off facts, figures, details and explanations with unassailable authority and then fixes us with a piercing gaze,

'Any questions?'

Having learnt in the last 30 seconds that the frog is a symbol of life, that this temple is dedicated to a sparrow-hawk as well as a crocodile, that women in ancient Egypt delivered babies in a sitting position and that in the mummification process the brain was pulled out through the nostrils, no one really knows where to begin.

Nile Cruising: Fancy dress night with Gerald and friend, Nigel goes native, a short break from reading. Aswan: Shehan's first customer for a year.

Day 59: Egypt

At 2.15 in the afternoon we reach Aswan, the capital of Upper Egypt, 550 miles from Cairo. The Nile begins to break up at Aswan, and will not, for several hundred miles, be the orderly river we've come to know and love. It is divided by the bulk of Elephantine Island, then broken by a series of cataracts and two dams.

My thermometer, laid out for five minutes in the sun, registers 121 Fahrenheit, 50 Celsius. The river seems busier here. Maybe it is because the town itself is bigger than Luxor, and contains modern high-rise blocks and a four-lane Corniche, or perhaps the narrowing of the river around the islands concentrates the traffic. Feluccas with weirdly misspelt English names, like *Hapey Tripe*, drift about, looking for tourist business.

Bid our farewells to Wahid and Abdul and Gerald and Pat and seek out the Old Cataract Hotel. Try out one of the fiacres lined up hopefully along the Corniche. My driver is called Shehan, and he's very proud of Abla, his black horse with white copper blinkers and the hand of Fatima on the saddle. Shehan says that the Gulf crisis has been very bad for business: 'For a year nobody come.'

I ask him what he did during that time.

'Sleep,' he replies, matter-of-factly. 'My horse sleep at my home. I sleep in the car.'

It's belly-dancing night at the Cataract Hotel. The audience consists almost entirely of tour groups, but Romany assures me that the belly dancer is the real thing. Every now and then she will lead some victim from one of the tables to dance with her. All this does is demonstrate that belly dancing is not something anyone can do after a few beers. One grey-haired man is so confused by the encounter that he wanders the room in a daze, unable to find where it was he was sitting.

Romany, who has already given Nigel a djellabah for his birthday, goes down to the floor for a word with the dancer, and glances over in our direction. Nigel disappears like greased lightning, not to be seen again until his birthday's over.

DAY 60 · ASWAN

There is a wide wooden balcony outside my room at the Old Cataract Hotel, and from it one of the most extraordinarily rich views one could wish for. It's a mixture of the mundane and the dramatic. Directly below me are the terraces and gardens of the hotel, lined with chairs, tables and sunshades. Below them, at the waterside, are the feluccas, their tall masts and angled sailbooms rising above the clusters of palm trees. Elephantine Island rises up in mid-stream, with the smooth granite rocks at its water's edge that resemble elephants bathing, and above them a collection of ruined buildings dating from as far back as the 3rd Dynasty – 4000 years ago – when Elephantine Island was the centre of the worship of the god Khnum, who, among other things, created mankind. Beyond the island is the desert. Low, bare, dusty hills, in the middle of which, solitary and exposed, stands the domed mausoleum of Aga Khan III, spiritual leader of the Ismaili Moslems, who died in 1957. The story goes that he suffered from severe rheumatism, and was told that a cure would be to rest his feet in desert sand. He came to Aswan, stuck his feet in the sand, was duly cured and gave orders that he be buried here.

I spend some of the day relaxing in a felucca, sailed at a leisurely pace by Captain Peckry, a 21-year-old Nubian. Clasping a cigarette between his lips, he moves the heavy single-sailed boat with some skill, but seems quite bored by the whole thing, only coming to life as we are heading back to shore. Out of the blue he asks if I would like to go to a Nubian wedding tonight.

'Will there be anything to drink?' I enquire, knowing the Moslem views on these matters.

'Beer, whiskey . . . hash,' replies Peckry, cheerfully. I feel rather pathetic for saying I might go and knowing full well I won't, but he has a felucca to recover in tomorrow, and we have a long, long way to go.

131

DAY 61 · ASWAN

 We are on our way out of Egypt at last. From tomorrow we shall cease for a while to be tourists and become travellers. Soon we shall exchange the cossetted comforts of Cataract Hotels and Hilton Cruises for the uncertainties of a public ferry into a country which my guide book describes as 'fraught with political turmoil, economic chaos, civil war, drought, famine, disease and refugee crisis . . .'

We travel in hope rather than certainty, having met people who have waited six weeks for the ferry into Sudan. We drive one last time along the Corniche, past acacia trees in bloom, and the Police Rowing Club, and the intriguing sign 'Pedaloos for hire', out of the town and along the first dam ever laid across the Nile, by the British in 1902.

The British dam looks like a toy now, compared to the Soviet-built monster which replaced it three and a half miles upstream, creating Lake Nasser which stretches over 300 miles, into the Sudan. The approach to the High Dam is beneath a web of overhead power lines, past soaring concrete monuments to Soviet-Egyptian co-operation, and all the trappings of modern military security – radar, anti-aircraft guns, camouflaged helicopters, silos, dug-outs, bunkers and early warning systems. This could be described as overkill, but, as someone chillingly pointed out, the dam at Aswan is 650 feet higher than Cairo and Alexandria, and if it were to burst Egypt would be virtually wiped out.

This complex is the nerve centre of Egypt, from which half of the country's electrical power and 99 per cent of its water flows. Its importance is colossal, but so is the investment needed to keep it going. Hamdy Eltahez, the Chairman of the High Dam Authority, who showed me round, was blunt about the need for outside help. A massive programme to replace all 12 Russian-built turbines with American models is currently underway. But there is now a new problem. The lake behind the dam is silting up rapidly. Since 1964, there has been an 82-foot build-up of sediment at the Sudani end of the lake. At this rate the water flow will be rapidly reduced and in some cases cut off altogether. Eltahez and Egypt are looking for a new international saviour, someone to invest in the vast costs of digging a by-pass canal around the silted up area. To invest in nothing less than diverting the Nile.

Some people question the wisdom of building the dam at all, pointing out that the yearly flooding of the Nile provided vital fertility, which now has to be provided artificially, which is expensive and destructive. The Nubians question why they had to lose 75 villages and have thousands of their people resettled to make way for the lake. But Eltahez is adamant.

The Aswan Dam saved Egypt in the nine years of drought between 1979 and 1988.

Whichever way you look at it, it is an extraordinary undertaking, the only project in modern Egypt to rival the works of the Pharaohs.

DAY 62 · ASWAN TO WADI HALFA

 At the gates of the Eastern Harbour, beneath an imposing sign announcing the jurisdiction of the 'Aswan Governate, High Dam Ports Authority', an official wearing a 'Port Police' armband attempts to hold the world at bay with a red loudhailer. Cars and trucks piled with crates and packing cases hoot their way past men and women piled with refrigerators, cabinets and bulging roped sacks. Porters, in frayed blue cotton jackets stand, confused and vacant, waiting to be shouted into action. A boy with a dustpan and long-handled brush dabs ineffectually around the feet of the throng. There is not a white face to be seen, and even Western clothes are a rare exception in a sea of chadors – veils covering the heads and bodies of the women – and grubby djellabahs, the long wide-sleeved robes of the men.

Slowly, patiently, this mass of people and possessions moves through the customs building and out towards a buff-hulled 160-foot ferry boat called the *Sinai*. It's a hard-worked, stocky, unglamorous vessel with an apparently unlimited capacity to absorb everyone *and* their kitchen sinks. The authorities, for their part, have done what they can to make getting aboard as difficult as possible. Passengers must squeeze between unloading trucks on one side and barbed wire, a link fence and sandbags on the other. Their progress is further impeded by an official of the Port Authority with wavy black hair and a wonderful repertoire of hand gestures who seems unable to communicate on any level less than uncontrolled fury. The slightest thing sets him off, igniting a Fawltyesque rage which quite cheers people up.

As this is the first ferry out of Aswan for two weeks it is full to capacity, which I'm told, with a vague shrug, is anywhere between 500 and 700 passengers, though I can see only two lifeboats, neither of which looks capable of taking 350 souls. We shall be on board for one night, covering the 186 miles to Wadi Halfa in roughly 15 hours.

There are three decks on the *Sinai* and the good news is that we have cabins to ourselves. The bad news is that it's almost impossible to reach them as the central companion-way fills up with crates, sacks, boxes and their owners. No one is able to move anyone else out of the way as there is nowhere out of the way to go. I walk up onto the top deck to watch the loading, but there is little shade and the temperature is over 100 degrees. Return to my cabin to read Alan Moorehead's *The White Nile*, only to find my cabin has filled up with some of the 30 boxes of drinking water we are carrying with us. Once I've sorted these and my bags onto the top bunk I lie down but the commotion in the gangway outside makes sleep impossible. There are no locks and every now and then an Arab face peers in before slamming the door again.

At 4.15 the barriers have gone up at the dockside and it appears everyone is aboard. The passengers, mainly Sudanis who have come to Aswan to buy things not available in their own country, sit, cocooned by their possessions, waiting patiently. Despite the overcrowding there is no feeling of pressure. People talk and joke with each other, and children play up and down the ladders. On the top deck prayer mats are being laid out and small groups (always of men) are gathering around the mullahs, as pupils before their teacher.

With an ear-splitting blast of the horn the *Sinai* pulls away from the jetty at a quarter to five, past one of the old ferries, of which only the bows can be seen, rising out of the water at an angle of 45 degrees.

We are on the waters of a lake that is younger than I am. Beneath the waves are the granite cliffs of the Nile Valley from which so many of the great monuments of Ancient Egypt were carved. Many of these monuments of the past, luckier than the Nubian villages of the present, were saved from the floodwater by a massive international aid programme to dismantle and re-site them. The Temple of Kalabsha, built around the time of Christ, is now perched on a headland close to the Eastern Harbour, after being moved 37 miles in 13,000 pieces. As we sail slowly away to the south the sight of its pylon and the columns of its Hypostyle Hall are a last reminder of the extraordinary and enigmatic power of Ancient Egypt.

At 7 o'clock the captain, Mahmoud il Sudani from Alexandria, turns muezzin and broadcasts prayers from the bridge. Almost 200 people gather on the deck, bowing, in ranks six deep, toward the low ragged mountains in the east, beyond which lie empty desert, the Red Sea, and the holy shrine of Mecca, 500 miles away.

Our own, polar, Mecca is still many thousands of miles off, but as the sun sets we cross the line of the Tropic of Cancer, and feel we are making progress.

Basil, busy avoiding the attentions of a mullah who is trying to convert him, has discovered the dining-room and with the proviso that we bring our own plates and cutlery is recommending it for dinner. Carrying my camp cutlery set (made in China) I fight my way to the galley only to find the door barred by a tall, be-turbaned figure with a gaze of dervish-like intensity. Like some *maître d'* gone berserk he occasionally emerges to deal very fiercely with the queue, thrusting them back and shooing them away. It turns out that the dining-room is also the immigration office and very few people are queuing

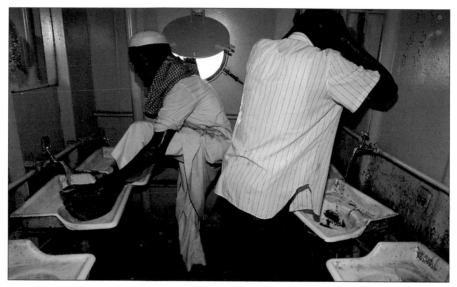

for the food. Chicken noodle soup, followed by macaroni (which I am assured is a typically Egyptian dish) with a pungent meat and tomato sauce, chicken, chips and fresh baked faturia – crisp, bap-like bread rolls – is eaten to the accompaniment of constant tapping at the portholes by those wanting to have their passports (pale blue for Sudan and green for Egypt) examined and processed.

Whenever I have ventured into the washing and lavatory area it has been full of people cleaning their feet before prayer, and now the basins are blocked and water sloshes around the floor. The squat toilets are foul smelling and permanently full.

To bed, climbing into my own sheet sleeping bag for the first time, and donning my head-torch to read about conditions during the siege of Khartoum in 1884, which don't sound a lot different from what we're undergoing now.

DAY 63 · ASWAN TO WADI HALFA

On the deck of the *Sinai*, directly in front of the bridge, is a three-piece suite, upholstered in claret velour, with worked wooden legs and decoratively curved arms. No one seems to know to whom this fragment of living-room belongs, but all sorts of people rest in it for a while. So it is that I find myself entering the Sudan on a sofa.

Sudan, the largest country in Africa, stretches from the Red Sea in the east to within a few hundred miles of Nigeria in the west, from the Tropic of Cancer almost to the Equator. Foreign visitors are not encouraged.

The first sight of its northernmost town, Wadi Halfa, is of an exposed rocky headland, on which stands a collection of open-sided tented structures, a handful of vehicles and a number of waiting figures, moving across the rocks as we approach. Their djellabahs are caught by a light breeze, giving their movements a dreamlike quality.

There is no port, and there are no other vessels. The Sudanese customs officers are slow and thorough, removing personal items and laboriously copying serial numbers. The cumbersome process of examination and paperwork seems to bear out the rule that the more forms you have to fill in the less efficient the country is likely to be.

In the end they confiscate two videos of *Around the World in 80 Days*, which are taken off for inspection, whilst we are allowed, after a three-hour wait, to step ashore and find transport into the town, which lies three miles away. Accompanying us are two minders from the Ministry of Information (and any country that has a Ministry of Information must have something to hide). I squeeze onto the back of a pick-up truck in which a dozen people are already standing, and we drive off across a sandy wasteland dotted with rocks and scrubby bushes. Then dwellings of the most primitive kind appear, some of them little more than cloth or skins stretched across four poles. They give way to small mud huts and eventually to a sprawl of long low painted buildings one of which is the Nile Hotel.

The hotel comprises a series of concrete courtyards with communal washing facilities – there is cold running water between six and seven, morning and evening – and basic rooms with brightly painted walls. It's plain and unadorned but a haven from the bleak and burning desert.

There will be no cold beers for a while as Sudan is run according to strict Islamic law, which forbids the use of alcohol. Nor is there any lunch at the hotel. We have to dig into the stocks of cheese spread, tinned tuna and Marks and Spencer chicken breasts, which Angela has assembled in what must have been the Mother of all Shopping Expeditions. I place my thermometer in the sunshine on the windowsill of my room where it registers 128 Fahrenheit, 54 Centigrade. I have been nowhere hotter in my life.

The proprietor of the hotel, Ibrahim Abbas, a tall, dignified, melancholy character, brings out two photographs, and I understand his sadness. One shows an elegant waterfront of distinctive wooden-balconied houses alongside a fine mosque with decorated minaret. The next shows nothing but water lapping around the pinnacle of the minaret.

'The waters come at night,' he remembers . . . 'pushed down the houses. It was terrible.' It was in August 1964 that Lake Nasser finally engulfed the old Wadi Halfa.

4 p.m.: I lie on a thin grubby mattress in my room. The air is unmoving. The thermometer shows 98 Fahrenheit, but it's dry, just bearable heat. Flies settle on my mouth and nostrils until I grow tired of waving them away and fall into a light sleep. The room seems hotter when I wake. I blink out at an implacable sky. Beside my bed my Braun alarm clock sits on a pink metal table next to a chair with a plastic strip seat. The walls are bare, with a pale blue wash over chipped and scuffed plaster.

Around 5 o'clock I hear the wailing sound of a distant locomotive, and within minutes the hotel is galvanized. This is the moment for which they have been waiting a month – the arrival of the Khartoum train. The hotel suddenly fills up – every bed, inside and outside, is mobilized.

Wadi Halfa, Sudan: The 'Nile Hilton' — reception and executive washroom, street life, an audience with the Governor, Nubian women.

Day 63: Sudan

At the cooler end of the day we pay a visit to the Governor of Wadi Halfa, an imposing, charismatic man with a greying beard who speaks good English in a soft deep voice. He has only recently been appointed. He is critical of the way things have been run.

'Since 26 years when old Wadi Halfa was flooded they have done nothing . . . only wait for the train and the ferry.' And, he might have added, the possibility of being flooded again if the water behind the dam should rise to 182 metres. It has once reached 178. But this governor is a quiet optimist and is pushing ahead with various projects to drag Wadi Halfa out of its lethargy, including an irrigation programme to help the town grow all its own wheat.

He offers us tea and sweets and talks of the diversity of these big African countries – there are 270 languages in the Sudan alone. The governor reveals that he was once Member of Parliament for Darfur in the far west, but concludes, 'I have enough of politics, now I like to work with the people'. I can't help feeling, as I leave, that this capable man has been sent as far away from the present government as possible, and that for a politician, Wadi Halfa is the Siberia of the Sudan.

The Nile Hilton, as the crew have christened our hotel, is packed tonight. There are bodies everywhere, and voices and shufflings and comings and goings, but the cold shower is spectacularly refreshing, and it's down to 92 degrees in my room. As I lie down to try and sleep I feel exhilarated but a little apprehensive. I have never experienced anything quite like this in my life, and I have the distinct feeling that there is worse to come.

DAY 64 · WADI HALFA TO ATBARA

POLE *to* **POLE**

Sleep is not easy at the Nile Hotel, what with the heat and the almost unbroken nocturnal soundtrack of rasping, hawking, spitting and snoring from just outside my window.

At one point in the night, despite stern instructions from my brain, my bowels are wide awake. I reach for torch and toilet paper, seek out one of the plastic jugs which are scattered around the hotel, fill it from one of the earthenware Ali Baba jars full of muddy Nile water, and, picking my way carefully between the sleeping bodies, head for the lavatories like a condemned man. There are fewer flies to contend with at night, but the smell is very bad, and it's best not to breathe through the nose if you can help it. This is not easy if you have to hold the torch in your mouth to keep both hands free.

Up at 7 o'clock. Fraser has found a scorpion in his room and killed it with a shoe. Wash at a communal trough, into which oozes a thin trickle of water. Breakfast consists of dark red beans, cheese, jam and two eggs sprinkled with turmeric.

The train leaves at 5 o'clock this evening, so I have time to stock up on some provisions for a journey that is scheduled to take 36 hours.

The desert begins at the door of the hotel. Across an empty expanse are houses surrounded by long low mud walls, the same colour as the sand and the hills, so all seem to blend together in one wide, dim-brown desiccated vista. No rain has fallen here since 1988.

In the market most people seem to be either eating or washing their hands. Dogs hang around waiting for scraps, children play with sticks and hoops, and the stalls sell onions, beans, some cucumber, dates, bananas, garlic and rice. Flies cluster round the already decomposing fruit.

As we film we seem to attract friends and enemies in equal measure. Among our friends is the customs man who returns my confiscated video of *80 Days*, grinning broadly, a little boy wearing an 'Egypt No Problem' T-shirt who attaches himself to us and a group of Sudanese from our hotel who invite me to share some fresh grilled Nile perch with them. Our enemies are sour-faced men who appear from nowhere scowling and finger-wagging. They have taken great but unspecified objection to our presence, and quickly gather around them a small angry group, swelled into a threatening crowd by curious onlookers. Their wrath can be insistent and disturbing. One of them takes a stick to Basil, and they seem to regard the presence of Patti and Angela, unveiled and working, as particularly provocative to Islamic sensibilities. Their own women keep a very low profile. I see one move swiftly past swathed in a 'World Cup 1990' sari.

At 4 o'clock we cross the sand to the station. Crowds are already milling around the long train, which is made up of three open service wagons at the front, 18 passenger coaches and eight freight cars at the back, a total of 29 vehicles behind one American-built diesel.

The Governor arrives to see us off. He's exchanged his robes for the characterless but ideologically sound safari shirts favoured by Kenneth Kaunda and others. He presents me with a box of dates for the journey, and smiles and shakes hands with us all most warmly.

'When the train leave you will see a sight,' he chuckles, and indeed as the whistle wails across the desert at 5 o'clock sharp and this huge, unwieldy combination begins to move, the low embankment is filled with a mass of running figures, hurtling toward the train, leaping onto the coaches and eventually clambering up onto the roof.

Apart from the Roof Class travellers who, if they are prepared to risk extremes of heat and cold and blowing sand, are not officially discouraged, there are three Classes on the train. Although we are in First it's quite basic – we are four to a compartment, few of the lights or fans work, and the basin in the lavatory has disappeared. The train superintendent, another big, friendly man, reckons there could be 4000 passengers altogether, though he doesn't know for sure.

A milepost in the sand indicates 899 kilometres (557 miles) to Khartoum.

The long, straight, single-track line was built on the orders of General Kitchener in 1897, to help in the relief of Khartoum which the Mahdi had seized from General Gordon twelve years previously. Despite the punishing heat and lack of water, the British and Egyptian forces laid track at the rate of more than half a kilometre a day, covering the 230 miles to Abu Hamed in 10 months.

Once the pride of the Empire, the Nile Valley Express is now much reduced. Nearly all the coaches are in need of repair, and the wooden struts of their frames can often be seen through the rotten panelling. Delays are almost obligatory, sometimes extending to days.

But for all its inadequacies, riding this train is an exhilarating experience. As night falls on the Nubian Desert and a pale half moon lends a ghostly glow to a landscape of silver sand and occasional low jagged peaks, I sit at the open door of our coach, with a little Van Morrison on my Walkman, and marvel at the sheer beauty of it all.

Twice we come to an unscheduled halt – once for a broken vacuum pipe, and once for 'engine failure'. As soon as the train stops, passengers on the roof jump down and curl up to sleep on the sand, usually in groups of three or four, with one person on watch in case the train should start. Some get out to pray, others to stretch their legs and cool off in the light desert breeze.

Then, miraculously, the train rumbles into motion and they all rush back as we continue into the night, shadows from lighted compartments forming an abstract pattern of cubes and squares on the floor of the desert and spent cigarettes flashing from windows like fireflies.

DAY 65 · WADI HALFA TO ATBARA

POLE *to* **POLE**

At some point in the night I wake feeling as if I have a rock lodged in my throat. Swallowing is piercingly painful, and only partly relieved by a swig from my water bottle. I'm relieved to find that I'm not the only one suffering. The cause is fine sand blowing off the desert and inhaled in sleep. There is dust over everything in the compartment, and only our precious bottled water to wash with.

At 6.30 a.m. Nigel, who must have been born on wall-bars, is already up on the roof filming the sunrise. Fraser is also up there and I know I shall have to join them. The train never moves at more than a steady 45 miles an hour but the scramble onto the top requires an act of faith in the shifting, creaking fittings between the coaches. There are about 20 people riding on our coach, and the atmosphere is friendly. Ali Hassan is young, maybe 18 or 19, travelling to Khartoum to study civil engineering. He seems surprised that people in England cannot ride on the top of trains. I explain about bridges.

We talk about the state of the country. He is optimistic. There is no famine any more and the civil war in the south is less severe than it was. I ask him if it is a religious struggle between the Muslims of the north (comprising about 70 per cent of the country) and the Christians and non-Muslims of the south. He says it is political. Garang, the leader of the rebels, wants to be prime minister, and if he would only content himself with a position in the existing government the war could be over. The Sudanese need no friends, he adds, they will solve their own problems.

Our roof-top deliberations are interrupted by the arrival of a robed bundle of a man carrying a huge kettle swathed in cloth, and a stack of glasses.

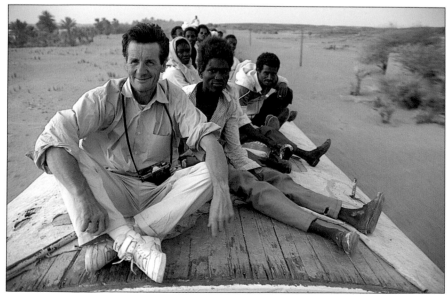

Ali Hassan insists on buying me a cup of tea, and a cloth bung is removed from the spout and my glass filled with a sweet but refreshingly sharp substance. I'm lingering over the pleasure of this unusual feat of catering, when I notice a bony hand impatiently extended. The tea-man wants the glass back so he can continue along the top of the train. He sways off into the distance and Fraser shakes his head. We'll get botulism, he declares, that's for sure. Still, that was the least of my worries when I climbed onto the top of a moving express.

At 8 o'clock we pass Station Number 6 (none of the stations across the desert have names). I remember a Sudanese butler in Cyprus insisting I visit his family here, but there seems no sign of life, family or otherwise for miles around. I make my way through the shredded and rusting remains of a connecting corridor to the dining car. There are six tables set beside dirty, shattered plastic windows and a number of empty wall-fittings where fans used to be. The breakfast of bread, chunks of beef, a boiled egg and lentils is not bad.

We reach Abu Hamed as the day is beginning to boil up. This is where the Nile, having completed a wide loop, turns south again.

The engine that has miraculously survived the night is taken off here, and whilst it is being refuelled, I walk down to the river bank. A number of long, low boats with outboard motors are filling up with passengers to cross to the far shore. I notice that the women travel separately from the men, as they are required to do on the train.

By midday my thermometer reads 100 degrees in the compartment. Outside the rock-strewn desert floor is bleached white. Inside I'm eating a tin of 'Stewed Chicken with Bone', canned in China, bought in Wadi Halfa. The rest of the crew are opting for health, safety and Sainsbury's tuna. No one has much energy left and when I squeeze a plastic tube of mustard so hard that the end flies off and covers Nigel in a pattern of yellow blobs, there is a sort of weary resignation that this is the kind of thing that happens on the Nile Valley Express.

About half-past one someone falls off the roof and the train backs up for half a mile to collect him. He was flat out at the time and the whole episode gives a new meaning to falling asleep.

Between Artoli and Atbara we run close to the Nile, which is thick and muddy here compared to Egypt. The villages are squashed along the bank, and there seems to be no systematic irrigation. The houses are square, of mud-brick, simple shelters from the sun. There are goats, but no vehicles. It looks a hard life out there despite such a bounteous river.

In the dining-car, desperate for anything to relieve the relentless heat, some people are drinking Nile water, complete with mud. I stick to tea, bought for me by three Khartoumers, two of whom are returning from a honeymoon in Cairo. One is an agricultural engineer, another a lawyer. They are anxious to tell me of the damage they think the present government is inflicting on their country. The fundamentalist hardliners are aggressive, they have killed many opponents and, says the lawyer with a frustrated shake of the head, 'They really do dislike educated people'.

As we step off the train in the cool of the evening at another Nileside stop, I watch a roof passenger unwind his turban and lower it down to a water-seller who ties it around the handle of a bucket which is then hoisted up again. Locals sit beside their wares with hurricane lamps burning, and little girls walk up and down with kettles kept warm on a base of burning charcoal. The river has a rich, sweet smell here and the bleached and silent rock of the desert rises, bare and uncompromising, against the last of the sun. As I'm thinking how utterly and wonderfully strange it all is I notice that the coach in which we have been travelling across the Nubian Desert bears the maker's name: 'Gloucester Railway Carriage Company, 1959'.

We reach the busy town of Atbara, 193 miles from Khartoum, 17 hours after leaving Wadi Halfa. From here we are to continue south by bus. I can remember only shadows, soft smells of cooking and a lot of carrying as we disembark. At a government rest house we celebrate the successful conclusion of a potentially very difficult stretch of the journey with a jug or two of karkaday, a pleasant Ribena-like beverage made from the hibiscus flower. Well, it's all there is.

DAY 66 · ATBARA TO KHARTOUM

 The room which I share with Basil has, like its occupants, seen better days. The washbasin sports hot and cold taps, but only cold water, and that flows into a basin covered in a thin waxy layer of coagulated dirt. The beds are narrow and the linen grey enough for me to bring out my own sheet sleeping-bag.

Surrounding the room is a wide balcony with a couple of cane chairs, and it is from here, soon after 6.30 in the morning, that I look down onto a green and pleasant garden, in which is a pair of security guards, fast asleep. They are not just asleep at their posts, they are asleep in their beds, at their posts.

Having packed my bags for the 35th time since the North Pole, I make my way to what is proudly signposted as the Dinning Room, and after a remarkably good breakfast, including porridge, we catch the bus to Khartoum. It is built onto a Bedford chassis, circa 1956, and richly decorated in bright primary colours, like some 1960s hippy caravan. It is 'air conditioned', which means open at the sides.

Our equipment is roped on top by a number of porter/helpers who travel with us. One is jovial and speaks good English. When I ask him how long the journey will take he says, 'Eight hours . . . ,' and adds with a twinkle, 'Eight *hard* hours . . .'

We are on our way at 7.15, to make the most of the cool of the day. This is a fairly hopeless objective as it is already 92 degrees. My excitement at being aboard such a colourful, ethnic form of transport is rapidly moderated by my acquaintance with the sticky plastic seats, leg room that would have tested Toulouse Lautrec, and the hard metal of the seat frames, which means that if I nod off I run the risk of splitting my head open.

Atbara is a railway town, the junction of the lines to Khartoum from Wadi Halfa in the north and Port Sudan on the Red Sea coast, and we climb up over lines and past sidings full of derelict steam engines before rattling into the shanty town suburbs, where mud walls give way to semi-circular constructions of the utmost simplicity, covered in rush matting, goatskin, cardboard or whatever is available. They sprawl across the sand like patchwork tortoises. Less than 30 minutes after starting off we leave the metalled road behind and, passing a huge open rubbish tip, we bounce into the desert. Bounce is an understatement. There are jolts of such severity that the whole bus leaves the ground, flinging us towards the metal roof. Away to the west a train passes, heading north, with a human crest stretching back along the coaches.

By 9 o'clock the temperature has reached 100 once more and huge stretches of silvery water and thick stands of palm tree fill the horizon – the most vivid mirages I've ever seen.

Our driver, Ibrahim, is laconic and has one white eye, which stares fixedly ahead. There is no visible road, but he concentrates on the rocky, sandy surface as if negotiating Piccadilly Circus at rush hour. Occasionally he reaches into a small plastic bag and extricates a wad of tobacco which he rubs, breaks and sniffs into each nostril. We pull up every now and then and Nigel, Patti, Fraser, Clem and Angela toil off into the distance to set up for a passing shot. The moment we stop an eager, bright-eyed young boy, who appears to live on the roof, leaps down, pulls open the bonnet and fills up the radiator with water before scampering back up among the cases.

Ibrahim cannot understand the need for all these stops, he just wants to get to Khartoum. It is Mohammed's birthday and there will be festivities tonight. My porter friend is much more chatty. He says he is a schoolmaster and asks me such imponderables as, 'Do you know Richard Burton?' I shake my head. There is a short pause. 'Do you know Roger Moore?'

We stop at a Nileside village. The river, swollen by the rains in Ethiopia, has risen 11 metres and will continue to rise until October. But the great, wide, generous Nile flows by on its way to make electricity for the Egyptians, leaving these Sudanese villages to try and extract what they can with, in this case, one steam pump and wooden sticks and boards to scrape out irrigation channels.

It's one of the puzzles of history that such hardship and poverty can exist in a land which over 2000 years ago was renowned for an iron industry and a rich agriculture. The area we are passing through still has some of the remains of the ancient kingdom of Meroe, including a group of broken and leaning pyramids, some topless, which stand in the desert like a row of bad teeth.

We reach the town of Shendi, 132 kilometres from Atbara, after six hours of hot and desperately uncomfortable travelling. With great relief we step down at the Taieba Tourist Hotel. This proves to be closed, the gardens overgrown and unwatered, the spacious public rooms empty and smelling of decay. We are allowed to use the toilets, from which a couple of mangy cats emerge and skulk away. This must once have been a fine riverside hotel. Now it gives pleasure to no one.

We find a café which serves cold Pepsi and a hot vegetable dip of okra, tomatoes, shallots and cucumber. Very tasty, though not all of us risk eating it.

At a quarter to seven, as lightning flashes on the eastern horizon, we are stopped beside a canal bridge at our third army checkpoint of the day. An hour later we are crossing the Nile at Khartoum. Someone is pointing out the confluence of the Blue and White Niles but I'm staring downstream, transfixed by what appears to be a thick cloud obscuring the rest of the sky and drifting rapidly over the river like a curtain being drawn across the city. Then suddenly we are surrounded by a rushing wind, breathtakingly cool, and a hissing, crackling shower of sand, which douses lights and whips into eyes and mouths. Those of us not already wearing them reach for the face-masks we were issued with at the start of the journey. We are in the middle of one of the violent local sandstorms called a haboub, sparked off by a storm out in the desert (the one we had seen earlier). It is an absurdly theatrical entry into the capital – on Mohammed's birthday with the wind whistling and the sand swirling round the lights and tents specially erected for the celebrations.

How the camera and the rest of the equipment will survive is another matter, and it's with considerable relief that we roll up outside the Khartoum Hilton 13 hours after leaving Atbara. The first white faces we've seen since leaving Aswan look apprehensively at us as we approach the reception desk, shabby, unshaven and caked with desert sand.

Never has a hot shower been quite as exquisitely welcome, let alone a double bed and a mini-bar – empty, but still a mini-bar.

The haboub is still howling round the building as I fall asleep.

DAY 69 · KHARTOUM

 After a weekend of recovery from the journey into Sudan it's now time to investigate how we are going to get out. This necessitates a visit to the Ministry of Information. We drive out along what was the Corniche and is now El Nil Avenue, beneath majestic mahogany trees and alongside colonial remnants like the Grand Hotel and the People's Palace – a much restored version of the building where General Gordon lost his life in 1885. Khartoum seems to be a city without an identity. It grew up in the 1820s on a curved spit of land between the White and Blue Niles which resembled an elephant's trunk, *khartoum* in Arabic. It prospered as a centre of the slave trade, a gateway to the vast human resources of central Africa. In 1885 the local hero, the Mahdi, took the city from Gordon and the British, but was defeated by Kitchener in 1898 after which Khartoum was rebuilt in the Western style even to the extent of laying out the streets in the form of a Union Jack. A pleasant, easy-going way of life was ensured despite the enervating climate and the centre of the city still resembles Greece and Rome more than Africa or Arabia. Since the pedantic but house-proud colonialists left no one seems to know quite what to do with Khartoum. There are not the seething millions here as there are in Cairo who energize the city by sheer weight of numbers, and the present government, a supporter of Saddam Hussein and the Generals' coup in the USSR, is not much interested in international appeal. All this, combined with a comatose economy (inflation is currently running at 240 per cent) leaves the capital city lethargic, a junk-shop of the past, lacking any internal dynamism.

The threat of violence is more real here than in any of the other countries through which we have travelled. The American ambassador was assassinated recently. In 1988, a bomb was thrown into the restaurant of the Acropole Hotel, a popular rendezvous for Western aid workers and journalists. Five people were killed. Last year a bomb was tossed into the lobby of the hotel at which we are staying. A notice by the lifts reminds guests that there is a curfew in the city between 11 p.m. and 4 a.m.

Despite the presence of tanks and troops at various points in the city, especially around the bridges, access to the Ministry of Information seems very relaxed. People come and go in the forecourt including a trim urbane gentleman with short silver-grey hair who turns out to be Sudan's leading film director, Jed Gudalla Gubara. He is a man of spirit and humour, fluent in English. He says he is shooting two films here at the moment. I ask him what they are. One, he says, is about National Savings, and the other about mining.

The news from inside the Ministry of Information is not good. They refuse to give us a permit to travel south. A state of civil war has existed there for years and they cannot guarantee our safety. Even if we were to fly into the southern capital of Juba, it is surrounded by Garang's SPLA (Sudan People's Liberation Army) fighters and it would be highly dangerous for us to try and get through to Uganda.

Our attempt to follow the 30 degree meridian, in which we have succeeded, give or take a degree or two, since reaching Leningrad 42 days ago, looks to have ground to a halt.

Back at the hotel we consider our options. There is no shortage of advice. The expatriate community here has grown close as it has diminished, and the lobby of the Hilton is one of the places where it meets the outside world. We talk to an Englishman who has worked here for three years and who thinks that if the present government continues its policies most of the aid agencies will be forced out of Sudan in the next year. He looks up with weary resignation, 'They don't like us'. The aid scams are a joke, he says. 'Twenty million pounds worth of stuff is unaccounted for.' He finishes yet another fruit juice. 'Welcome to the Sudan,' he keeps repeating with a shallow laugh.

Still feeling low on energy, I content myself with a game of table tennis, a lazy swim and a wander round the undernourished hotel bookshop, which must be the only one in the world which has Jilly Cooper next door to *The Cultural Atlas of Islam* and Jeffrey Archer side by side with *The Sudanese Bourgeoisie – Vanguard of Development?*.

I finish Alan Moorehead's *The White Nile* looking out across the river itself, swollen and grey, inundating fields and trees a few hundred yards from my window. If I could follow it, it would lead me due south across swamp and desert to the Equator and the Mountains of the Moon, the very centre of Africa, to which the great names of Victorian exploration, the Spekes and Burtons and Stanleys and Livingstones had been drawn 130 years ago. Now it seems that my hopes of seeing any more of the White Nile must be abandoned – a casualty of war.

DAY 70 · KHARTOUM

There may be a way out of our predicament. Clem has made contact with a group of Eritreans who are experienced at cross-border transport. Where, when and whether they'll take us will depend on a meeting later today. Meanwhile we go to film in Omdurman, across the Nile.

The British never bothered to incorporate Omdurman into their new plan for Khartoum and it remains very much an African city, without high-rise buildings or great monuments.

In the souk – the market – there is every small item one might want. These are essentials, not luxury goods. Spices, oil (for cooking and lighting), piles of metal buckets, cooking utensils, cloth, cottons and food – bananas, limes, lemons, mangoes, dates, onions, huge bowls piled high with nuts.

On one side of an open area a line of men are sat crosslegged on the ground. Each one has the tools of his trade arranged neatly in front of him. One has a short spade on a bridge of bricks, another a light bulb on top of a tool bag, another a bag of paintbrushes with a plasterer's trowel on top. They are waiting to be hired for work and seem to be quite placid and patient until we raise the camera, when all hell breaks loose. A man with a pick axe gestures at my head so graphically that I automatically shield myself. He smiles broadly at this, thank God.

The absence of any form of tourism in the Sudan results in many small pleasures, one of which is to be able to watch the extraordinary skills of the felucca builders beside the Nile without having to buy model boats or 'I Have Seen . . .' T-shirts. A thick trunk of mahogany is hoisted by as many as ten men onto a frame about 6 feet off the ground. Then two men, one on top and one underneath saw down through the trunk until it falls neatly apart into four planks. Apart from the back-breaking work involved in sawing manually through mahogany in conditions of extreme heat, the two men are shaping and curving the wood as they cut through it, making precise calculations without benefit of any instruments except their own eyes. What comes out at the end of this remarkable toil are boards perfectly fashioned to the shape of the hull. They can build a felucca from mahogany stump to sailing vessel in 45 days.

Our meeting with the Eritrean transport contacts is set for the afternoon, back across the Nile, in Khartoum itself.

A neat modern villa is the incongruous headquarters of the EPLF – the Eritrean People's Liberation Front – and also of Ayusha Travel, an organization set up to capitalize on the experience gained driving to and from Northern Ethiopia during the 30-year war which ended with the overthrow of Colonel Mengistu only four months previously. On the walls of the bungalow are murals depicting idealized freedom fighters – women, armed to the teeth, about to hurl grenades, tribal warriors brandishing spears, and the skulls of enemy dead grinning grotesquely. Hassan Kika shows me into his office. He is a soft-spoken, quietly authoritative man. It's much easier to think of him as a transport manager than a freedom fighter, though he does have things like bomb fragments on his desk, and talks of the '10,000 martyrs' who died fighting for Eritrea against Ethiopian dictatorship.

Now the victory they always believed in has come and in two years time there will be a United Nations sponsored referendum in Eritrea to decide whether it will become a new independent state. Hassan Kika thinks the result is a foregone conclusion.

I put our more mundane problem to him and we look at the map together. There is a way he can take us into Ethiopia. It would involve a six or seven hour drive on a good road to Gedaref, and from there on what he calls 'rough roads' south to the border crossing at Gallabat. He cautions that the rainy season has been much later this year and parts of the road could be washed away, but with his Landcruisers he doesn't anticipate a problem. I ask him if there is still any fighting across the border.

'No . . . no, I don't think so, no. The TPLF (the Tigrayan Forces who defeated Mengistu) was controlling all this part of Ethiopia. But there are some, you know, who doesn't want to join with them, so they have made their own band.' Bandits? He smiles, but not very convincingly.

'The people in the village will chase them out you know.'

Hassan Kika and the Eritreans appear to have saved our bacon. They say that they can let us have the vehicles we want by the weekend. They estimate it will take us about three days to drive from Khartoum to Gondar in Ethiopia.

Back to the hotel, much relieved, only to have my enthusiasm dampened by an English couple who have just spent five weeks in custody in Eritrea after their yacht strayed into a restricted area. They were not treated well. There had been some 'physical stuff' and no legal representation.

'And don't believe any estimate of time they give you.'

The couple, who are on their way back home, have with them a white parrot called Gnasher, who is a Category B protected species, so all sorts of export licences are required. They now have the paperwork but Air France will only take him in a special box, which they are having made at the moment. Meanwhile Gnasher is getting very twitchy and nibbling at anything he can find.

'I've already had to pay for two pairs of curtains he's eaten in Asmara,' says his lady owner resignedly.

Never a dull moment in the Khartoum Hilton. And it's British night tonight in the buffet.

DAY 71 · KHARTOUM

The modern British presence in Khartoum has dwindled to a handful of aid workers and teachers. Since the Gulf War even the embassy has been reduced to fewer than 10 people. There remains the Sudan Club, once open only to those of British and British Commonwealth nationality, now extended to include anyone from an EEC country. It occupies a villa in the middle of the city. It has a swimming-pool, squash courts, a pale green lawn and a membership that has shrunk to 230 from a colonial high of over 1000. I meet Alan Woodruff for lunch here. He is Professor of Medicine at the University of Juba. He's 70 years old and plays tennis three times a week.

Talking with him offers a bracing corrective to any dewy-eyed nostalgia for a British Sudan. I ask him what it was like during the Gulf War, when Sudan took Saddam Hussein's side and most European governments advised their nationals to get out.

Professor Woodruff brightens visibly at the memory. 'Well, I . . . I had the whole place to myself . . . dined in state, on my own!' He says he felt quite safe and secure. The country's myriad political problems and the fact that he is, as he admits, living in a 'war situation' does not seem to worry him half as much as the salad.

'Maju' . . . he calls to the waiter, 'you know I never eat salad!'

He turns to me forbiddingly, 'Salad is one of the worst ways of contracting dysentery (I presume he means one of the best). One of the first principles of keeping fit in the tropics, is that you avoid salads.'

He claims he has not lost a day's work in 10 years here, so I move my rather succulent plateful of tomato and onions as far away from me as is politely possible. I would think the rest of the menu, which contains items like Scotch egg and Twisted Fish could be a problem, but not for the professor. Anything that is served hot, out of the Club's kitchen, is safe. Twisted fish?

'Very good, fillets of fish twisted round and fried.'

The 1500 students of Professor Woodruff's beloved University of Juba were recently airlifted from the south when the war made it impossible for life and work to continue. He has high praise for his students, and says the Sudanese make very good doctors. But there are not the resources to train enough of them. 'The World Health Organization recommend that there should be one doctor for every thousand of the population – in the Sudan I think it is still one doctor to ten or twelve thousand.'

Later, and much against my better judgement, I'm lured into a game of squash with Noshir, an Indian working here in Khartoum. He is clearly used to

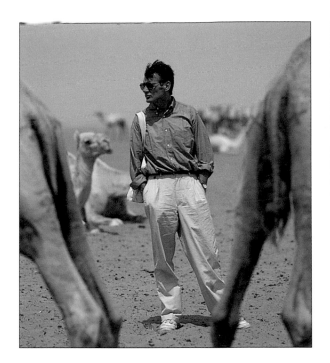

playing in the heat, and is very understanding when I am reduced to a state of total collapse after less than 10 minutes.

'It must have been about 100 degrees in there,' he says consolingly. May and June is the hottest time. His wife, he recalls, once left some eggs in the car by mistake and they were boiled when she came back.

He is happy in Khartoum. He sends his children to the local schools and thinks it is a good thing that they have to learn Arabic.

'It's nice out here, you don't have a drug problem, you don't have mindless violence, and the family gets together.'

On my way out of the Sudan Club I stop at the notice board. There's a Disco Buffet on 4 October, an International Swimming Fun Day, a European Quiz Evening, even a Halloween Fancy Dress Ball. To the outside world Khartoum is the sluggish centre of a war-torn, famine-ridden country on the brink of economic collapse, but to those living here, the Noshirs and the Professor Woodruffs, it is, for better or worse, the centre of their world. For them, and even for me after half a week here, Khartoum ceases to feel remote or difficult or dangerous. It is where we are. It is home.

DAY 73 · KHARTOUM

Still no sign of the permits we need for the journey south. Pass the time with a visit to the camel market, out in the desert. Huge numbers of cattle and camels gathered here from all over the country, accompanied by herdsmen who have walked with them for hundreds of miles. I ask how much it would cost to buy a camel – one owner, good condition – and am quoted twenty-five thousand Sudanese pounds, which is a thousand sterling.

On the way back we run into trouble. We have stopped in one of the featureless desert settlements that border the city. Our several minders have gone to buy drinks. Through the car window Basil photographs a beautiful robed figure against a background of drifting smoke. His camera is spotted and two or three men approach the car pointing and demanding the film. Basil refuses to hand it over. A crowd gathers and soon the atmosphere is as hot as the day itself. Arms stretch into the car in which we are sitting, fingers jab at the camera. Someone shouts to us not to get out of the car, as if we could. We are surrounded and people are banging on the roof. All the fuss is because they thought that Basil was snapping not a fine figure of a Sudani but the rubbish tip in the background. With a smart piece of sleight of hand Basil passes over to them an unexposed film.

We end up filming the least provocative thing we can think of – the point where the waters of the Blue and White Niles meet.

A group of pelicans bobs obligingly along the line where the waters merge, and, yes, it is possible to distinguish the different colours. The White Nile is clearly grey and the Blue Nile undoubtedly brown.

To bed with another sandstorm howling into town.

DAY 74 · KHARTOUM TO GEDAREF

Woken at 5 o'clock. The permits have arrived at the eleventh hour and we must load the vehicles for departure as soon as possible. The Eritreans turn up with three spanking clean Toyota Landcruisers and a smaller Nissan Patrol to take our baggage. Water, food, fuel and some of the camera equipment are roped expertly onto roof-racks and we are on our way by 7.30.

After the bouncing desert ride from Atbara to Khartoum, our progress toward Gedaref, 260 miles south-east, seems almost serene. The powerful, well-sprung vehicles glide along the metalled highway that is Sudan's vital supply line, connecting the capital with Port Sudan, on the Red Sea.

The scenery is as flat as Lincolnshire and wide green stony fields on either side of the road continue to invite the comparison. Tall minarets dot the countryside like church spires. There is industry here, in the shape of cotton and flour mills and factories producing medical packaging, glucose and glass. A grey Mercedes 500 with the red stripe of the government, races past, cutting in front of an advancing truck by a narrow margin. My immediate thought is that it must be another president fleeing, and that the Sudan, like the USSR, is collapsing beneath us.

10.20 a.m. Petrol sprays out across our windscreen and we pull to a stop. The carburettor has come loose and the engine is awash with precious fuel.

After some time spent trying to mend it with rope, it's decided that a spare part is required. Fortunately we are on the outskirts of the town of El Hasaheisa, and our driver Mikele goes off to locate what is required whilst we wait beside a brown, burnt earth roadside ditch topped with a row of usha bushes, whose fruit looks rich and seductive but is deadly poison. A group of children gather to stare. My unbounded confidence in the Eritreans has taken a bit of a knock.

12.30 p.m. We are on our way again.

Just outside Gedaref is a huge refugee, or 'displaced persons' camp, housing 22,000 Ethiopians. It has been here for 16 years. The Sudanese pursued a benevolent but not altogether altruistic policy of support for those fighting the government of Colonel Mengistu and these camps, filled largely with political refugees were recruiting and training centres for the Tigrayan resistance. This one is as big as a small town, and well laid out with long lines of circular huts capped with conical thatched roofs, and surrounded by high fences. A big crowd gathers around us. I have the feeling that visits such as ours are a spot of welcome entertainment in an otherwise confined and routine existence. The presence of the camera is also an opportunity to air grievances and appeal to the world. Refugees, some wearing 'Desert Storm' and 'Rambo' T-shirts, tell us that there is not enough food, that they have to do the most menial jobs for the Sudanese in order to make money to live, and that now the war is over they want international pressure to be used to get them back home again.

'What can you do for us . . . ?' 'What can you do for us?' they keep repeating.

The worst part is leaving. Being able to leave.

In Gedaref we are quartered at another government rest house. Our shared rooms are set off a verandah which is screened with netting to keep out mosquitoes. The floors are covered in badly-fitting vinyl, the walls are bare and plastered. There is a fan that doesn't work and basins with no running water. It is a cheerless place. We sit, before supper, with glasses of lemonade, feeling like occupants of an old folks home.

DAY 75 · GEDAREF TO KANINA

 Alarm sounds on the chair beside my bed at 5.15. Slept well despite a rich assortment of noises off. Dogs barking, cockerels crowing from an indecently early hour, cats, crickets and muezzins. It was as if someone had broken into the BBC Sound Effects Library and put on all the African tapes simultaneously.

The dawn temperature is a refreshingly cool 80 degrees, and an encouraging contrast to the stuffiness and claustrophobia of the night before. There is no breakfast, so after a bracing argument over the bill, we pack up the vehicles, in which our Eritrean drivers have spent the night, and head for the border. It'll have to be another Sainsbury's picnic on the way.

Surveying my Michelin map (Africa North East and Arabia), I notice the road to Gallabat is clearly marked but lined with a series of blue notches. The key reveals these to indicate 'roads impassable in the rainy season'. The rainy season, though late, is past, but its aftermath is the only thing that seems to cause the Eritreans any concern.

We are only 96 miles from the frontier, and with luck, could be in Gondar, Ethiopia by this evening.

Fifteen minutes later comes the first, ominous sign that things might not be so easy. We pull up at a crossroads in the centre of Gedaref. The town is already full of people, buying bread, selling hot corn on the cob or just hanging around. A shabby group gathers curiously by the vehicles, peering in. Normally we'd either get out or wind the window down but this morning we want to keep moving. Instead the drivers are consulting, pointing and arguing. It's clear that they're already lost. After a few minutes they climb back in and haul us round in a bad-tempered U-turn.

We follow an unmade track, the rain-softened soil already churned up by trucks from the border. This is where the drivers earn their money. They must be able to read the tricky surface ahead, riding in the grooves when there is clearance enough to do so and switching onto the ridges when the grooves run too deep. The driver must match decisiveness with delicacy – as if the walls of hardening mud were made of eggshell.

As happens in Africa, there are people walking in the middle of nowhere and Mikele stops twice to give rides – once to an old woman and her daughter, and further on to a farmer whose name is Ibrahim. He is going to visit his fields in the village of Doka. He has 20 cows and also grows *sim-sim*, which I'm told is sesame. He wears a crisp white djellabah and a neat lace takia and argues loudly with Mikele about religion. Arab versus Christian.

We pass the carcass of a cow, picked clean by the birds of prey. Yellow butterflies flutter about the bones and alight on the skin, which has shrunk in the sun and now looks like an inadequate blanket, put there by someone trying to conceal an accident. Nigel films it and Fraser dangles his microphone boom over it. Basil asks Fraser why he is recording the sound of a long-dead animal. Fraser seems genuinely hurt by the question: 'The flies are alive!'

Ibrahim chews tobacco and displays a surprising knowledge of idiomatic English.

'What is it you English say . . . ?'

'About what?'

He shifts a wad of tobacco across his mouth and back again.

'. . . you say about English ladies . . .'

I crane back to try and catch this over the revving of the engines.

'What do we say, Ibrahim?'

'All the same with the light off?'

He giggles helplessly. I'm quite shocked.

We have been travelling for nearly six hours when we reach Ibrahim's destination. His parting shot is to tell us that in his opinion we shall not reach Gallabat before dark. The drivers laugh this off, but it raises awkward questions for us. Transport from the Ethiopian side is to meet us at the border this evening and we have absolutely no means of getting a message to them if anything goes wrong.

We move on, encouraged by a faster, more solid surface out amongst the corrugated iron shacks of the village.

Then we take a wrong turning. There are no signposts and the Eritreans have not a map amongst them. Eventually we find what appears to be a dried-up river bed. We drive along it until the Nissan gets stuck and has to be towed out by Mikele. Then Mikele gets stuck and has to be pulled out by the Nissan.

The landscape is changing from semi-desert to savannah. Acacia trees proliferate. At a village where we stop to fill the radiators the look of the people has changed too. There are fewer djellabahs and more colourful robes and cloths as well as armlets and necklaces and other ornate jewellery.

The track is now so badly pitted and potholed that our drivers are forced to seek the drier, less well-used ground on either side. It is less well-used largely because it is planted with crops, and as we charge through, flattening maize and sesame, I try not to think of the grossness of our action.

As the sun declines the colours of the countryside become more beautiful. The blackness of the soil contrasts with the pale lemon of the grass and the glowing russet of the eucalyptus tree barks.

When our drivers are not pulling each other out of the mud they are questioning anyone who goes by. Little children, old women bearing piles of wood, young girls, all are asked with increasing desperation, 'Gallabat . . . Gallabat?'.

Night falls and one of the Landcruisers is stuck at an angle of 45 degrees, another sprays an arc of mud from its back wheels as it tries to drag the beleaguered vehicle onto the level. A donkey trots quietly past bearing an elderly man who gives a hint of a sad smile as he overtakes us and disappears into the distance.

7 o'clock. One Landcruiser is now seriously damaged with a crack in the suspension. This necessitates much unloading and redistribution of baggage amongst other, already crowded vehicles. It is pitch dark. As we are doing this three figures appear from the undergrowth. One of them is a little boy holding a candle. Behind him the horizon is momentarily illuminated by a flash of lightning. We are tired, dusty and saddle-sore but there is something about this moment which is unforgettable.

By 8 o'clock, after 13 hours driving, we find ourselves in a small settlement. There is no electric light, just a collection of dimly-lit huts and dogs prowling about beside a smelly stream. We are told this is the village of Kanina. Being near the frontier it has a police presence. Their advice is that it would be highly dangerous to travel further tonight and they agree to put us up in the compound of the police station. They gather beds together and by the light of oil lamps and torches we rustle up a meal of cheese spread and pressed chicken and other slithery things out of tins. The 'bathroom' consists of a large urn of water in one corner of the mud-floored compound. The lavatory is outside. Anywhere.

DAY 76 · KANINA TO SHEDI

In Kanina the dawn chorus lasts all night. Never have I heard such a symphony of grunting, chattering, hooting, whooping, howling, barking and honking. And that was just the crew. The village by daylight looks quite pleasant and green, a mixture of straw-thatched conical huts and more substantial structures roofed in corrugated iron settled in a hollow.

Once again we decide to move on as early as possible and stop for breakfast after we have covered some ground. It's still frustratingly difficult to gather any accurate information but Gallabat is said to be no more than 30 kilometres (18 miles) away.

We leave at ten to six, just before sunrise. Dust and dirt of travel is ingrained in everything — our bodies, clothes, bags and bedding. The Landcruisers that were gleaming and pristine 48 hours ago are unrecognizably filthy.

The Eritrean drivers, who have worked much harder than ourselves, are a little chastened this morning. After yesterday's unproductive free-for-all they have developed a system which involves following rather than racing. The lead driver goes ahead and inspects the route, then comes back to give instructions. The problem, however, remains fundamental. There is no road to Gallabat. There is not even a continuous track to Gallabat. Whatever track there might be is likely to be obscured by an ever-thickening carpet of low trees and undergrowth. The dark shape of the Ethiopian highlands remains elusively distant.

We carry on where we left off yesterday, bulldozing through fields of maize and millet, and sliding and swerving onto the thick mass of trenches ground into the mud by vehicles much heavier than our own. Though Mikele and his team ride the ridges bravely, flicking into four-wheel drive and plunging ahead at full throttle there is more sound and fury than actual progress. The pervading smell of burning rubber and freshly-gouged earth merely underlines the fact that we are in the wrong place with the wrong kind of transport. Not only does the earth seem stickier and heavier, but trees are flicking at us through the windows, and as I am helping push out the Landcruiser for the umpteenth time a thorn bush drags me back. I survive but my trousers are ripped like paper.

By 10 a.m. we have moved seven and a half miles in four hours. This is our 14th day in the Sudan and the country seems increasingly reluctant to let us go.

The police escort given to us by the authorities at Kanina, has now broken down. As they struggle to fix a water-pipe, an army unit draws up, insisting that we take armed guards with us to the border. They say there are men from Mengistu's recently defeated army roaming the hills, 'living off their wits'. Now we have in addition to our own damaged vehicle a disabled police escort, and two soldiers to fit into an already overloaded convoy.

An hour later, about midday, the scenery is becoming more picturesque and we stop to allow Nigel to climb a low hill and get some shots. The soldiers become very agitated and order him back. One of them, who is travelling with Angela and Patti, has told them both that these hills are full of armed men who will not hesitate to shoot on sight.

The main road to Ethiopia: Transport, modern and ancient, morning preparations at the police station, Kanina.

We pile back into the vehicles only to find, round the next corner, an upended truck with its load of salt sacks scattered onto the road. This, it turns out, is the first sign of a northbound convoy which pins us down for an hour or more as 40 or 50 trucks and tractors pulling trailers trundle past us. These swaying, overloaded old Austins and Bedfords, all of which have five or six armed men travelling on top of the cargo, make light work of the road conditions, but I feel sorry for Mikele as he looks balefully at the deepening ruts they leave behind, over which he and the others will have to return.

At 3 p.m., having moved 14 miles in 9 hours we emerge from the trees into a collection of army huts at the top of a hill. Down below us is Gallabat.

Like Wadi Halfa the town itself is endowed with less than its oft-quoted name might suggest. But for us Gallabat and its Ethiopian counterpart of Metemma on the other side of a shallow valley is the Promised Land, the end of the worst stretch of the journey since leaving the Pole.

Our battered convoy rolls down the hill towards a collection of thatched huts and crowds of people milling around a small grubby building marked 'Democratic Republic Sudan Customs'. It all looks unfamiliar and potentially threatening but to our enormous relief our Ethiopian contacts – Graham Hancock, a journalist and Santha Faiia, a Malaysian photographer who has lived a long time in the country – are there to meet us. They bring the welcome news that we are cleared through Sudan customs and there are no customs on the Ethiopian side before Addis Ababa.

The Sudan–Ethiopia frontier is a stagnant creek, over which a concrete bridge has been recently erected. It doesn't surprise me when Graham warns that it is an area of high malaria risk.

I walk across, through a jostling mass of donkeys, trucks and curious faces, into Ethiopia, where, as they use the Julian calendar and not the Gregorian, the year is 1984, and the month, I think, January.

Whilst the load is moved onto a new set of Landcruisers, I revel in the pleasure of the first beer since Aswan, just over two weeks ago. It is almost body temperature but quite wonderful.

Because it's now so late in the day we are advised not to attempt to reach Gondar, as the roads pass through bandit territory, and we put up for the night at a village about 25 miles from the border. I don't think any of us care much where we stay so long as there is a comfortable bed and some hot water. There are neither in Shedi. The accommodation, though looking quaint enough by candlelight, is rougher than anything we've experienced so far. My room is reached through a small dimly-lit bar which gives onto what smells and feels like a farmyard. In the middle of it are people sitting around a fire, and off to the sides are rooms that look like rough stables. Mine has an earth floor and wattle and daub partitions. There is a corrugated iron door and ceiling. The proprietress finds me a chair and a couple of stones to wedge one of the legs of the bed. Cockroaches and beetles scuttle away in the torchlight as I unpack. Electric light would be terrifying here.

This 'hotel', in which only Basil and I are quartered is nevertheless more luxurious than the rest, in that it sports a shower. This consists of a large plastic drum with a supply valve controlled by a piece of wire. The stream of cool water is heavenly. Not so the lavatory next door. I have become used to the squat technique, so I'm not unduly worried to find myself poised above a shallow hole filled with sawdust. It's when the sawdust starts to move that I feel just the slightest bit queasy. What I thought was sawdust is in fact a cauldron of maggots, over which the occasional cockroach stumbles.

Despite this revelation I partake heartily of Fray Bentos corned beef, Garibaldi biscuits and several Ethiopian beers before turning in.

DAY 77 · SHEDI TO GONDAR

I don't sleep for long. I don't think any of us does. Though I remain wrapped tight in a sheet sleeping-bag, and covered up from head to toe, I cannot reconcile myself to the fetid smell from the sticky rough cloth of the mattress, the treasure trove of insects concealed within it and the presence of bodies only a breath away on the other side of the thin mud wall. Because of my protective cocoon I become very hot and push open the door to let some air in. I must have dozed and wake to find a face peering down at me and a moment later the door slamming shut. When I do nod off I'm woken sharply by a peculiar, violent and inhuman sound. It sounds like a donkey having a nightmare.

I've never risen at 5.15 with less reluctance. Splash a little bottled water on my face and tiptoe to the door, only to find it has been locked on the outside. Fortunately Basil is within shouting distance. We assemble in the pre-dawn light and recount our various experiences in this most ethnic of stopovers. Angela had an armed guard in her room, though not all night, I'm assured, and Nigel's nerves of steel were shredded when a cat jumped onto his bed in the small hours. For once Fraser seems to have found nothing in his shoe, ear or any other orifice.

We set off for Gondar before dawn. The roads are straighter and in better condition than in the Sudan, but the river beds here are not dry and consequently must be crossed with greater care.

I travel with Graham who fills me in with the history and politics of the country, as we pass through scenery which resembles the Welsh borders. He says it's a good time to be in Ethiopia, in the euphoric aftermath of the fall of Mengistu's government and just after the rains have turned the countryside green.

Colonel Mengistu had ruled the country for 16 years, after deposing Emperor Haile Selassie who had ruled for 57 years. Under Mengistu poverty and corruption went hand in hand with totalitarianism and an irrelevant pro-Soviet policy. The Eritreans opposed him because they wanted independence for themselves and the Tigrayans opposed him because they wanted political change in Ethiopia. In the end it was a people's army from Tigray in the north-east that formed the driving force behind the EPRDF (The Ethiopian People's Revolutionary Democratic Front) that swept through the country and forced Mengistu to flee to Zimbabwe just over four months ago. Thirty-five-year-old Meles Zenawi became head of the new government. It is, as Graham says, a young revolution.

'People between 16 and 30 have completely changed the face of this country in the last six months.'

The soldiers who are travelling with us as protection are part of this volunteer EPRDF army – paid only in cigarettes, food and accommodation. The emblems on their tunics are inked in by hand, they wear cut-off jeans and carry Kalashnikov AK-47 rifles. They are probably 15 or 16 years old.

The scenery outside is now almost alpine. Green meadows are filled with the short-lived but intense yellow flower called maskal which is the national emblem. There are butterflies and gold and green weaver birds and brilliant red bishops. A Soviet-built tank stands abandoned in the long grass. It looks idyllic out there but there have been frequent attacks on the road since the end of the war and our escort slips a bullet into the breach and pokes his rifle out, looking watchfully around at the mountains.

We stop at a village for refreshment. We buy some tea whilst our guards sit talking quietly with colleagues. I'm impressed that they don't swagger or behave loudly or aggressively. They sit there quite gravely, as if prematurely aged by their responsibility as liberators.

There are casualties of war. The children have had no schooling here for several years. A number of them are pitifully thin. Often their heads have been shaved, and their pointed faces and big eyes bring to mind pictures of concentration camp victims. All this in surroundings that resemble Switzerland.

Graham sees cause for optimism, 'The former government structure was one of total control of the whole country . . . they had their cadres in every village . . . neighbours were encouraged to spy on each other . . . these rebels fought to get rid of that . . . at every level people are more free than they were before.'

By mid-afternoon we have reached the village of Aykel, which is entered through a tall, ungraceful metal arch bearing slogans like 'People's Power' and 'Ethiopia Shall Be The Home Of Heavy Industry'. Below them a cluster of wretchedly poor children gather around us.

'You! . . . you!', they shout, holding their hands out for anything. I give one of them a 'Wet One' – one of the cleaning tissues we carry with us – and mime what to do. He is still vigorously wiping his face with it when we leave 20 minutes later.

Beyond Aykel we follow a stony track over a wide upland plateau.

Thunder has been rumbling and clouds building and finally the heavens open and down come hailstones the size of marbles. It is hard to believe that ice is falling on us less than 24 hours after we were sweating our way out of the Sudan.

It is a wonderfully refreshing deluge and as the clouds pass on and the sun begins to come through we find ourselves on the outskirts of Gondar. Our three-day journey has turned into four hard-travelling 15-hour days and everyone is tired, crumpled and desperate for a creature comfort or two. As we drive into this sizeable town, 7000 feet above sea-level and for 200 years the capital of Ethiopia, we come up behind a large and forlorn crowd of men who look in a worse state than ourselves. They are walking disconsolately down the hill carrying cans or plastic containers. Apparently they are some of the 70,000 government troops garrisoned in Gondar who surrendered to the EPRDF without a fight. Deciding what to do with them is one of the problems facing the new administration – Mengistu had one of the biggest standing armies in Africa and there are an estimated 400,000 to 500,000 of his men still in custody, and 2 million of their dependents neglected.

The Gohar Hotel is spectacularly sited on a bluff overlooking the city and the wide panorama of mountains that encircle it. We have been nowhere like this. Built for a tourist industry that never happened, the hotel combines a museum, a repository of local arts and crafts with tall, interestingly designed public spaces and a decently-stocked bar.

There is a sign on the back of my door which could be an offer or a dire warning. 'Room Service. Express snakes available at all times,' it reads.

Apart from the danger of express snakes the chief delights of the Gohar Hotel are electric light, hot water (for a whole hour in the evening) and a freshly made bed. It is chilly enough for me to huddle to sleep beneath two blankets.

DAY 78 · GONDAR TO BAHIR DAR

A cool morning. Mist clings to the mountain ranges, enveloping all but the tallest ridges and summits. The only other people staying at the hotel are a couple of Red Cross workers and 10 EPRDF troops who are quartered in one wing free of charge.

In the foyer there is evidence of the stillborn attempt to bring tourists here. 'Ethiopia, 13 months of sunshine', reads one poster, playing on their calendar difference. Another extols the wonders of the nearby Simian Mountains . . . 'The splendid Roof of Africa – peak after rugged peak stretching away to the limitless horizon; pastoral scenes of shepherds and their flocks, carpets of Alpine flowers.'

Down to the centre of town. The place looks better from a distance. Below the picturesque patchwork of red and grey roofs are streets thronged with people, most of whom look downtrodden and threadbare. The djellabah, a simple, sensible economical garment is hardly worn here, partly because of the climate and partly because only 15 of the country's 45 million people are Moslem. Here they seem to wear whatever they can get their hands on. One little girl appears to be dressed in a nightie, another a torn crocheted sweater. Some have shoes, many don't. Food is stacked next to open drains, and it's easy to see how disease thrives. A lot of the children quickly gather round us, despite the efforts of some of the older men who try to clear them away by throwing stones. They look very unhealthy, with bulging stomachs and sores on their faces around which flies gather. They watch us quietly through big protruding eyes. One or two of the livelier ones try to interest us in packets of American army rations which found their way here after the Gulf War. I'm offered freeze-dried 'Cherry Nutcake', 'Tootsie Roll', 'Tomatoes au Gratin' and 'Beef and Rice Meatballs', all in identical grey sachets.

One boy, Mohammed Nuru, speaks English well. He is one of a family of seven. Large families are common in the poorer parts of Africa as they represent an economic asset – a family work-force. He has lost friends and family in the war. He is Moslem but many of his friends are Christian and the two religions get on well here.

English is taught in schools as a second language and Mohamed listens to the BBC World Service.

'I have a great chance to listen for football . . . particularly England football . . . club football. Every Saturday from 4 to 6.'

His favourite team is Manchester United, but I try to put him right.

One thing there is no shortage of in Gondar is sewing machines. A line of machinists stretches up the hill and all seem busy. I take one of them my trousers, severely ripped in the cause of leaving Sudan, and within 90 seconds of work on his foot-pedalled Mansukh machine he has restored them to full health.

To get away from the relentless pressure of the market Graham and I go off to look at Gondar's fine stone-walled castles. The first one was built by the Emperor Fasilidas in 1635 when Gondar was made capital because of a superstition rife at the time that the capital should begin with a 'G'. The five emperors who followed him all built their own castles, in the grounds, as it were. The distinctiveness of these dark towers has much to do with Ethiopia's curious history. It is unique in Africa in having been ruled by a direct line through 45 generations, and though these fortified palaces reveal a distinct European influence, Ethiopia was never colonized. The link with the Jews is fascinating. Graham has a well-researched theory that the Ark of the Covenant is held in a chapel not far from here, and he has just completed a book on his findings.

In one corner of the grounds there is a cage and in it the first lion I have seen in Africa. His name is Tafara and he once belonged to Haile Selassie – the last Emperor. Selassie died a year after he was deposed by Mengistu, in 1975, and with him died Imperial Ethiopia. Tafara, the lion that was the symbol of his power lingers on, an embarrassment, one feels, to almost everybody. His cage is small and he paces it restlessly, with only flies for company. There are raw wounds on his back and legs. He had a partner who has long since died. Now he is 20 years old and one can only hope that he does not have to suffer this indignity much longer.

By the time we leave Gondar darkness is falling, and we are soon in the thick of a tremendous electrical storm, the longest and most spectacular I've ever witnessed. Torrential rain pounds the vehicles, and for over two hours fork and sheet lightning rip and burst across the sky. The flashes occasionally reveal dramatic pinnacles of rock and abandoned tanks by the side of the

Northern Ethiopia: On the castle battlements at Gondar, 'Graham Hancock, I presume', the road through the mountains.

road, frozen into negative for an instant by the intensity of the lightning. At other times they reveal my suitcase, riding uncovered on the roof rack of the vehicle in front. This is the sort of test they write commercials about.

We arrive at the town of Bahir Dar, 110 miles from Gondar, at 10 o'clock at night, having dropped about 2000 feet in the process. The rain has stopped. The storm has passed on. There is a chain barrier across the road, and after some moments a bleary soldier wrapped in a pink blanket with a rifle over his shoulder emerges and looks at our safe passage note. I can tell by his face that he doesn't understand a word of it. He stares hard at it, then back at us, yawns powerfully and waves us on.

My suitcase hasn't survived the onslaught. Red dust and rain have turned some of my shirts an interesting colour.

DAY 79 · BAHIR DAR

 Our hotel gives onto the placid grey waters of Lake Tana, which is considered to be the source of the Blue Nile. It has taken us the best part of a month to follow the river down from Cairo. The gardens running down to the lake are rich with hibiscus and poinsettia and the approach to the hotel is dominated by a flowering euphorbia, a goblet-shaped tree that looks like a giant cactus.

We gather at 9 a.m. to make an expedition to the Blue Nile Falls, or the Tissisat ('Smoking Water') Falls as they are known locally. Leaving Bahir Dar we pass a huge and graphic anti-Mengistu painting by the roadside. Leering horribly, he has one arm raised in a dictator's clenched fist salute, and the other securing a crutch beneath his armpit, as the lower part of his body decomposes onto a heap of skulls.

Outside the town a pair of storks rise lazily from the fields and away over a road busy with groups of people carrying bundles of wood into town. These resilient figures are of indeterminate age, with legs as thin as the sticks they carry.

At the village of Tissabay, 18 miles from Bahir Dar, we have to disembark and walk the last mile to the falls. We are not to be alone. No sooner have our vehicles been glimpsed than we are pursued by a crowd of boys waving and shouting. They all want to be our guides. Their technique is to press long sticks into our hands and as soon as anyone should grasp one, to stand proprietorially beside them. After much heated and exhausting negotiation we choose a group of guides and bearers and set off across a difficult stony path through the fields. Tadesse, 25 years old, and Tafese, a couple of years younger, are my 'guides' and I am their 'foreigner'.

'He is *our* foreigner!' they shout at anyone who tries to muscle in, and to me, solicitously, 'How you are now? Fine . . . ?'

What with our bearers carrying the film equipment, and me in my Turkish straw hat, we must look like every clichéd picture of the Great White Explorer. We cross a picturesque, four-arched stone bridge.

'Bridge built by Portuguese,' Tadesse tells me, a few seconds before Tafese tells me the same thing, 'Cement made of egg yolk and sand' . . . 'of egg yolk and sand,' echoes Tafese.

It's hot and increasingly clammy, as, after a 45-minute walk, we climb a long green slope, mount the brow of a hill and look down on one of the greatest natural spectacles I have ever seen. It is the central of the three falls that catches the eye. An immense torrent of water is plunging over it, a cascade so massive that it appears solid, as if the land itself is crashing downward. A continuous subterranean rumble seems to shake the ground. Locals say they have not seen the falls so full in their lifetime.

I'm aware of Tadesse looking expectantly towards me:

'How you find it? Attract . . . ?'

'Oh yes, attract all right . . . sublime, stupendous and stunning.'

'So . . . you like?'

A rainbow hangs over the gorge and the clifftops below us are covered in tropical jungle, a mini ecosystem created by the billowing clouds of spray. An explorer called James Bruce came here in the 1780s and described the sight as 'stupefying'. He claimed to have been the first white man to see the Falls, but two priests challenged his claim. Queen Elizabeth came here in 1965, and they built a viewing platform specially for her. Today there is nothing between ourselves and a 100-foot drop, except slippery grass. Patti nearly goes over, taking most of her guides with her.

2.15 p.m.: At lunch in the Fountain of Life Restaurant beside the lake there is a loud crack on the plate glass window. We dive for cover, but nothing has broken. A huge hornbill has flown into the glass and now lies stunned and flapping feebly on the patio outside. It flies off but only as far as the water. Santha and one of the waiters rush out and help it onto the bank, where it all but attacks them.

The sky is darkening over the lake this afternoon, and it looks as though we shall have our third storm in three days in Ethiopia. But the wood collectors still cross the water in their distinctive narrow papyrus boats. These delicate, insubstantial craft also service the islands of the lake, about 20 of which contain monasteries. Some of these are closed off to the outside world, many more will only allow men to land.

The storm never comes today, but the low dark clouds make Lake Tana even more mysterious and secretive.

DAY 80 · BAHIR DAR TO ADDIS ABABA

POLE *to* **POLE** Six times in the last seven days we've been up before dawn, usually to catch the coolest time of day. This morning it is because we have a very long drive ahead if we are to reach Addis Ababa on schedule. The capital is 300 miles away and we are taking a gamble by using a subsidiary road for the first 160 miles to avoid the busy truck route. My Michelin map has the first part of our journey picked out in yellow and white stripes, indicating, elegantly but rather unhelpfully, 'road liable to be impractical in bad weather'. As there is also a rumour that a bridge is down this could be quite an adventure.

We leave at a quarter to seven, apprehension mixing with elation at the prospect of a great step forward. If we can reach Addis by tonight we shall be less than a thousand miles, on long straight roads, from the Equator.

At the first checkpoint, we ask a soldier with boots, but no laces, if he knows anything about the bridge being down. He shakes his head, which is very confusing. A mile further on Sayem, our driver, pulls up and there is much argument between him and his colleagues about fuel. As in the USSR and Sudan petrol is strictly rationed here and cannot be acquired without coupons and permits. Sayem is worried that the garages on our back road will not know anything about our permits. Bearing in mind the misfortunes that have attended our transport from Khartoum he's right to worry, but calculations are made and we all start off again. A few yards later we stop again, this time to interrogate a bus driver as to the state of the suspect bridge. Smiles all round – the road is passable.

Once clear of settlements we are into a beautiful, Arcadian landscape of green terraced fields, with a silver river winding its way down through the valley, toward ragged mountain peaks half hidden in haze.

It's a stick culture here. Everyone we pass seems to have a stick – for rest, for protection, and for herding the sheep, cattle and goats, which are constantly on the move by the roadside. The silhouetted, walking figure, stick slung across shoulders, could be the trade mark of pastoral Africa.

In the villages the main street is always full. Men, women, children, donkeys and dogs mill about and our driver blasts his horn and ploughs into the middle of them. South of Mota, where Mussolini's six-year occupation of the country has left behind some chunky and incongruous European-style public buildings, we climb onto a broad and grassy plateau from which distant mountains rise to 12,000 feet. Chocolate-coloured streams drain away some of the billions of tonnes of rich Ethiopian soil which will eventually end up behind the Aswan dam, clogging the desert waters of Lake Nasser. Up here the wood and thatch dwellings are often surrounded by carefully cut and dressed dry stone walls, but the villagers are very poor. Clothes are patched up and threadbare. Trousers are worn into strands, boots have holes in them. There is no sign of the pick-up trucks and tractors which could still be seen in the poorest parts of the Sudan. Graham thinks the explanation for this lies in foreign reluctance to invest in Mengistu. Under his communist regime Ethiopia received the lowest per capita amount of development aid of any country in the world. Long-term development aid, as opposed to short-term emergency aid, is what really matters to a country, though often it is strung around with so many conditions and debt repayments that it ceases to be of real help.

We reach the junction with the main Addis road after six hours of bumpy but uninterrupted progress, and are soon descending through a patchwork of green and yellow fields into the Blue Nile Gorge, where the south flowing river has cut a mile down into the rocky massif before slowly turning west and north into the Sudan.

The heat rises, trapped by towering red sandstone walls. When we stop for lunch beside a lazy waterfall my thermometer shows 100 degrees and the cool, clear air of the highlands is a just a happy memory. As we dip once more into our dwindling supplies of peanut butter, Treacle Crinkles and Fruit Rustics, we are not alone. From somewhere on the cliff wall above us, come high-pitched, almost human cries and an olive baboon lopes away along a rocky ledge. Graham says that there are few wild animals left in Ethiopia now. They have been hunted to extinction.

At the bottom of the gorge a single-span steel bridge crosses the Blue Nile, flowing fast and muddy below. This bridge is such a vital link between the north and south of the country that it has apparently never been filmed. Under Selassie and Mengistu it was strictly out of bounds. It is our good fortune to have come along so soon after the liberation, and instead of hostility and secrecy we are greeted with curiosity and co-operation. This EPRDF army seems to feel so secure in it's achievements that there is no need for striking poses of aggression or intimidation. It must be unique in the world, an army that smiles.

Taking full advantage of their helpfulness we end up driving across the bridge four times. The soldiers look increasingly bemused as we keep coming back through the check-points, grinning manically.

About 3 o'clock in the afternoon we drive up the steep hairpin bends to the south of the gorge, and take one last look at the Nile which has led us two and a half thousand miles into Africa. Once over the mountains and beyond Addis we shall pick up another natural route – the Great Rift Valley – to push a thousand miles further south, into the heart of the continent.

As we near Addis the road surface is increasingly cracked and broken, the result of the enormous movement of troops down from the north in the

Roadside life on the way to Addis Ababa. The Blue Nile Bridge –
as never seen on television.

Day 80: Ethiopia

last months of the war. A lot of military hardware, mainly personnel carriers, armoured cars and tanks, has been left by the side of the road. With the sky darkening behind them, a hyena loping across the road in front and lightning once again splitting the western horizon it is an apocalyptic sight.

Darkness falls, and it is after 8 o'clock when we first see the lights of Addis. The drivers have been at it for 13 hours, which is quite a feat of concentration on damaged, unlit roads.

The last plateau we crossed was 10,000 feet and Addis Ababa, at 8000 feet, is one of the highest capitals in the world.

There is a smell of wood smoke in the air, and for the first time in Ethiopia I notice private cars. A burned-out tank, slewed half-way onto the pavement outside the Presidential Palace, is a reminder of the resistance the EPRDF encountered when they took the city. Between two and three thousand were killed here when the Presidential guard put up a last fight.

Culture shock as we arrive at the Addis Hilton, into a world of white faces, blond hair, thick legs, full bellies. Curfew from 1 a.m to 6 a.m., but telephones and mini-bars. Gorgeous, sensational and wonderful shower. The dust runs off in muddy channels. My eyes are red-rimmed and sore, and I have picked up a cluster of flea bites from somewhere but I suppose that's a small price to pay for what we've just been through.

Can't help noticing that the only postcards available here carry fine colour photos of the Blue Nile Bridge – the bridge no one had ever filmed.

DAY 82 · ADDIS ABABA

Addis Ababa was chosen by Emperor Menelik II to be his capital in 1887. The name means 'New Flower' in Amharic, the official language of Ethiopia, which is a Semitic language, closer to Arabic and Hebrew than anything African. It is a nondescript city set handsomely in a bowl of mountains but reflecting no great sense of civic pride. Under Mengistu it was adorned with roughly-painted metal arches and towers celebrating communism in Ethiopia. This morning one of these towers is lying on its side on a road close to the hotel. Men in green overalls dismember it with hammers and oxyacetylene torches. The thin panels offer little resistance. A severed red star is flung into the back of a truck.

We make our way down the hill, past the grand but overgrown gates of the old Palace of the Emperors, and the empty plinth where a 30-foot-high statue of Lenin used to cast a beady eye in the direction of Revolution Square. Lenin has gone and Revolution Square is now Maskal Square. We approach it through an arch bearing the green, yellow and red colours of Ethiopia and surmounted with the faded legend 'Long Live Proletarian Internationalism'. It is a wide, long, rectangular space with a grassy bank, ramparts and a city museum on one side and dull modern constructions on the other.

Children wearing 'New Kids on the Block' T-shirts shout 'Money! . . . money!' at us. Above their heads hammer and sickles in lights still hang from the lamp-posts.

Rumour reaches us that a big crowd is heading for the square to demonstrate in favour of the United Democratic Nationals, a party opposed to the government's plans to allow self-determination to Eritrea and any other independently minded provinces. A couple of police jeeps with machine-guns mounted in the back cruise anxiously by. Any form of public protest has been unheard of for so long that the general mood in the approaching crowd seems celebratory. But as the first flag-waving rows of demonstrators reach the square, there is a sound of crackling gunfire. Some people throw themselves to the ground, and we make a brisk retreat towards our vehicles.

Gunfire breaks out again, and for a moment it looks as if there will be panic. Members of the crowd are running toward the centre of the square. Whoever, or whatever tried to stop them has been silenced. Apart from a lady from Agence Presse we seem to be the only foreigners present. As our brief is to get to the South Pole in one piece rather than be Kate Adie we leave the field open to Agence Presse. There are no further incidents but over 10,000 are later reported to have protested against the new government.

DAY 83 · ADDIS ABABA

It's a damp morning with light rain and moderate temperatures as we make our way past the hillside of corrugated iron roofed huts behind the hotel to the big, hexagonal and corrugated iron roofed church of St Michael. Crowds move slowly through the rain towards the church. Umbrellas are up, salesmen are out offering candles and tapers. Beggars line the path, and a number of people are standing up close to the church wall, their lips moving urgently in prayer. A stand of eucalyptus trees, tall and tired, surrounds the building, adding a little gloom.

There are 25 million Christians in Ethiopia, out of a total population of 45 million, and church attendance is taken very seriously. The services are long – this one began at 6 a.m. and will last three and a half to four hours, after which there will be a ceremonial breakfast followed by another service. Serious worshippers are expected to attend twice at the weekend and on ceremonial days, when services can last up to six hours. There is a mixed bag of ages and sexes in the congregation (many of whom never get into the church itself), including elderly men in army greatcoats, young girls in white robes and young men in headscarves who stand, eyes closed, chanting to themselves. Someone estimates that there are at least 1000 people here.

We have to remove our shoes before going inside the church, which is arranged in a series of concentric circles running outwards from the holy of holies at the core of the building. There seem to be separate sections for men and women. One arcade is full of the elders of the congregation – white-robed men holding sticks with a crosspiece that I notice is often of ornately worked silver. The colours proliferate as you go further in, in fact the centre resembles a fabric warehouse. Elaborate use is made of curtains and carpets and fringes and pelmets, and the priests themselves wear highly decorative robes and capes, often in shimmering brocade. The walls, when not covered with cloths and rugs have painted scenes; some show Christ's miracles, others the Virgin Mary and one St George plunging his spear into a dragon's mouth. It's reminiscent of the services in Cyprus and Leningrad and again indicates Ethiopia's links with the North and East rather than the rest of Africa.

Ceremonial is very important, as are props. A Bible, said to be 300 years old, with pages of skin, not paper, is paraded around in a gold frame. Worshippers touch it with their forehead and then kiss it, and when it is read it is in the ancient language of Ge'ez, which is not commonly understood outside the priesthood.

The most extraordinary part of the service is the music which is played on three big barrel-shaped drums, 'kebros', accompanied by sistras, which are small wooden-handled instruments on which a line of silver discs is shaken to produce a sound not unlike that of a castanet or tambourine. The three drummers and 20 other musicians slowly build up a rhythmic counterpoint to the increasingly fast and strident chanting of the priest, and as they do so they begin a swinging forward movement with steps to left and right. It is an hypnotic routine and presumably intended to play worshippers and participants into some heightened state. We leave after nearly three hours of the service. The charismatic and indefatigable chief priest is in full flood at an open balcony as the rain drips past him off the roof and onto the patient crowd below.

If all goes well I am to travel into southern Ethiopia with an Oxfam team, and this afternoon I go out to meet them at the home of Belai Berhe, who has worked with Oxfam since it began operating in Ethiopia 17 years ago. He has a comfortable, sparsely furnished house on the outskirts of the city, and while I talk with him and Kiros, a water and wells specialist, Neggar, who designed the new village wells and Nick Rosevear, the only Englishman of the group, Belai's wife performs the coffee ceremony. It's not a ceremony in the sense that it is done on rare and special occasions, in fact it happens several times a day in nearly every household in the country. The Ethiopians adore coffee and grow some of the best in the world.

It is about as far from instant coffee as you can go, and involves first roasting the beans over a charcoal burner. A bracing, pungent smell rises from the fire as the white beans turn brown. When the beans are roasted they are offered round for us to smell then pounded in a wooden mortar with what looks like a spider wrench from a car kit. The grains are then laid out on a straw dish, before being squeezed into a tall elegant coffee pot with a narrow head into which is poured boiling water and the jug then placed back on the coals to keep warm.

The coffee, needless to say, is excellent, sharp and fresh and powerful.

The ceremony, Belai tells me, should take an hour – 20 minutes over the preparation and 40 minutes over the drinking. We spend at least 40 minutes drinking and talking over the recent 'take-over', as people here prefer to call it. Someone points out that the removal of Mengistu was not a revolution, that the revolution happened in 1974 when Haile Selassie was overthrown. What happened in May was just putting it back on course.

Neggar is optimistic that things will get better particularly if farmers are allowed to farm their own land and sell their own produce but at the end of it all Nick sums up the difference between now and then.

'Six months ago we couldn't have sat here and talked like this. Under Mengistu Ethiopia was to all intents and purposes a closed country.'

Belai's hospitable wife and family have prepared supper for us as well and it's my first experience of a staple of the Ethiopian diet – injera. Injera is made from a low grade cereal called tef, and it is not unlike a rubber mat in size and consistency, sour to the western palate but very useful for mopping up the various side dishes – an all-purpose spicy stew known as a 'wat', spinach, and a feta-like cheese. A meady liquor called tej completes a collection of unfamiliar tastes.

DAY 84 · ADDIS ABABA TO LAKE AWASA

 Clusters of small, deep red spots on my arm, stomach and around my ankles indicate, according to Dawood (*How to Stay Healthy Abroad*), the activities of *cimex*, which sounds like a Swiss drug company but is in fact the Latin name for bedbug. I found it in the chapter entitled 'Fleas, lice, bugs, scabies and other creatures', which I defy anyone to read without scratching. After a lot of misunderstanding I manage to persuade hotel housekeeping to come up and spray my bed.

'Make the bed?'

'No . . . no . . . the bed is made, but it has some bugs in it, which need to be removed.'

'You want your bags removed?'

The combination of bugs in the bed and a bug in my digestive system has meant little rest, but nothing much has gone right here. The management even chose our day off to empty the swimming-pool.

Now, a little after seven in the morning, we are leaving Addis, to no one's regret, and heading south again. I am in an Oxfam Landcruiser, accompanied by Nick, with an Oxfam helper, Tadesse, at the wheel.

The road out of Addis is metalled and we make good progress. We pass factories and power stations on the outskirts of town. Nick reckons that the industrial infrastructure is enough for Ethiopia's needs, but is run at only 30 per cent of its potential.

Most Ethiopians are farmers anyway – 92 per cent of the population in fact. Of these, 89 per cent are subsistence farmers, growing only what they need for themselves. Our journey from the Sudanese border has been through the provinces of Gondar, Shewa and now Arsi, the only three that produce a surplus. The other 11 provinces survive at a basic level or in the recent cases of Wollo, Tigray and Eritrea not even that.

This is the grim background to Oxfam's 17 years of work out here, but Nick is hopeful that the Ethiopians will be able to solve their own problems.

'If one thinks about the fact that more than half of the gross national

product, for the last 17 years . . . has been spent on the civil war, that is an awful lot to ask of anybody, let alone a country where there are such intractable problems.'

If the new government can give some encouragement to farmers to grow for profit, he believes that Oxfam, along with other non-government agencies, could help the country to a stage at which, as he puts it, 'Oxfam hopes to do itself out of a job'.

The landscape is changing again as we come down from the plateau and into the Rift Valley, part of a 4000-mile split in the earth's crust running from the Red Sea to Mozambique. Acacia trees have replaced fig and eucalyptus, their flat tops reflecting the flat, wide, plain between distant mountain ranges. The dusty terrain is studded with termite mounds – white, chunky blobs like the droppings of some giant creature that has moved across the countryside.

Outside Meki we pass two priests standing beside the road beneath wildly colourful umbrellas. For a moment it looks as though they're hitch-hiking, but in fact they're collecting for church funds. As a vehicle goes by they upturn their brollies and people throw money in.

At Bulbula, cattle are being driven down to drink at a palm-fringed pool fed by a narrow river and here we encounter our first baobab tree. These ancient growths are sometimes referred to as 'Upside-Down' trees and with their wide, stumpy trunks and scrawny branches do indeed look as if they have been thrust into the earth the wrong way up.

By lunchtime we've covered 150 miles with ease and have reached the noisy, vigorous road junction town of Shashamene. Kites and eagles circle above a busy main street with video stores, garages, stationery shops and public table tennis by the side of the road. Little children chew sugar cane, whilst their older brothers and sisters sell corn on the cob off charcoal fires. A huge parked Mercedes truck offers shade to a sheep suckling its young, a sleeping dog and, under the back axle, a cow, possibly hiding away from the legendary Ethiopian butcher's shops in which you can order a slice of raw flesh off the carcass and eat it then and there. We look into one. A huddle of men in the back of the shop are chewing away surrounded by walls of meat. Roger is very keen for me to join them but they are, thank God, not the least bit interested in appearing on television. We encounter similar resistance from the voluble and entertaining spokesman of a Rastafarian community in the town. Maybe it's because he's from Peckham in South London, but Tony, who talks to us outside a neat and well-kept collection of plain wooden huts with washing spread out on the grass to dry, is paranoid about the media. He's also fascinated by the media. His heroes are John Arlott, the cricket commentator and Max Robertson. He is canny enough to know that people are curious about a Jamaican who supports Manchester United and claims to be a member of one of the lost tribes of Judah. He is also convinced that for some reason we will misrepresent him.

'You people! . . . What can you ever know or understand about what we do here!'

Understanding only comes from knowing but Tony is adamant:

'Come back in three years when we have got it together.'

Janet, also from Peckham, smiles helpfully, says she can't change his mind, but she does recognize me from Monty Python. I feel our stay at Shashamene has been in the very best Python tradition.

Having failed with raw meat and Rastas we fetch up for the night at a lakeside hotel in Awasa. It's rather like checking into a zoo. A monkey sits at reception chewing the rubber off a pencil. In the grounds a pair of black and white Casqued Hornbills crash about in a cover of lush and exotic trees.

A tunnel of hibiscus bushes leads to a pair of old iron gates that give onto Lake Awasa itself. The water is fringed by a reed bed in which Nick points out to me at least four varieties of kingfisher, an African Jacana, or Lilytrotter – an Audrey Hepburn of the avian world – and a tall, red-necked

Goliath Heron who appears to be monarch of all he surveys until with a rush of black and white and a brief cry of protest he is seen off by an African Fish Eagle.

The hotel bar fills up at dusk with locals and the ubiquitous aid workers or 'aidies' as they're known here. Unfortunately the beer runs out and not many people are left when at 10 o'clock there is an English language news programme on the television, preceded, inexplicably, by a short film on ankle injuries.

Our dinner conversation is becoming increasingly dominated by bowel talk. Since the crossing into Ethiopia all of us have been afflicted in some way. Is it the beer? Or the hotel salad? Nick can cap all our stories with his experience of *giardia lamblia*, which sounds like the ultimate in these sort of problems. I look it up in Dawood before I go to sleep and wish I hadn't.

DAY 85 · LAKE AWASA

Out today to see Oxfam's water resources programme at work. Like many people I have contributed to Oxfam for many years and it's rare to have a first-hand chance to see how the money is spent. We head for Boditi, a small town, two hours drive away along dirt roads.

Oxfam's programme is designed to require the minimum amount of cost and technological expertise. There is little point in pouring money into sophisticated technology unless the local people can use it and repair it when it goes wrong. The village well that Kiros and Nick take me to see uses a simple pump with only two replaceable parts, which can be installed with nothing more than a spanner. It has been dug 90 feet down to tap an almost infinite source. A possibly tainted water supply from a river two hours walk away has been replaced by a safe, regular supply of pure water in the centre of the village, at a cost of around £2000, provided, in this case, from Comic Relief funds. It's too early to tell how significant a difference it will make to the lives of these 600 villagers but aside from the obvious health advantages Nick thinks that one of the chief benefits will be to the lives of the women of the village whose job it traditionally is to walk to the river to collect and carry back the water. Suddenly they have three or four hours a day given back to them.

There is some bad news waiting for us at the hotel. Monty Ruben, a friend who had looked after us in Kenya when I was filming *The Missionary* there nine years ago has been taken to hospital after a heart attack. He was to meet us at the border and guide us to Nairobi, but now we must make alternative plans, and quickly too, for we should cross the border in two days time.

DAY 86 · LAKE AWASA TO MOYALE

Scatter the monkeys from the vehicles at 7 o'clock as we load up once again. It's our eleventh day in Ethiopia. By tonight we hope to be in the border town of Moyale, 325 miles away. We pick our way through the Awasa rush hour, in which we are about the only vehicles. Everyone else is walking; schoolchildren, farmers, soldiers, workers on their way to the textile factory or the production lines of the National Tobacco and Matches Corporation.

There is not much public transport down here. People either walk, or pack into the back of precarious and over-laden pick-up trucks, which travel at lethal speeds. There is the occasional bus, so occasional that it is usually packed to the gunnels. The only other alternative is to hitch a ride on top of a truck. This sounds to me a novel way of seeing Africa, which is why I end up jostling with banana sellers in the main road at Yirga Alem at 9 o'clock on a Thursday morning. After a half-hour wait we persuade a small truck packed with sacks of kef to take us some of the way to Moyale.

The roadside buzzes with life on this stretch of green, fertile, lushly tropical valley, and besides the usual firewood and charcoal vendors are small children waving sugar canes four times their own size, and squatting figures laying out white peanuts to dry on the hot road surface.

Pedestrians – mostly women – toil by with enormous loads on backs or heads. A mountain of cut grass almost obscures the old lady beneath it, giving the impression that it is moving up the road of its own volition.

We pass a crowd of people on a bridge staring down into the gully below. A truck has plunged 20 feet and lies there on its back, wheels still spinning. An hour later on a deserted stretch among acacia scrub a pick-up truck which had earlier roared past us packed with standing figures, lies flipped over on the road, its cab crushed, and two of the passengers dead.

By early afternoon the countryside has changed from the fertile valleys to a scrub-covered semi-desert. I've seen camels for the first time since the Sudan and the termite architecture is increasingly Gothic. One mound, at least 15 feet high, is the most extraordinary feat of building I have seen since the Hypostyle Hall at Karnak.

The people are changing too. We are now in the land of the Borena, animists and gatherers. The women are very beautiful, exotically dressed in bright swirls of jade green, deep blue and lemon yellow. They smile broadly as we pass.

At 5.30 a rattling truck takes us through the last of the army checkpoints and into the town of Moyale. The barrier – a bar stretched across the road and weighted at one end with an old cylinder block – is raised and lowered by one of the boy soldiers holding a length of rope.

Moyale is divided into Ethiopian and Kenyan Moyale by a muddy stream and some sophisticated link fencing on the Kenyan side. Judging by the lights and the noise and the crowds in the street, Ethiopian Moyale is the hotter of the two spots. It has the rakish brashness and heightened energy of a frontier town. Arguments are louder here, drivers more impatient, demands more urgent. Music blares out from shops. Graceful pale blue jacaranda trees add a little style to its streets, but really, the place is a mess.

At the Bekele Molla hotel we are greeted by the good news that Monty Ruben is not seriously ill and that Abercrombie and Kent, the safari people, have at the last minute organized alternative transport for us to Nairobi.

Our hotel is described by its manager as the best hotel in Moyale. I cannot imagine what the opposition must be like. The rooms are set off a yard in motel style. I *do* have a double bed with slightly damp but, I think, clean sheets and there *is* electric light, but the bathroom has no running water or flushing lavatory. A half-full plastic bucket of water must serve all my needs. The curtain is a fragment of torn sacking and there is a heady smell of stale urine.

I'm told that there is a serious water crisis in the town. Wells have been sunk but the water is brackish. Southern Ethiopia and Northern Kenya are becoming part of the Sahel – the sub-Saharan area that is turning rapidly into desert. This information only serves to turn my particular gloom into a general gloom. So little of what I have seen so far in Africa can by any stretch of the imagination be described as progress, with the possible exception of

Overleaf: Into country number eleven: Last sight of Ethiopia at
the Moyale border post, Kenyan immigration, Wendy prepares lunch,
Ahmed's descendants at Marsabit, rare Grevy's zebra,
Northern Kenya — the long unwinding road.

Days 86 and 87: Ethiopia to Kenya

the pump and well I saw yesterday near Boditi. Maybe 'progress' is a Western concept, irrelevant in African terms. Talk of 'solutions' and 'ways forward' may make us feel better but can mean nothing until the yawning gap between Western and African culture begins to narrow and that probably requires a lot more listening and a lot less talking.

I finish the day writing up my notes in my hotel room. I feel a light tingling on my left arm and look down to find that I have diverted a column of ants off the wall and across my body.

Later. After a last taste of injera and wat at a restaurant in the town, I have doused myself with Repel, lit one of the spiral anti-mosquito burners provided and taken a large swig of Scotch. I hope my dreams of Ethiopia will not be affected by this grim place, for so much of what I have seen of the country has been a rich and surprising revelation.

DAY 87 · MOYALE TO MARSABIT

Wind rose during the night. I rose several times as well. It seems that the restoration of digestive stability after Addis was only temporary. My alarm sounds at six. Reach for the light, but there is no electricity this morning. Wash in mineral water as my bucket supply has all gone.

After breakfast we climb into new vehicles marshalled by Wendy Corroyer, an impressively competent lady from Abercrombie and Kent. There are four altogether, Landcruisers again, but larger than we have had previously, bought as one-ton trucks and converted into sturdy, elongated jeeps for work on safaris. My driver is short, muscular and middle-aged. He smiles easily, but cannily. His name is Kalului. Our other drivers are Kabagire, a young, slim, shyly handsome man, George, and William whose T-shirt reads 'Born to be on Vacation'.

At half-past eight we roll down the hill out of Ethiopia. Out of 1984 and back into 1991.

As the Kenyan customs officer plants an entry stamp on a fresh page of my passport I remark on how odd it is that it should be seven years later here. He looks across the page at my Ethiopian visa and nods sagely, 'They will never catch us up.'

Further up the hill, in the main square of Kenyan Moyale, we wait for the armed guard who will accompany us as far as Isiolo. This is the third country in a row to have bandit problems. Here the blame is laid on Somali guerrillas.

We are now in Swahili-speaking Africa and I can dust down my Jambos (Hellos) and my Akuna Matatas (No Problems). Less auspiciously for us Pole Pole in Swahili means Slowly Slowly.

This does not deter Kalului from setting off like a man possessed once all the border checks are completed. Unfortunately the British were never as keen on road building as the Italians, and the smooth tarred Ethiopian road north of Moyale becomes dirt track to the south. A fine dust soon settles over everything and I now know why they laughed when I appeared at breakfast in a clean white shirt.

Every now and then we hit a run of shallow ruts and for 15 seconds it's like being in a cocktail shaker. I cannot imagine how the vehicles survive this kind of treatment. The answer is they don't and at 11.20 we have our first puncture.

Wendy is philosophical about the delay. She has been in the safari business for years and as she says cheerfully, 'I haven't lost anyone yet.' Born in South Africa and now living in Kenya she describes herself unapologetically as 'an old colonial'. She thinks that there have been many improvements in the country, but the fast-growing population has brought problems. Wild animals are now increasingly confined to expensively maintained reserves, with results that include the sharp growth in elephant numbers. From being almost an endangered species elephants are now in danger of damaging a fragile environment. Richard Leakey, the Director of Kenya's Wildlife Services, is, Wendy reckons, facing a tough decision.

'We made this stand on the elephant poaching and burning all that ivory, so now we have got world attention, we've got to think of a solution other than culling.'

Apart from the security checkpoints – nail-studded wooden strips laid across the road – there are few breaks in this silent wilderness.

After an incongruous picnic of Brie cheese, frankfurters and fresh pineapple, we rattle and roll on toward our goal for the day – the town of Marsabit, 155 miles south of Moyale.

Scrub gives way to desert. We cross a desolate coverless landscape of black basalt rocks called the Dida Galgalu – the 'Plains Of Darkness' – and then, as we begin to climb out of the plains and up onto the 6000-foot plateau of Marsabit, the 'Place of Cold', the scenery changes dramatically. We begin, at last, to see wild animals – such as dik-dik, the tiniest of the antelope family, gerenuk, which stand on their hind legs to nibble thornbush branches and apparently never need to drink and the ubiquitous Grant's gazelle, poised and graceful. Higher up, at the rim of a magnificent volcanic crater, we are watched closely by a greater kudu, a fine, tall antelope with lofty spiralling horns.

Our resting place for the night is the Marsabit Lodge, set in rich green woodland beside a crater lake within the National Park.

No sooner have we arrived than a slow procession of elephants – three adults and three young – emerge from the trees and make their stately way round the lake towards us. They are the descendants of the magnificent Ahmed, the only elephant to be protected by presidential decree. He used to live in this park, constantly attended by his own personal rangers. To sit with a beer at sunset watching a young descendant of his being taught how to flick earth onto its back is well worth the price of the ticket. On the tree beside me hangs a sign, 'Animals are requested to be silent when people are drinking, and vice versa'.

By a stroke of luck there is a complete power failure in the hotel. We eat by candlelight and sit afterwards beside a log fire. Sprawled out in front of us is an unkempt and indolent hotel cat. Now and then we can hear from out of the darkness a tearing of undergrowth as the elephants plod slowly about, feeding voraciously. The combination of cats at the hearth and elephants in the garden outside is quite surreal, and oddly comforting.

DAY 88 · MARSABIT TO SHABA

 At first light we are on our way up the bumpy tortuous track and out of this mountain-top forest, passing by some extraordinary trees with sinewy roots twisting down the outside of the trunk. Wendy tells me these are Strangler Figs. They are seeded by birds and grow around an existing tree becoming stronger and stronger until they kill off the host.

The road south – still no more than a dusty track – descends from Mount Marsabit to the hot and rocky plain. We pass a group of Rendille tribesmen, tall and very straight, wearing head-dresses, bare-chested apart from coloured beads around the neck, taking their cattle to water. One carries a gun, another a stick tipped with a plume of ostrich feathers, a sign that they come in peace – unless you're an elephant. One looms close by and the men fling stones at it to keep it away from their herd. A little while later a group of Rendille women pass. These nomadic people walking barefoot along the dusty rutted tracks of Africa look as effortlessly graceful and immaculate as anyone on a *Vogue* cover. From a band around their heads hang discs of what looks like gold or silver, their long necks are held erect by a stack of beads, and they wear loose flowing garments of red and white striped cotton. They lead donkeys hung about with every kind of plastic container. They're looking for water.

Weaver birds nest in the low flat-topped acacias. Those with tidy nests are the Sociable weavers and those with the scruffier nests, constantly having to rebuild, are known as the Sparrow weavers. Two white-bellied turacos, known, because of their cry, as the Go Away birds, shriek at us from a high branch.

We are now entering the land of the Samburu, or 'Butterfly' tribe. They are a branch of the Ma people, of whom the best known are the Masai, who many years ago split from the Samburu and went south. The Samburu remain, like the Rendille and the Borena in southern Ethiopia, a colourful, un-Westernized tribe still practising male and female circumcision. They love dress and display, especially favouring ear ornaments – rings in top and bottom and lobes pierced then stretched into holes an inch wide.

I have fond memories of filming *The Missionary* in Samburu territory – at the village of Lerata. We built a mud and wattle chapel, complete with stained glass windows, in which I played 'From Greenland's Icy Mountain', which the local children specially learnt for the occasion. Our construction crew put a new roof on the schoolroom, and I wanted to return and see if it had survived and what, if anything, they remembered of us.

It is baking hot again – 112 degrees in the sun – as we reach the village. The schoolchildren, neatly turned out in gold and blue uniforms, have obviously been told to expect a celebrity, and as soon as we stop they crowd around Wendy, chanting, smiling and clapping. When eventually they are pointed in my direction they are confused and cannot whip up quite the same degree of enthusiasm. But Henry the teacher is still there and so is the schoolroom roof, and beneath it I tell the children about the journey I am doing with the aid of the inflatable globe that stood me in such good stead on *Around the World in 80 Days*. At the end I donate the globe to Lerata School, which they all seem to think is wonderful and proceed to play football with it.

A boy called Tom, who remembers singing in the film, has come all the way from Eldoret University in the west of the country where he is a sociology student. We look at photos taken during the filming, whilst the bonily photogenic elders of the village debate how much it will cost for them to be filmed.

This is a poor part of the country and the liveliness and eagerness of the children is moving. Henry, who is the sort of opportunist the place needs, tells me they are building a dormitory for children who have to come in from a long way. They have everything but the roof.

By the time I leave Lerata they have money for another roof.

As we drive away, a dust devil, a column of dust whipped up by the wind to a height of 30 or 40 feet, snakes out of the bush and across our path. It seems an appropriate image for our visit to Lerata. A rush of hyperactive whites, a windfall and we're gone.

At 4 o'clock we are staring into the eyeless sockets of two massive water-buffalo skulls which mark the entrance to the Shaba National Reserve, 160 miles from Marsabit and not much more than 50 miles from the Equator.

The Shaba Lodge is a wonderful hotel, unashamedly modern but not ostentatiously luxurious, skilfully landscaped among tall trees along the Vaso Nyiro River. Last night at Marsabit we had water but no electricity, the night before that we had electricity and no water, tonight we have a swimming-pool, double beds, mosquito nets, a bedroom and a sitting-room. But the shock of comfort brings with it less pleasant shocks. One is the realization that, for the first time since leaving the Old Cataract Hotel, Aswan, we are back on the tourist trail — back in the world of aimlessly pointing video cameras, bandy white legs and loud complaining voices.

'Where are those bats coming from?'

'I don't know where they're coming from.'

'They came right down and zoomed my head. It was horrible!'

I have to physically restrain myself from shouting, 'Then why come here? Why ever leave home at all?'

Maybe it's just that I've been away from home too long.

DAY 89 · SHABA TO NAIROBI

A significant day ahead. By the time it's over we should be in the Southern Hemisphere, over half-way to our goal after three months travelling.

Wendy thinks we should be up at 5 a.m. if we want to see the summit of Mount Kenya before the clouds form over it, but long-term fatigue wins the day over short-term shot-chasing and we gather for breakfast soon after 6 o'clock. Sparrows and starlings are already in attendance in the dining room. The sparrows are familiar but the starlings here look a lot sharper than their British counterparts. They're known as Superb starlings and are luridly turned out with metallic blue backs and chestnut bellies.

The Shaba Lodge has a bookshop and whilst we wait to leave I'm able to acquire the indispensable *Field Guide to the Birds of East Africa* (650 species described) and the equally illuminating *Mammals of Africa*.

Straightaway I'm able to identify a Greenbacked Heron (rare) and the more common Marabou Stork. Two of these are moving, with measured strut, along a sandy spit in the middle of the river. Seen from behind, with their heads down and their voluminous white wings clasped behind them they look like a couple of elderly dons debating some fine point of moral philosophy.

Isiolo is a place of mixed blessings. Roads from predominantly Moslem Somalia and predominantly Christian Ethiopia converge here, on the northern edge of the prosperous colonial heartland around Mount Kenya. A fine mosque, with delicate filigree work around the windows and a cluster of beautiful domed alcoves atop the minarets, shares the main street with a branch of Barclays Bank, video stores, one-room hotels and churches of the Seventh-Day Adventists and many others of the 140 religious sects alive and well in Kenya. The roadside salesmen are hard and aggressive, but at least the going is softer, with the road metalled again after 320 miles of dirt-track.

Lying between here and Nairobi, and forcing a long detour to east or west is the soaring bulk of the Mount Kenya massif. The highest of its ragged peaks, Batian, rises to 17,000 feet. It is the second highest point in Africa, after Kilimanjaro, and was first climbed by a Westerner, Sir Halford Mackinder, in the last year of the nineteenth century. Even from the hot plain beyond Isiolo one can make out the glaciers and ice-fields at its summit, which ensure that there is always snow at the Equator.

As the road climbs, I can see that Wendy was right – a helmet of cloud is beginning to form around the top of the mountain and may well have concealed it altogether by the time we are close enough to film.

The scenery has once more undergone an amazing transformation. We could be in the American Rockies, with the towering crags of Mount Kenya on one side and rolling prairie on the other.

A Secretary Bird, quills bristling, struts self-importantly through a fresh-cut cornfield, an Augur Buzzard beadily scans the terrain from the top of a telegraph pole. Higher up fat, fluffy flocks of sheep graze in the shadow of the mountain.

'Great sweater country,' says Wendy. We grab a shot of the summit with seconds to spare, and the road coasts downhill to the town of Nanyuki, passing signs for 'Jack Wright Ltd Family Butcher', 'Modern Sanitary Stores', 'Kenya Insurance', 'Marshall's Peugeot' and finally, 'The Equator'.

Clem and Angela have driven out from Nairobi to surprise us – and a lot of onlooking souvenir salesmen – with a bottle or two of champagne. This reunion of the entire crew not only celebrates a certain achievement, it also averts potential anti-climax, for the Equator line, marked as it is by power-cables, a main road and an electricity sub-station, could just as well be in Croydon as Kenya.

In the ruins of what was once the Silverbeck Hotel, which straddled the Equator and offered punters the prospect of buying a beer in the Northern Hemisphere and drinking it in the Southern, a young African called Peter demonstrates the Coriolis effect by which energy in the Northern Hemisphere appears to be directed to the right, and in the Southern to the left. Peter drains a bowl of water in the North, and, by means of a floating stick, we observe that the water drains away in a clockwise direction. Then we, (myself and a group of American tourists) wander with Peter, his stick and his plastic bucket into the Southern Hemisphere where we observe that

in exactly the same operation, the stick turns anti-clockwise. On the Equator line itself, the stick doesn't turn at all.

Peter politely acknowledges our expressions of wonder and then prepares for the next demonstration whilst we collect certificates to show that we have seen what we have seen.

For a proper celebration of Sunday at the Equator we adjourn to the unashamed luxury of the Mount Kenya Safari Club. Here, amidst immaculately coiffeured lawns, patrolled by ibises, cranes, peacocks and marabou storks, is a sign telling us we are eating our Sunday joint on Latitude 00.00, Longitude 37.7 East, at 7000 feet.

The run into Nairobi is full of reminders of a way of life very different from what we have seen in our last six weeks in Africa. Tribal costumes give way to T-shirts and jeans. There are traffic jams of private cars, road signs, newspapers, irrigation sprinklers, villagers on bicycles (why were there so few bicycles in Ethiopia and Sudan?) and polite notices at the end of towns and villages saying 'Kwaheri'. Goodbye.

For us it's goodbye to the Northern Hemisphere after three months on the road. I don't really think about what's to come. It's hard enough to accept that we have to do that distance all over again.

DAY 95 · NAIROBI

 It seems to be an odd psychological and physiological fact that on a journey like this time off is trouble. The system, geared up to movement and rapid adjustment to changing conditions, is caught off guard and may begin to wind down, thinking perhaps that it's all over. The adrenalin is switched off and all sorts of little ailments appear. I have the feeling that after five days break in Nairobi all of us will be very glad to be on the move again. We all know that the only way back home is via the South Pole.

This morning I'm to be fitted for an outfit in advance of the next stage of our journey – an Abercrombie and Kent safari into the Masai Mara game reserve. I'm collected at the hotel by a London black cab. President Arap Moi was so impressed with them on a visit to Britain that he allowed them to be imported into Kenya free of duty, and there are now over 100 operating in Nairobi. I ask Michael Nqanga, my driver, if anything has ever gone wrong with his vehicle. 'Not exactly,' he replies, but doesn't elaborate.

Downtown Nairobi is compact and modern and not particularly beautiful. Bland concrete blocks are being superseded by bland aluminium and glass blocks. The reflecting walls of Lonrho's new headquarters dominate the skyline. If cranes and scaffolding are a sign of confidence then Nairobi appears to be doing well, though local people I have spoken to regard Moi's

maintenance of a one-party state as a source of weakness and potential future chaos. Opposition is tightly muzzled, both by the imprisonment of its leaders and restriction and censorship of the press.

But at Colpro, safari suppliers to the rich and famous, it's business as usual. Well, not quite as usual, for as Chetan Haria, the proprietor, tells me, the tourist market still hasn't recovered from the Gulf crisis. There was a time, he remembered fondly, when 270 Americans came in at once, 'all wanting to look the same'.

His family began the business as an army surplus store 30 years ago and it has grown to be the leading supplier of safari gear, much of which is based on military uniform. Now that the Hemingway days are over and hunting is strictly controlled the outfits are a mass of anachronisms, a matter of fashion rather than practicality. The jacket design seems entirely pocket led. Some models have as many as 12 in various places. What earthly use, I ask Chetan, is a pocket sewn into the lining in the middle of the back? He glances towards the door.

'There are thieves outside,' he confides darkly.

I settle for what is described as a 'photo-journalist's jacket' as I know it will be good for a laugh from the crew. It is.

A photograph of Prince Charles – a previous customer – is tacked onto the wall beside the changing booth from which I eventually emerge with my ensemble – a cotton shirt with a map of Kenya printed on it, my photo-journalist's jacket and a pair of trousers which can be unzipped at the kneecap should I prefer shorts.

Apart from being an extremely helpful place, Chetan's store displays none of the colonial snobbishness I had associated with safari-ism. He is just as happy to sell you a tape of local tribal music, or a 'Wild Thing' T-shirt, or a 'Horny Friends' bag.

Outside, many of the city's buildings are being draped in the national colours for Kenyatta Day, tomorrow's national holiday in honour of the man who led Kenya to independence from the British 28 years ago.

Like Colpro the outfitters and the Republic of Kenya, Abercrombie and Kent have been in business for almost 30 years. Their safari stores are located in a solid stone-walled building in one of the burgeoning industrial estates around Nairobi. Here two Isuzu trucks are being loaded up with the eleven and a half tons of equipment we shall need over the next three days. Travel-hardened wooden and tin crates are filled with everything from toilet paper and fresh-cut flowers to hot-water bottles and cases of Blanc de Blancs. In the storeroom are rows of trestle-tables, bed-frames and barbecues, sackfuls of mallets, shelves of hurricane lamps and coat hangers, piles of doormats and shovels and lavatory seats. There is even a wood-framed double-bed. 'Usually reserved for honeymooners,' explains Martin, who is in charge of our preparations.

The drive to the Mara can be tricky, with dirt roads for most of the way. Martin is anxious to get the big trucks off as soon as possible.

'In the last four years the rains have gone crazy.' (They call rain 'rains' out here, but elephants they call 'elephant'.)

This year they are expected two weeks early, which could mean tomorrow, and an eight-hour journey to the camp can take as long as four days in bad weather.

DAY 96 · NAIROBI TO THE MASAI MARA

Up at 5.15. On the move, away from the world of CNN and English newspapers and telephone access to life at home.

Pulling back the curtains I can make out the dark clouds which have hung over the capital these past few days with still no sign of them emptying. Below me a border of white, purple, orange and blue bougainvillea almost obscures the chain-link fence which, like the corridor outside my room, is patrolled by guards with nightsticks.

I'm reunited with Wendy and Kalului and our caravan sets off at 6.30. The streets of Nairobi are quiet on this Kenyatta Day holiday, but as the sun rises and we head north along the Trans-African highway, the roads soon fill up with the tearaway minibuses they call Matatus, whose names indicate

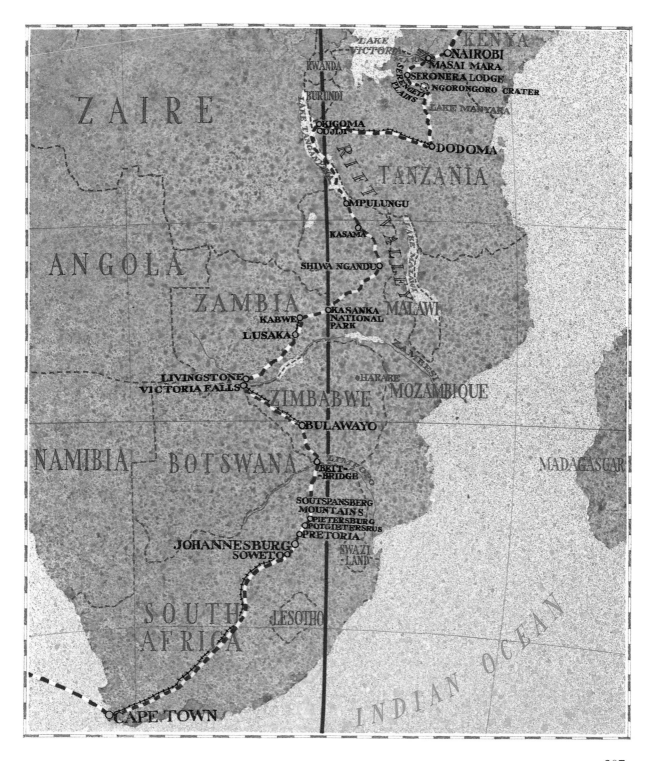

their driving style – 'Exocet', 'Sidewinder', and most ironic of all in view of their appalling accident record 'Gateway to Heaven'.

Up and over a string of fertile valleys and cultivated hillsides, where roses, carnations and poinsettias are grown to be sold in Europe. Behind neatly trimmed hedges is a picture postcard tea plantation, with rows of green bushes radiating from a cluster of low red-roofed buildings. It looks like a country without a care in the world, yet so many here feel it is heading into serious political trouble.

We climb to the top of the eastern wall of the Rift Valley, about 8000 feet above sea-level. There is an almost dizzying view of a great expanse of sunlit plain dominated to the north by the grey deeply fissured walls of the extinct volcano Longonot.

The valley floor is rich ranchland, and when, in the film *Mogambo*, Clark Gable looks out over this same view and shouts 'Gorilla!', every true Kenyan cracks up. The nearest gorilla is at least 500 miles away.

Our reverie is broken by the roar of a Mack truck on its way from Ruanda in central Africa to the port of Mombasa. It barrels dangerously down the hill, sending up a shower of dust and stones around the words on its tailgate – 'Praise The Lord. He is Merciful'.

We stop to buy a late breakfast of fresh grilled corncobs from some children at the roadside. A troop of baboons is scattered across the road, extracting bits of corn and wheat grain that have, literally, fallen off the back of a lorry. Some have their young slung beneath them, where they remain until five weeks old, after which they're transferred onto mother's back for three months and only much later allowed to run and play on their own. Wendy says that most safari tours miss all this. They are air-lifted straight out to the Mara.

The entertainment goes on. Giraffe glide with effortless grace through the pale gold grass. Hartebeest and Thomson's gazelle graze beneath the predatory eye of vultures, kites and buzzards. A black-tailed mongoose scuttles across our path. As we climb the western wall of the Rift Valley we come upon a flock of 50 or 60 goats who have mounted the bank at the side of the road, nuzzling the earth and sticking their heads into a honeycomb of small holes, from which they are trying to extract salt.

We are now running west, back a little way toward our 30 degree meridian. At Narok we leave the metalled road again and are soon bouncing our way over mercifully dry tracks, past tall, long-striding Masai, usually wearing red cloaks or blankets across one shoulder. Their villages, enclosed by a stockade fence, are known as manyattas. The men maintain the fence leaving the women to the less glamorous job of coating the stick-frame houses with dung.

By late afternoon we have covered about 145 miles from Nairobi and are crossing into the Masai Mara National Reserve. Unlike the Serengeti to the south, the Mara is not a National Park and the Masai farmers are allowed to graze their flocks here. This mixture of the wild and the domestic, cows and sheep grazing alongside giraffe and elephant gives the Reserve a special, Noah's Ark quality.

But man is now very much a part of the Mara, and as we near the river, the afternoon session of tourists are being transported out of their lodges in a fleet of open-topped minibuses.

Wendy is a bit sniffy about them, 'If you've been to Africa and stayed in a lodge, you've been on a holiday, if you've been to Africa and stayed in a tent you've been on safari.'

When we reach our campsite by the banks of the Mara River, the tents have only just been erected and lavatories not yet dug nor beds erected. Patrick, the *maître de camp*, who has safaried with Hemingway, but still looks only 25, welcomes us, quickly introduces the staff of 13, makes us cups of tea and leaves us to look at the local river life. This consists of a colony of around 30 hippos puffing and wheezing like a lot of old men in a club after lunch. They apparently spend most of the day there, emerging at night to feed, and I'm told, wander through the camp. 'It's perfectly all right so long as you stay in your tent,' Martin advises, cheerfully.

We are on what is known as the 'Out Of Africa' safari – one up from the 'Hemingway', which is one up from the 'Kenya Under Canvas'. This certainly isn't how I remember school camp. The tents are spacious. At the back, and under cover, there is a sort of dressing area, with a table and mirror, and a plastic toilet over a freshly dug hole. Beside the hole is a pile of earth, a small spade and a sign: 'Hippos cover it up, will you do too.' I have an old-fashioned bed, a solar-powered light and a rail for my clothes, and outside the roof of the tent extends over a washstand and a couple of canvas chairs, excellent for sitting out in before supper, and drinking a Scotch to the accompaniment of awfully rude noises from the river.

Dinner is served after a slight delay owing to the activity of baboons in the kitchen. Martin tells the story of one guest who felt a baboon against the side of his tent and whacked it with a heavy torch. It turned out to be a hippo, which charged off through the kitchen tent, which offered little resistance, and the hippo vanished into the bush with the kitchen wrapped around him.

10.20 p.m.: The river is silent. A big moon casts a silvery light across the trees and banks of the river. A group of Masai from the local manyatta guard the camp, sitting by a wood fire and talking quietly. One of them, an elderly man with close-cropped grey hair, walks up and down between our tents and the river, ear-ringed, blanketed and carrying a spear. I feel very strongly that I am in a dream I once had, a long time ago.

DAY 97 · THE MASAI MARA

Roars, splashes and hippo hoots mark the end of the night and I'm already awake when I hear the first human cry.

'Jambo!' comes from outside a nearby tent, followed by the sound of a door-flap being unzipped and bleary greetings from the occupants. It's 6 o'clock. There are no lie-ins on safari.

I'm Jambo-ed a minute or two later. A flask of tea, a plate of biscuits and milk in a china jug are set down by the bed and hot water poured into the washing bowl outside.

Dressed in my Colpro safari outfit, looking, and feeling, like a cut-price David Attenborough, I set out at 6.45, with the sun struggling to make an impression on a cloudy lifeless sky.

We make our way along the damp uneven track from the riverside toward the tall slope of the escarpment, passing zebra, impala and a grazing warthog. Warthogs – ugly, endearing creatures – live in the remains of anthills into which they insert themselves backwards. For some reason this makes me even more fond of them.

Six elephants, mighty ears flapping and trunks ripping at the croton bushes, move down the hill away from us. They only sleep about two hours a night, I'm told. Kalului, who has an extraordinary sixth sense about the presence of animals spots a lion couple, way in the distance. As we drive closer they turn out to be a somewhat battered male and a lethargic female. Neither seems to bat an eyelid at the circling presence of three vehicles and a clutch of cameras only yards away. The female, after washing and yawning, unhurriedly raises herself and the male immediately follows. He is limping. Lions spend about a week together mating, sometimes coupling as much as 80 times in 24 hours, but this affair looks to be over, if it ever began.

Meanwhile, in another episode of the Masai Mara soap opera, a male ostrich is doing his best to attract the ladies' attention. He cannot rely on subtlety as his legs turn pink during the mating season, so he goes for broke with an outrageous fan dance, a wonderful spectacle of feather control, which does seem to have several female beaks turning in his direction.

In the midst of life we are in death. We pass Nubian vultures tearing away at the corpse of a zebra. These birds are known as the butchers, the only ones with necks and beaks powerful enough to open up a carcass. The coarse grass of the plain is littered with skulls, bones and skins, and the constant presence of vultures, eagles, buzzards and land scavengers like jackals, with their sharp faces and big ears, is a reminder of the precariousness of life.

Our feeding is a little more decorous. We are treated to one of the set-pieces of an A and K safari – the 'Out of Africa' breakfast. Whilst we have been ear-wigging lion couples, the staff from the camp have set up a long table, complete with fresh flowers and cut-glass butter-dishes, on the top of the Olololo escarpment. Eggs, bacon and sausage are sizzling on an open fire and the waiters are in dinner-jackets. The plain stretches away, flat and wide, between the escarpment walls of the Rift Valley, south toward Tanzania. A thousand feet below us the sunless Mara, which we know to be teeming with living things, looks grey and empty, except for a Second World War DC-3, which makes a wide, banking turn before settling down onto the airstrip, only a few hundred yards from where we watched the lions.

Later in the day grey clouds have filled the sky and the rain comes in, straight and heavy, putting an end to safari for the day.

Our journey through Africa has been planned to tread a fine line between the rainy seasons, but nature has not played along. The late rains in Sudan and now early rains in Kenya will not make our progress any easier.

The temperature falls to 63 Fahrenheit – the coldest we've experienced since northern Norway. There isn't much to do but sit and watch the water drip off the tents and listen to the blowing, wheezing, gasping, gurgling pleasure of the hippos.

Later some of the local Masai come to the camp to perform a traditional dance which tells the story of a lion hunt. I ask one of them afterwards if this is all now a thing of the past. He shakes his head firmly. Although it is not officially permitted to kill a lion in the Reserve, he and his fellow villagers recently took the law into their own hands after a lion had persistently attacked their goats. They hunted the lion down and killed it, with spears and arrows, not guns. Would he do it again? He nods, equally firmly, but says that the leader of their manyatta has now been recruited by the conservation people. 'This makes life more difficult for us.'

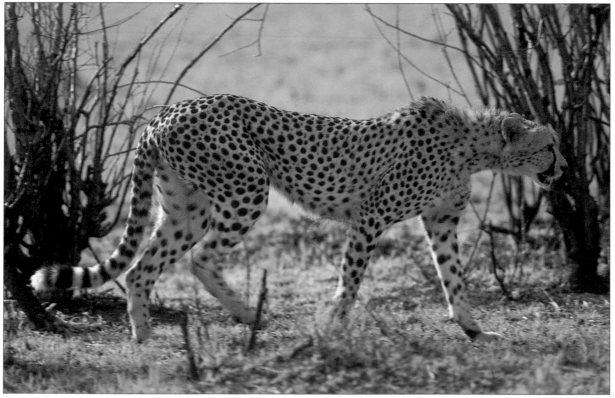

DAY 98 · THE MASAI MARA

Wake to a sky of cloud and drizzle, which is unfortunate as we are to begin the day with a balloon ride over the Mara.

It's chilly and still dark when we arrive at the launch area, at a place called Little Governor's Camp. Surrounded by trees and stone-built, thatched cottages with hanging baskets by the doors it is not unlike an English village green, on a wet morning in November. However, the rain is not strong enough to abort the trip, and as a glum sunlight struggles through, instructions are given to fill the envelopes – the gasbags – of the two balloons. The envelopes are made by Thunder and Colt of Oswestry, from six and a half miles of polyester fabric, and are thought to be the largest in the world. By the time they are inflated, each with 330,000 cubic feet of air, heated to 100 degrees Centigrade, they will stand 90 feet high. Dawn breaks to the roar of the burners, their piercing yellow tongues of flame and the slow tumescence of the multi-coloured giants.

Each balloon can carry a dozen people and an apprehensive mixture of English and Americans is gathered in the half-light. I feel a sharp sting at the back of my leg, and turning to scratch, I notice that everyone else is doing the same thing.

'Safari ants,' says an Englishman cheerfully. 'Touch them and they bite.'

As a large number of them are half-way up my trouser leg, and the ground is full of reinforcements this isn't particularly helpful, and trying to extricate myself from them is like a coping with a series of very light electric shocks.

Eventually the towering balloons are ready and we climb into our baskets. Each one is traditional, made of wood and cane, and divided into partitions, so once inside we must look a little like milk-bottles in a crate. Most of my co-passengers are American but the pilot is very British.

'My name is John Coleman and I'm your pilot this morning. As you can see I have three stripes on my epaulette – one for each laundry.'

He keeps up a steady stream of such observations as we rise slowly into the sky above the murky treescape below.

'If you feel a little frightened, don't worry. I get scared whenever I fly. Chicken in the basket.'

The Americans are a bit bewildered by all this and also a little disappointed at the lack of wildlife talent this soggy morning.

Still, they point in hope.

'Hey, look at that bird!' 'Look down there, there's one of those things . . .'

As John Coleman steers us along the tops of the trees, we learn from

216

him that the hippos who keep us awake at night are amongst 2500 in the reserve, that the lungfish survives in the ox-bow lakes of the Mara River by burying itself in the mud during the long dry season and re-emerging when the rains come, and that elephants can drop their blood temperature 11 degrees just by flapping their ears.

Coleman takes the balloon down until we are almost on the ground, slowly skimming the surface at animal height, but not having found much he climbs swiftly to 1500 feet. He makes it all look very easy, but as he says, this is good ballooning country, no power cables or barbed wire fences to worry about and a climate good enough for 350 days a year operation. The only danger is to stray across into Tanzania and have to put down there. It's easily done and recently a balloon safari was arrested and held by the Tanzanians for illegal entry.

The landing is a bit of a drag and a bump, but not uncomfortable, and we find ourselves within cork's distance of another Masai Mara champagne breakfast. Our glasses of pink champagne match the legs of a randy male ostrich racing about in the distance, but otherwise our bacon, egg, sausage, mushroom and croissant 'kill' is observed only by a Yellow-Bearded Kite, a predator kept from the long, low breakfast table by a line of spears.

Coleman brings the proceedings to a close with a toast to wives and girlfriends – 'May they never meet' – after which we collect another certificate.

I feel as though I've done a day's work but it's not yet 10 o'clock as a pale sun at last begins to warm the grassland and the indefatigable Wendy leads us off on another grand nature ramble.

We return to the donga, which is the Swahili word for the small overgrown creek, where yesterday we saw the two lions conspicuously not mating. Today things have changed. Same lioness, different lion – probably the brother of the failed suitor. This time they are obviously interested in the same thing. They sit eyeing each other until, as yesterday, the female gets up and strolls off. As if on an invisible lead her partner follows and waits for such time as she squats down. This is the signal for him to settle on top. They couple for no more than 25 seconds, to an accompaniment of low growling and neck-biting. Then the male stands back and the female rolls over onto her back. After a decent interval of 9 or 10 minutes the whole thing starts again.

Then, from down amongst the undergrowth, another lioness appears, leading four very young cubs. (Wendy estimates them to be about six weeks old, and probably out in the open for the first time.) One stays close to his mother, but looks bright and adventurous, two others follow a little further behind, but number four is clearly the runt of the litter, unable to keep up. Meanwhile, up on the low hill, uncle and aunt are at it again. They all seem quite oblivious of each other and of the intrusion of a half-dozen telephoto lenses. More distressingly it seems at one point that the mother is oblivious to her fourth cub who is floundering way behind in the long grass, but just as we thought she'd forgotten, she raises her head, turns, pads slowly back down the hill, picks the runt up in her mouth and carries it back to the family. It's mesmerizing activity and we remain absorbed for the best part of an hour. By which time, as I calculate it, the happy couple have mated six more times.

A short while afterwards we come across a stately column of giraffe moving across the landscape in what appears to be slow motion. At the back of the procession is a smaller, lame giraffe walking awkwardly, and falling further behind. This time it doesn't look as if anyone is going back to help.

Wendy shakes her head . . . 'They just carry on, it's the survival of the fittest. That's why it's probably better if some predator comes along . . . they wouldn't be able to kill them standing up like that . . . they'll wait till they lie down.'

Birth, reproduction and death. We've been close to it all today.

Though it doesn't actually rain again, the grey clouds pile up to bring on a premature dusk. Sweaters come out and the camp staff light a fire beside the river for us. I wander round to the kitchen. A big pizza is being loaded into the oven. Patrick is busying around and I probably get in the way, but I can't leave here without talking to someone who's been on safari with Hemingway. Was Hemingway as good as he said he was? Patrick nods.

'He must have learnt to shoot with the American cowboys. Some shoot in the stomach or the leg, but not him. He was good.'

Others of Patrick's illustrious companions were not as naturally gifted. President Tito generally had to be assisted . . . 'We had some problems . . . he doesn't shoot on the best part.' Prince Charles, whom he accompanied on a camel safari up to Lake Turkana, wasn't interested in the hunting but was himself nearly hunted.

'He stepped on the back of a crocodile thinking that it's a stone, or a log lying by the sand. Then this crocodile started moving – he was frightened!'

I have the impression that Patrick preferred the old days, when risks were greater but groups were smaller, when you ate what you hunted and slept in the open.

Now that tourism has taken a firm hold here it seems that safaris have become a parody of themselves. We dress like white hunters. We are treated like white hunters, brought whiskies at sundown and bacon and eggs for breakfast, yet we hunt with Canon cameras from within solid vehicles. Maybe one day visitors will be able to see, enjoy and learn about animals in the wild without having to go through the pretence of being latter-day Hemingways.

But for now we remain pleasantly cossetted. After a farewell barbecue dinner of impala and hartebeest the staff bring in a cake for us and dance around the table singing 'Jambo Bwana'. It may all seem a bit colonial, but they have made us very happy here and I don't think they've hated it any more than we have.

DAY 99 · THE MASAI MARA TO SERONERA

 Of course, the day we have to leave our camp is better than any since we arrived – clear skies and a fine sunrise to shave by. A generous, traveller's breakfast including fresh pine-apple, melon, porridge and all sorts of cholesterol, and fond farewells to Patrick and his staff and particularly to Wendy who has been such an excellent and informative companion and guide – giving us just about the right balance of carrot and stick. Addresses are exchanged and family safari holidays promised. Not that we shall be leaving Abercrombie and Kent behind altogether. Kalului and Kabagire have agreed to drive us down through the Serengeti to pick up the train at Dodoma, in Tanzania, over 450 miles to the south. Craig, a young, athletic Kenyan, will be taking over Wendy's role as trouble-shooter and animal-spotter. Craig was born and raised in Kenya of white, English parents.

'Over here they call us Vanilla Gorillas,' he grinned.

We leave the Hippo Riviera at a quarter to eight, heading south and east toward the Tanzanian border.

Our 30 degree meridian remains elusive, as Lake Victoria, with irregular and unpredictable ferry crossings, blocks our way to the west. The good news is that this morning I exchange the dusty, threadbare map of 'Africa North East and Arabia' which has accompanied me for seven weeks – since Port Said – for a crisp and pristine 'Africa Central and South'.

I have a feeling it will be worn in very quickly as we venture into rarely visited territory to complete the last thousand miles of our sweeping detour round Southern Sudan.

Animal-spotting is every bit as obsessive as train-spotting and one of the gaps in my book is filled after little more than half an hour's driving when we catch our first sight of a cheetah. It's a solitary animal but its presence has a magnetic effect on the supporting cast. Thomson's gazelle grazing nearby freeze in mid-mastication. Impala's heads turn and stare as if hypnotized. There is very little point in trying to run away from an animal whose 'maximum speed in emergency' can, according to my book, 'reach 110 kph'. The cheetah looks made for speed. Its head is small, body long and powerful, legs lean and slender. Cheetahs stalk their prey with infinite care and patience, moving to within a hundred yards before attacking. The suspense is so sustained, the build-up so painstakingly slow that in the 15 minutes we are there nothing moves except eyeballs.

Near the border we catch our first sight of migrating wildebeeste. They are returning south in long columns after feeding on the short rich grass of the Mara. We have to wait 20 minutes for one procession to pass across the track. They seem in good spirits, butting each other playfully, cavorting, facing the wrong way and generally displaying all the characteristics of a school outing on the way home. I can't imagine why these heavy-shouldered grey-pelted beasts should be quite so happy. A quarter of a million of them die on the migration each year. Some die natural deaths, but many more perish from drowning whilst crossing the river, snakebites (those carcasses are left untouched by other predators, who can tell there is poison on the body), and the activities of lion, leopard, cheetah, serval and others.

A little further on we come across two hyena shuffling off with a piece of wildebeeste. They are shifty looking creatures, round-shouldered and surly. I rather like them. They'll never get a decent part in a Walt Disney film, but they do keep the place tidy and I'm rather endeared to the fact that they giggle so much when they've made a kill that they give away their position and are often dispossessed by more lugubrious beasts.

Close by the Kenyan border-post a solidly built, light blue truck is stuck in the mud. A small group of young whites stand looking dolefully at it. They are mostly Australians, New Zealanders and Brits on an overland adventure tour from Nairobi to Harare, Zimbabwe. Their leaders are a short, smiling young man with a *Just William* shock of hair and a girl called Dave.

'German . . . built for the Russian front,' says the young man jabbing a spanner at the beached vehicle.

Despite its bulk Kabagire manages to pull it out of the mud with his Landcruiser. The overlanders remount and the truck slowly and unsteadily heaves itself up the last few yards to the border leaving behind a pair of deep trenches and a baboon sorting through the remains of their campfire with the meticulous care of a forensic scientist.

After passing through customs and immigration without incident we run a short way downhill to a bridge across the Sand River and up a rocky slope past a sign 'Welcome to Serengeti National Park'. Elephant herds, bigger than anything we saw in the Mara, crowd the brown-gold grassland studded with enough trees to give them cover and food. A family of warthogs sprints across the road in front of us, tails hoisted in unison. Nigel is particularly soppy about warthogs, and the sight of baby ones is almost too much for him. We'll probably find rolls of film full of them.

1.20 p.m.: At the Bologonja border station. Set between solid stone posts topped with massively horned buffalo skulls is a gate with 'Tanzania' written on it. This is the first country I've seen with a gate and makes me rather warm to the place. It's 140,000 square miles bigger than Kenya, though a minnow compared to Egypt, Sudan and Ethiopia. Once a part of German East Africa, it became the independent republic of Tanganyika in 1962 and merged with the People's Republic of Zanzibar to form the name on the gate in 1964.

We have a three and a half hour wait at the thatched bungalow that is the border-post, and we are still there, having all our permits laboriously described in longhand, when the overlanders catch us up. The truck has had no further mishaps, but they have to keep its engine running as the starter motor's gone.

Once through the gate, we appear to be in a garden of Eden with trees, lush green grass and streams bubbling through, but this soon gives way to the Serengeti proper, a 57,000 square mile expanse of scrubland. Unlike the Masai Mara it is a park set aside for wild animals only. There are no cattle or herdsmen here. We pass more lion, this time about 10 of them at a kill. A wildebeeste is the victim and by the time we arrive the male lions have already fed and are lying, panting in the shade, whilst the females dismember what's left. A macabre chorus of 30 or 40 quarrelling vultures and Marabou storks stand some yards away waiting for the pickings.

Finally a very young lion approaches the stomach which has been left intact. Though I will him not to, it's all that's left to him and he picks it up. Half-digested grass spills from the gut as he drags it along between his front legs, away to his own private place.

The altitude dial on Basil's watch reads 1750 metres (5500 feet) as we cross the Seronera river into a green cover of mahogany, fig and umbrella acacias, amongst which are set big smoothed boulders of the sort that John Wayne chased Indians through. Our hotel is built around one of these outcrops, and offers the serious pleasure of being able to stroll across the rocks at dusk and watch the light fade over the Serengeti as a colony of hyrax – rabbit-sized furry creatures that look a little like draught excluders – scuttle about in the background. A full moon slowly rises as the immense plain merges with an immense sky.

DAY 100 · SERONERA TO LAKE MANYARA

 Pull back the curtains at 7 a.m. to find myself staring into the wide curious eyes of a vervet monkey, nose pressed up against the window, watching me unblinkingly. I admonish him sternly.

'You monkey!'

Basil thinks this is very funny, but we have been on the road for three months.

Day 100: Tanzania

Across the Tanzanian border: Masai cattle and the Ngorongoro Crater, view from my window of Lake Manyara.

It is a clear, fresh, glistening morning and I cannot quite believe that I am alive and in the Serengeti and only hours away from the Ngorongoro Crater, the second largest in the world. And me a schoolboy from Sheffield.

Just then I hear, from the passageway, the unmistakable sound of other ex-schoolboys from Sheffield.

'Hurry along Clifford!' . . . An early morning chorus of Yorkshire accents recedes towards the restaurant. Later I see them being squeezed into a fleet of white mini-vans and driven off to the lions.

Twenty-five per cent of Tanzania is apparently turned over to conservation, a higher proportion than anywhere else in Africa. My driver Kalului worked here in 1960 and remembers when the Serengeti National Park was created and hunters were turned into poachers overnight. He was a ranger and responsible for apprehending those who didn't understand that their livelihood was now someone else's. Later he became a guide and has many tales of near disaster. I had noticed that whenever we have stopped in the Serengeti, Kalului very carefully examines the surroundings before letting us out of the vehicle. He has learnt by experience to be very careful.

Once, he recalls, he had checked the area around a tree before laying out a picnic only to find, half-way through the picnic, that a leopard was actually in the tree above them finishing off its kill. Someone noticed, screamed, and that brought the leopard tearing down.

I confess to him that my only disappointment of the safari has been an absence of rhino and leopard. Kalului attempts to redress this by an amazing park-full of impersonations from leopard to rhino to tortoise to jackal, mating wildebeeste and the animal he unhesitatingly names as the most dangerous of them all, the buffalo.

'Many times buffalo is chasing me . . .'

I ask him what he does in such a case.

'I running . . . up the tree!'

He grins broadly, almost as if remembering one of life's forgotten pleasures.

Kalului, small and wiry, with his energetic, humorous face that can easily turn truculent has become too close a companion to submit tamely to an interview, and when we do get him in front of the camera he has fun turning some of my questions back on me . . . 'What tribe are *you* from?' he asks.

'British Middle Class,' I reply staunchly. It doesn't have quite the same ring as Akamba.

We drive on south-east passing the end of the Olduvai Gorge, in which Louis and Mary Leakey, and more recently Donald Johanson, found some of the earliest human remains on the planet, including, at nearby Laetoli, a 3.6-million-year-old footprint trail, preserved in solidified volcanic ash.

We wind up from the plain to the rim of the Ngorongoro Crater, almost 6600 feet above sea-level. Spectacular views unfold, of the Serengeti on one side and the vast circle of extinct volcano on the other.

A group of Masai herdsmen approaches from along the ridge, preceded by the soft, delicate tinkling of cow bells – what Wendy used to call 'the sound of Africa'. They are young, mostly teenagers, dramatically turned out in ostrich-feather head-dresses, enormous wooden earrings and cloaks of intense purple and deep red. They are not unselfconscious. I notice one of them adjusting his outfit in the reflection from the car window. Nor is their initial friendliness and curiosity unprofessional. If we want to take a photo of them, or even of the crater below them, we must pay.

We continue on the road around the rim. All the way along are groups of children, decked out in beads, faces painted, holding spears and ready to go into a parody of the Masai dances for anyone with money.

Crater Lodge is a spartan, tidily laid out collection of huts which resembles an army camp, but is in fact a hotel with one of the finest views in the world. Spread out below us is the mile-wide crater with trees around a small soda lake at the bottom. A pelican, legs dangling lazily, glides in the thermals. The habitat inside the crater looks less dark, secret and Lost-World-like than I had expected. In fact it looks suspiciously as though there is a car park down there. Certainly I can see more minibuses than I can see wild animals. But then it could be the effect of the deceptively strong beer I've been served. I look at the bottle for guidance but it has no label, only the words 'Beer Only' embossed on the side.

A Kenyan expatriate, working for the hotel, berates me for not going down into the crater.

'The Eighth Wonder of the World,' he announces, spreading his hand out to the view, before fixing me with a withering glance . . . 'You have seen it, but you have not *experienced* it.'

The truth is that I know what he means but I am a traveller not a tourist. I'm more concerned with the sailing date of the ships from South Africa than the departure of the next safari bus to the bottom of the crater. I'm trying to get to the South Pole, dammit, not Tanzania.

Not that I say this to him. He might ask why. And then I'd be floored.

Reluctantly leaving behind the second largest crater in the world we descend southwards through thick tropical rain forest and into a network of Mulu villages connected by red earth roads in poor condition.

At 5 o'clock we reach our destination for the night, another hotel with a stupendous view, this time from the top of the Rift Valley across Lake Manyara. A series of short, steep rivers, with mantra-like names – the Yambi, Endabash, Ndala, Chemchem, Msasa, Mchanga and Mkindu – drain off the spectacular western wall of the escarpment, through a forest of fig, mahogany and croton into the long slim lake 2000 feet below. The garden of the hotel is dominated by the vivid red and green umbrellas of three flame trees whose blossom looks even more striking tonight against the slate grey skies of an impending storm. From my balcony I watch the storm approach, trailing curtains of rain across the lake. Then a fork of lightning slices the grey haze, dust from the shore is caught by the sudden fierce wind and swept in clouds up towards me. Wind rattles and batters at the glass, then the rain comes and after the rain a double rainbow arches over the north-eastern shore.

Life indoors is a bit of a let-down after this. The hotel is full of Western tourists and the food is a bland chicken and leek soup and roast lamb.

To sleep over Hemingway's *Green Hills Of Africa*, a well-written, but relentless account of his hunting prowess. I should think there was nothing more dangerous in the African bush than our Ernest on a day when he was out to prove himself.

DAY 101 · LAKE MANYARA TO DODOMA

We've 250 miles ahead of us today, so up at 6.15 for an early start. Peer out over the balcony to see baboons swarming all over the place, taking apart the ornamental gardens.

Leave an hour later, taking the right turn at the end of the hotel drive. The safari traffic turns left and I feel a quite poignant sense of regret at leaving the animals behind.

A rough track, uncomfortably negotiated, brings us out onto the main road from Dodoma to Arusha. This is a fine, recently constructed highway. It even has white line markings. We sizzle along it for 15 miles, as far as a large phosphate factory at Minjingu. I know it's called Minjingu because it's written several times on a roadside hoarding: 'Have You Applied Minjingu Phosphate Fertiliser?', 'Have You Taken Your Sample?' and finally 'Bon Voyage from Minjingu'. It's quite the opposite as it turns out. Mal voyage from Minjingu to Dodoma, on a road surface, once metalled but since left to break up into a cracked and pitted mess.

We're out of the dramatic scenery and bumping along between dry straw-coloured fields through which bare patches of an ash-grey rock can be glimpsed, with only the occasional 'sausage tree' to enliven the view with its long, cylindrical fruit dangling from the branches.

The villages are plain and poor, growing staple foods like banana and papaya and tomato. At the junction town of Babati we buy samosa and bread for lunch. Even the children here seem to view us with caution, a sort of guarded suspicion which we have not met anywhere else but Sudan, where xenophobia seemed like government policy. What have the children been taught here? I know that Julius Nyerere preached self-sufficiency and non-alignment which may have delivered national pride but not much in the way of economic self-confidence.

For five or six hours we progress along a winding ridge, densely wooded with acacia resplendent in colours of deep green, pale brown and golden yellow, a splash of Vermont in the fall. Then we're running down onto the plain and the baobab trees are the star turn. Some of them are believed to be 2000 years old, massively built, 20 or 30 feet around the trunk, with flanks the colour and texture of gunmetal. Birds love them and owls, hornbills, bats and buffalo weavers nest amongst them.

Over 10 hours after leaving Lake Manyara we finally reach the outskirts of Dodoma, a city of only 45,000 people, not even among the ten largest cities of Tanzania, but plum in the middle of the country. It is announced by a faded sign beside a broken road, 'Welcome to Dodoma, Capital City'.

This is strong missionary country. On the way in we come across the incongruous sight of orderly rows of vines, tended by the Passionist Fathers, and producing Dodoma Red, which I am warned against.

The Vocation Centre of the Precious Blood Missionaries and the Assemblies of God Bible College beckon with their signs as does the New Limpopo Bar. A stretch of dual carriageway around the refreshingly modest Parliament building passes the Roman Catholic bookshop, the Paradise Theatre – Elliott Gould and Kate Jackson in *Dirty Tricks* – and the headquarters of the ruling CCM party (attached directly to the Parliament) before depositing us before the colonial façade of the Dodoma Hotel. Considering this is the best hotel in a capital city it's disappointing that there is no hot water on tap, but a bucketful can be brought to you on request. In the public rooms fat armchairs with their stuffing leaking out are set around an old John Broadwood piano with middle C missing. The food is dull but the beer is cool and welcome. My bed has a huge mosquito net, though I point out to the attendant that it has three very large holes in it. He smiles helplessly and produces a can of fly-spray the size of a bazooka which he uses so freely that I am unable to breathe inside the room for at least ten minutes.

There is a disco in the hotel tonight and it's a measure of how tired I am that the music blasts me to sleep.

DAY 102 · DODOMA TO KIGOMA

I've noticed that everything in my room from the grey pillow that I didn't dare lay my head on to the mirror I don't shave in front of because there is no hot water is stencilled with a long serial number and the initials TRC – Tanzanian Railway Company. It's appropriate I suppose, for our destiny is now in their hands from here to Mpulungu in Zambia – 800 miles through the heart of Africa.

When nine years old or thereabouts . . . while looking at a map of Africa, and putting my finger on the blank space then representing the unsolved mystery of the continent, I said to myself with absolute assurance and an amazing audacity which are no longer in my character now: 'When I grow up I shall go there'. I read this last night as mosquitoes poured through the holes in my net and, although it is Joseph Conrad's recollection of his childhood in Poland, it could as well have been an expression of my own boyhood fascination with somewhere as remote from my domestic surroundings as it seemed possible then to be. Lake Tanganyika, the second deepest lake in the world (after Lake Baikal), set in the centre of the African continent, surrounded by mountain and jungle and God knows what is, I'm sure, what I was thinking of. It's now one railway journey away.

I like Dodoma. It's not beautiful but the people are pleasant. Tanzanians don't intrude, they aren't curious or reproving or obsessive starers. They quietly go about their business, which might include selling wooden whistles outside the Parliament building.

'How much?'

'400.'

'I only have 200.'

'I'll give it to you for 300.'

'I only have 200.'

'All right. 200.'

Now that's the sort of haggling I like.

I meet an Englishman, a university professor checking out Tanzania prior to some investment from the World Bank. He is in despair over the paperwork needed to get anything done here. He shakes his head in disbelief:

'They have a saying in this country that bureaucracy is like God. It's everywhere.'

The servants of God are certainly here in force. Religion seems to be the growth industry. On one of the major intersections the Indian Christians' huge domed neo-classical château stands next to the sweeping modern red-brick lines of the Lutheran cathedral, which in turn faces across to the squat polygonal towers and domes of the Anglican Church.

The English language *Daily News* has a sports headline with a familiar, almost nostalgic ring. 'Angry Fans on Rampage.' Football is popular here with a big match in prospect tonight as Black Fighters of Zanzibar take on Railways of Morogoro, whose players most likely have TRC stencilled somewhere on their bodies.

At ten minutes after midday a large metal cylinder hanging outside the office of the stationmaster at Dodoma is rung loudly, and the purveyors of nuts, eggs, bananas, dried fish, sweet potatoes, rubber sandals, fresh water, loaves of bread, toy aeroplanes and other traveller's fare edge closer to the railway track. Beginning as a distant shimmer, a diesel locomotive with a red cow-catcher and a distinctive yellow V on the front slowly materializes, bringing in the express from the port of Dar es Salaam, 280 miles to the east. It's an enormous relief to see it. This and the boat down Lake Tanganyika are two of the essential connections on the journey. Neither is easy. There is an element of uncertainty about our rights to seats on the train as none of our bookings has been confirmed, and indeed, all our compartments are occupied. Polite persuasion is not enough and we just have to move in and hope that the sight of 30 boxes of film equipment will put the skids under anyone. An emotional farewell to Kalului and Kabagire who have looked after us since the Ethiopia border. I leave Kalului my Michelin map – Africa North and East and Arabia – which I know he coveted.

The train is not in good shape. Most of the windows are broken, and that's only in First Class. There are, considerately, two types of lavatory, announced on their doors as 'High Type' (European) and 'Low Type' (non-European). Once we are under way, I approach the High Type, prepared for the worst, only to find that it is not there at all. The High Type has vanished, leaving behind only a hole in the floor.

It's seven in the evening. To the restaurant car for dinner. Hot and crowded, but there's something familiar about it. A metal manufacturer's disc by the door reads 'BREL, Derby 1980'. Of course, these battered coaches rolling across the East African bush, are exactly the same design as British Inter-City stock. They may look as if they've had it but they're 30 years younger than those which many London commuters travel in.

Chicken or fish with rice and potatoes. Run DMC rap music sounds loudly from the next door table, making it difficult to hear my dining companion who says he is a footballer with CDA Tabora. CDA stands for Capital Development Authority. Not an easy one to chant on the terraces.

We stop frequently, and I wish I hadn't eaten on the train. By the line-side is a feast of food – tables set up with chicken stews and rice and beans, all fresh from voluminous saucepans. Kebabs and live chickens and even a duck are bought and sold through the windows. At all these stops I've been aware of a persistent clicking sound. I thought it might be cicadas but now I see it is made by children who carry their wares – cigarettes maybe, or bananas – in one hand and click loose coins in the other to attract business.

Craig and Nigel have ears pressed to a radio at the window, trying, in the midst of this line-side cacophony, to pick up the sound from Edinburgh where England are playing Scotland in the Rugby Union World Cup semifinal.

Nigel suddenly turns from the radio with a look of total disbelief: 'They've gone to the *news*! . . . They've gone to the news with two minutes left!'

As we pull away from Itigi, 105 miles beyond Dodoma, Mbego, our coach attendant, a wraith-like figure in white cap, blue tunic and trousers, appears dragging a shapeless green canvas bundle from which he extricates my bedding which he lays out with infinite care and precision. Later I see him sitting at the open door of the train gently and ruminatively stroking the head of a young man next to him.

Night falls and the electricity supply fails. To sleep reading *Heart of Darkness* by torchlight. Outside is Africa . . . 'its mystery, its greatness, the amazing reality of its concealed life . . .'

DAY 103 · DODOMA TO KIGOMA

Dream of thousands of shuffling feet, a babble of strange voices, baby cries, chickens clucking, heavy objects being dragged close by me, clicks and curses and strange cries. My eyes are wide open, but I can see nothing. My window has been boarded up. The noises continue, growing in intensity.

Dawn. In the Low Type, which is filthy and caked with un-flushed waste, a sign reads 'The co-operation of passengers is required to prevent waste of water and the misuse of this toilet compartment'. There's no water to waste.

Something is different about the train this morning. It's shorter for a start, and the restaurant car is different (the clock has stopped at 8.10 rather than 1.05). Over breakfast of fried egg, boiled potato, bread, marge and three cups of sweet tea, I hear the explanation of my dream last night. Soon after midnight the train stopped at Tabora in order to be split up and re-grouped into three separate trains. Patti and Craig had to spend three hours on the platform making sure our equipment was not sent north to Mwanza or south to Mpanda. Apparently Patti received one proposal of marriage. Craig none, sadly. Angela tried to help out with her torch until she found out that the entire shunting manoeuvres at Tabora were being co-ordinated by torch signals.

Later, to the restaurant car for elevenses. It is closed. All the windows have been covered up with some kind of material. Rueful smiles all round. No one seems particularly worried, except me. I try again in half an hour only to find the rueful smiles turned to wholehearted joy at the continued closure of the restaurant. Then a soldier emerges from inside, positively wreathed in smiles.

'It is a girl,' he announces.

It must be almost as we touch the 30 degree meridian, for the first time since the Mediterranean, that a little girl is born in the restaurant car of the Dar es Salaam to Kigoma Express. It is certainly the best thing the restaurant car has provided so far and I take it as a very good omen for the rest of our journey.

Mercury being well out of retrograde at the moment things do seem to be going, if not comfortably, at least smoothly and we are on the final curve into Kigoma by late afternoon, only three and a half hours behind schedule on a 27-hour journey. A lush, thick, heavy heat spills in from the open doorway. Children run out from groves of bananas, papaya and mango to wave at the train. Mbego sits on the step at the end of our coach, unselfconsciously tickling the ear of his friend. There is a marked absence of the heightened stress and strain that usually grips arriving passengers.

Kigoma Station is a fine old colonial building, and looks as though it could be North Italian with its arches and loggia. Its grand clock, in the fine tradition of TRC, is stopped. Useless Facts Department: from a hanging sign above one of the doors I learn that the Swahili for Stationmaster is Steshinimasta.

We are driven to our lodgings by a soft-spoken middle-aged man in a well-kept Toyota Corolla, with a transfer of the Pope on one window. He turns out to be a doctor as well as a taxi driver and apologizes for not taking the direct road to the hotel.

'There are large holes in it, you understand.'

Our detour bounces us along a red earth track, scattering chickens and goats, which leads to the low, nondescript façade of the Railway Hotel.

We unload for the 53rd time. Kigoma, elevation 2541 feet, population 50,044, is just about bang on course at 29.36 degrees East. We have completed our long, enforced eastern swing from Khartoum in 30 days, and hopefully we've made it in time to make the infrequent but vital ferry connection to Mpulungu and Zambia.

Clem, who should be feeling very pleased with himself, appears from hotel reception looking quite the opposite. Apparently no one knows anything about our bookings, and they do not have enough rooms for us. Kigoma is by no means awash with alternative accommodation so this is a cruel blow. As Clem and Angela embark on the slow process of sorting out the reservations, I walk across a bare and uninviting lobby to be confronted with the sort of view that lifts the spirits however low they might have sunk. A descent of chipped concrete steps leads down to a grassy bank, studded with tables and parasols, beyond which the waves of a wide blue-green lake spill lethargically onto a beach of coarse red sand. Lake Tanganyika, confined here into a small bay between low, grassy headlands, stretches away, across to the hazy cliffs of Zaire, once the Congo, Conrad's Heart of Darkness.

It is a breathtaking revelation of scale and space, as if I had opened a door onto the centre of Africa.

'*When I grow up I shall go there . . .*'

Well, I've had my cosmic moment and now the reality must be faced. The Railway Hotel, Kigoma is not the heart of darkness. It is more like a cross between a pub in Earl's Court and a minor Hilton. Encamped on the thick unmown lawns are two dozen Australian and New Zealand overlanders drinking beer. A Japanese film crew are at work in the lake and another harassed European rushes past us clutching a sheaf of papers.

After hours of patient negotiation we are all found rooms. They are arranged in unglamorous functional blocks which do no justice at all to the splendour of the location. Mine has a small bed with a frame for a mosquito net, but no net. A concrete floor extends into a washing area with a shower and basin, but no hot water. My lavatory is of the High Type, but the cistern overflows gently and persistently. As if to further mock my dreams of solitariness and isolation, all I can hear as I unpack is a radio crackling out the last seconds of commentary from the Rugby Union World Cup followed by a roar from the darkness outside as Australia defeat New Zealand.

Later I settle down with Conrad on my narrow bed, and read myself to sleep to the sound of 'the howling sorrow of savages' and the gentle lapping of an overflowing lavatory cistern.

DAY 104 · KIGOMA

Day of rest and recuperation at the hotel. I have fixed the cistern by jamming a lavatory brush beneath the ballcock. Examine myself in the mirror (Serial Number TRC HOT GM NM 024) to see whether three and a half months of travel have left any damage. I gaze into dull weary eyes set in sun-reddened features. A bleached immobility of expression. I look like a survivor from some awful natural disaster. Laugh at the thought, and only then do I recognize something of myself.

At breakfast – omelette, chips and sliced white bread – the manager apologizes for the lack of facilities:

'We have hot water boilers and supply all ready, but no one comes to fit them' . . . He rubs a handkerchief across his face and shakes his head . . . 'They are simply standing in waste.'

A few African horror stories with our omelettes . . . Craig tells us that in his opinion electric shocks are the best cure for snake-bites. He recounts the story of someone whose life was saved after a bite – from 'some sort of cobra' – when he was wired up to an outboard motor.

'Put the earth in one hand and the live wire on the bite. Five applications in 15 seconds. Oh sure, his hair stood on end and he was lifted a foot or two off the ground, but the doctors said it saved his life.'

After breakfast, having ascertained that the risk of bilharzia is low as the water is not stagnant, that crocodiles would not come in this far and sea serpents are all I have to watch out for, I take a cautious bathe. The water is clear and cool, the surroundings quite beautiful. No sailing boats or water-sporters to disturb the peace. Only the barely perceptible wake of a passing dugout troubles the placid water. And I can tell my grandchildren that I swam in Lake Tanganyika.

Dry out in warm sun with a cold Safari Beer. At the bar is a small, straight-backed European who turns out to have spent 19 months in Antarctica. Had he enjoyed it?

He pulls fiercely on a cigarette, scouring it for every last ounce of

nicotine, before answering, with eyes narrowed against an endless exhalation.

'Put it zis vay . . . it is an experience you should go through.'

He knows the MV *Agulhas*, the ship we hope to take to Antarctica, and asks me to remember him to the captain.

'Sure . . . your name?'

'Doktor Brandt,' he replies after an inexplicable hesitation.

I ask him what he's doing here in Kigoma.

'Teaching blacks to use the telephone,' he replies crisply.

Having nothing better to do, I begin to suspect him of being involved in some sort of racket and later I find that I could be right, when I overhear him asking the manager, *sotto voce*, 'Any news?'

This surely is the stuff of Conrad. At last a whiff of intrigue and corruption in the heart of darkness.

It turns out that he is enquiring as to the whereabouts of his lavatory seat.

The manager spreads his arms helplessly. 'We wait for them . . .' But the Doktor is not in a mood to be trifled with.

'Vy cannot you take the lavatory seat from 14 and put it in 15?'

I rush to make sure my door's locked against possible loo seat predators.

Round off a bizarre day eating goat stew and drinking Primus beer from Burundi in a local restaurant in the middle of a power cut. Our host is the taxi driver-doctor, whose name is William, who has become our self-appointed guide to Kigoma. The restaurant, or what I can see of it in the lamplight, is rough and ready, with an ancient, almost biblical feel to it. Above the doorway is a large hand-lettered wooden board, like a pub sign. I presume that to be the name of the restaurant and ask William for a translation.

'It says "Pay Before You Leave".'

Anyway, the goat is excellent, and best of all, it is not the property of Tanzanian Railways.

DAY 105 · KIGOMA

Another day to kill before the ferry leaves. Take a boat to Ujiji, a few miles down the coast. Once the centre of a thriving slave trade it's also the place where Livingstone and Stanley met in 1871.

The location of this historic meeting is now a small museum in a well-tended garden on a hill above the busy waterfront. A forbidding, lumpish grey monument, 'erected by the Government of Tanganyika Territory' in 1927, stands beneath two mango trees said to be descendants of the one under which Livingstone and Stanley met. On it is carved a map of Africa with a cross incised into it. It's a brutal and arrogant

image. The only visitor besides ourselves is an Englishman from Leicester, looking very red and unprotected in the sun. He is in his fifties and had decided, after reading a book about Cecil Rhodes' plan for a railway from the Cape to Cairo, to do the journey himself. Today he had only one thing on his mind:

'All I'm looking for, Michael, is a cold beer.' I suggest he make for the Railway Hotel, Kigoma.

Things are more light-hearted inside the museum, despite its depressingly empty rooms and smell of disuse. Most of the work is by a local schoolteacher, A. Hamisi. There is a series of paintings of the great moments in the life of Livingstone – 'Dr Livingstone saving Chuma and Others from Slavery', 'Dr Livingstone Sitting Under the Mango Tree Thinking About Slavery in Ujiji'. Beside these are two life-size papier mâché models of Livingstone, looking like Buster Keaton in dark blue three-piece suit, raising his peaked cap to a Stanley looking like Harold Macmillan in light blue safari suit and pink face. These are also the work of A. Hamisi of Kigoma Secondary School. There is nothing else in the museum.

We drive out of Ujiji, up Livingstone Street, then right at Lumumba Road, and back via Mwanga – home of 'Vatican Enterprises Hardware Supplies' and 'Super Volcano Tailoring' to the busy mango and acacia-lined main street of Kigoma – also named after Patrice Lumumba, one of the great heroes of African independence who was assassinated in 1961.

At the Railway Hotel, half an hour before sunset. This is a magic time as the sun sinks toward the lake and the mountains of Zaire, always grey in the haze, sharpen to a deep black. At the lakeside tonight Australians and New Zealanders, Dr Brandt, erect and smoking powerfully, two Dutch boys, the Japanese underwater cameraman, even my friend from Leicester gather to watch the sun go down, and for a few minutes every sound, even the cries of the naked children plunging into water nearby, seems to grow distant.

239

DAY 106 · KIGOMA TO MPULUNGU

Down to the waterfront at 9 a.m. to join the queue for tickets on the ferry which runs to Mpulungu once a week. Ahead of me in the line is Francis, a farmer from Karema, one of the stops on the way down the lake. I explain to him what we are doing, and, with more difficulty, why we are doing it. He listens carefully before asking, politely, 'And will your film help to solve the problems it exposes?'

The MV *Liemba*, 800 tons, her lines as straight as the back of a Prussian cavalry officer, is said to be the oldest passenger ship in regular service anywhere in the world. Judging by her history she could have been better named the MV *Lazarus*. Built as a warship in Germany, she was carried in pieces overland and assembled on Lake Tanganyika in 1913. At the end of the Great War she was scuttled by the Germans, and lay on the bottom of the lake until raised and refitted by the British in 1922. She was in regular operation as a steam ship, before being converted to diesel in 1978. After 80 years she remains the only way out of Kigoma to the south or to the west. If we had missed today's sailing we would almost certainly have missed the sailing from Cape Town to Antarctica in a month's time.

We pull away at 5 p.m. The Australian and New Zealand overlanders have taken over the stern deck, and the locals crowd into the bows or the lower covered decks, squashing in with their boxloads of plastic sandals, pineapples, and even Lion Brand Mosquito Coils – 'Keep Out of Damp' – and with apparent good grace accepting the presence of two white-owned Land Rovers, which further reduce the space. At least we can all feel ourselves better off than the several hundred tired and confused occupants of the *Kabambare*, a barge just arrived from Kalemie in Zaire. They are refugees from the inter-tribal violence which has recently flared up in their country. They do not know if the Tanzanian authorities will accept them.

A last look at Kigoma from the departing ferry. I had come here expecting dense jungle, snakes, monkeys and swamps. Instead the town at the centre of Africa resembles a small port on a discreet Scottish loch, with the railway line running picturesquely between the water and low grassy hills – reassuring, comfortable, rendered exotic only by the bright slash of purple from the jacaranda trees on the shore.

My cabin has the stamp of Tanzanian Railways all over it. It claims to be air-conditioned but the fan is missing. There is a basin but no water, hot or cold. All but one of the light bulbs is missing.

Three hours out from Kigoma I am unenthusiastically facing up to a plate of rice and scrawny chicken leg, when the engine note changes down an octave, the ship slows and within seconds the night air is filled with a growing clamour of voices. They grow louder and more insistent, and are mingled with the splash of paddles and the thudding of boats against the hull. Out on deck in some alarm to witness an extraordinary scene. Flooded by powerful shipboard lights, a dozen or more dugouts are clustering around the *Liemba* like maggots at a corpse, filled with vendors of every kind of food, families trying to get themselves and their belongings aboard and water taxis touting to take people off. Everyone is screaming to make themselves heard, as a forest of hands extends from below decks, waving, beckoning, holding out money, helping some people aboard and others down into the bobbing mass of boats below.

Every boat is vying with its neighbour to get close to the *Liemba*. As soon as the tiniest gap is glimpsed paddles are applied furiously and very often one hull will ride up over another, until with cries of protest, the offending canoe is thrust back. Babes in arms are passed to the hopeful safety of outstretched hands. Small boys frantically bale out their boats.

This is African business. The whites can only watch and photograph. There is an urgency about it all that is spellbinding and exhilarating and exhausting. And I'm told later that what looked like a fully-fledged native attack is just one of 15 scheduled stops.

DAY 107 · KIGOMA TO MPULUNGU

Aboard the *Liemba*, Lake Tanganyika. The last day of October, 1991. Have taken a capsule of Imodium as a prevention against having to make use of the toilet facilities. I know it is unwise to meddle with my metabolism but the alternative is too frightful to contemplate.

It has rained before dawn and I step out of my cabin onto the head of a sleeping figure swathed in cotton robe and woollen shawls. I needn't have bothered with my profuse British apologies as he doesn't wake up. A row of passengers is sheltering beside him. Their heads turn towards me, defensive and unsmiling. My hot and airless little cabin may not be the last word in comfort but it is First Class, and I know that by the time I return from breakfast the officious policemen on board will have shooed these people back down below.

Later in the day the captain agrees to be interviewed. His name is Beatus T. Mghamba and he lives on the bridge deck, which is nearly always empty apart from the lifeboats (made by Meclans Ltd of Glasgow in 1922), a jolly group of ladies and a hard-drinking Englishman. At the appointed time for the interview – about five in the afternoon – I knock on Captain Mghamba's door. After some time it is answered by a handsome dreadlocked lady who

Day 107: Tanzania

Kigoma to Mpulungu: On the Liemba, *the Dutchman's Land Rover comes aboard, the floating wedding party, one of the 15 stops.*

is obviously surprised to see me. I ask for the Captain. She disappears into the cabin. There is a long wait and some muttering before she returns.

'He is asleep.'

She bats not an eyelid, and as I utter the immortal phrase, 'When he wakes up, tell him the BBC are waiting', she closes the door on me.

The Captain finally appears, dishevelled but surprisingly cheerful after his sleep. I ask him about the problems of running an 80-year-old ship.

'The ship is big, but the engine is small . . . manoeuvring is a little bit difficult.' He shrugs. He has no chart of the lake.

'We are sailing this through experience. If you are one mile away from the shore you will be safe.'

The *Liemba*, he tells me, is registered to carry 500 passengers and 34 crew, 'but sometimes, in summer seasons where we find that these people along Lake Tanganyika are harvesting their crops it can be more.'

'How many more?'

'Up to a thousand.'

At one of our 15 stops a wedding party paddles out to welcome guests off the ship. Huge brightly-coloured flags and banners stream in the wind

and there is great singing and chanting as they circle the ship. The progress of the *Liemba* reminds me of the Hurtigrute service which took us up through the Norwegian fiords three and a half months ago. In both cases the service is the only lifeline for communities unreachable by road or air. There the similarity ends. I cannot imagine the manic, uncontrolled exuberance of the *Liemba* surviving long in the cold Protestant waters of the North Atlantic.

As we progress south, some Zambians come aboard. Tomorrow they are voting for a new government, and I am quite shocked to hear that Kenneth Kaunda is so unpopular that he may well be unseated after 28 years in power. I always had the impression that he was one of the most secure, successful and responsible of the post-colonial leaders, but Japhet Zulu from Chingola, who describes himself as 'a simple businessman', thinks Kaunda has ruined the economy and he will not be voting for him.

At dusk, unobserved, except by me, one of the policemen who chases steerage passengers off the upper decks has removed his hat and boots and is praying towards Mecca. The sight of this man of authority so completely prostrating himself before a higher authority is oddly moving.

DAY 108 · KIGOMA TO MPULUNGU

Have taken another Imodium. This is quite definitely not wise, and may have contributed to a general feeling of malaise as we approach Zambia. The ship has emptied overnight. Apart from the crew there are now only ourselves, Japhet and his friend and 25 overlanders left on the *Liemba* as we cross the border into our 13th country.

A new country and a new month, our fourth on the road. The small deficiencies of Tanzania have begun to grind me down, and the prospect of a hot bath and clean clothes and a bed away from heat and mosquitoes is a more alluring prospect than the network of forested bays and islets that is the coast of Zambia.

'It's the first day of spring,' I hear someone say as we crowd at the deck rail.

'Don't be stupid . . . ,' another retorts, 'It's November. Spring starts in September.'

Of course, they're Australians. Or New Zealanders. Looking around at them I do not see the faces of explorers but of pale, tired children. They look as if they might have got lost on a hike from Sydney to Brisbane or Auckland to Wellington rather than being in the centre of Africa. They wait patiently for sight of their truck, which has been driven overland from Kigoma, and should be waiting for them on the dockside. Their journey will cost them £1000 or thereabouts and they sign on for nine weeks. I admire them. It isn't the easiest way to see the world, but it may be the one they will remember most.

We bid them farewell as we disembark at the small dockside of Mpulungu. Looking back on it from a distance, with the chunky, upright *Liemba* and its attendant crane nestling among wooded cliffs, surrounded by a stack of oil drums and building materials, it looks like a set in a James Bond film. The sort that is about to be blown sky-high.

New customs and immigration to be gone through, a new production team – Roger and Mirabel take over from Clem and Angela – and new guides and fixers. For once I don't feel I have the energy to respond.

The thick woolly heat seems to be inescapable down here by the lake, and I miss the openness and space of Kigoma.

Lunchtime: Feeling much recovered. We are lodged at a small collection of rondavels set in a tree-filled garden and run in easy-going fashion by Denish, an Indian of unforced charm and dazzling smile who came to Mpulungu for a 10-day holiday and was so captivated that he stayed and built this place – for himself, and any guests who might drop by. The first people we saw as we drove in were the overlanders, already pitching their tents on the grass, washing out clothes and forming a queue for the lavatory and the thin trickle of cold water that is the shower.

I'm sitting in the shade of an orange tree being fussed over by Jake da Motta, an engaging Hong Kong-born Englishman who, with others of his team, is in charge of our welfare over the next few days.

Up here, among the stone-walled huts and the hibiscus and the gentle breeze Mpulungu has taken on an unexpectedly Provençal aspect. This is soon to be quite rudely shattered.

Roger, naturally, anxious to get to work, has booked me an appointment with the local witch doctor.

After lunch we drive away from Denish's sanctuary and down a track which curves round the bay, away from Provence and back into Darkest Africa.

A crowd of people cluster around one of the more substantial bungalows in a lakeside village of thatched huts scattered messily about a patch of rising ground. Some of them are on tiptoe, straining to see through a window. Inside, I'm told, is an effiti, a man charged with being a black witch, or warlock, who is thought to have secured the deaths of five or six people. The witch doctor, or inganga, has been to the man's house and found a leather bottle in which a mixture of blood and poison was found. This is thought to be the blood of the victims.

The room where the investigation is being carried out is not, at first glance, in any way sinister. At one end, where the pale light from an overcast sky spills through a wrought iron window grille, is a plastic-covered sofa and matching chair. The floor is bare concrete, the walls plastered and painted grey. Two half-deflated beach balls hang from the ceiling, and on one of the walls are pictures of footballers and a BP Zambia calendar. On a small table is a line of six doll-like figures, one of which I notice is a white woman, with a short skirt wrapped around her.

Huddled in a corner, looking pathetic and helpless, with glazed eyes and glassy stare, is the accused. He wears a thin brown shirt and trousers, black moccasin shoes and a fat wristwatch. He bears an unnerving resemblance to Nelson Mandela.

The witch doctor, Dr Baela, is a young man from Zaire. He has pouting lips and big lazy eyes. He wears a head-dress of genet fur, a pink tunic with his name on the back and a pair of welding goggles. In one hand he holds a heart-shaped mirror with a border of shells and in the other a small pot with a mirror set into it. His helpers wear white cotton robes with red crosses on them.

It may be the effect of the presence of a camera, but they all look sheepish and rather awkward, like children at the start of a school play.

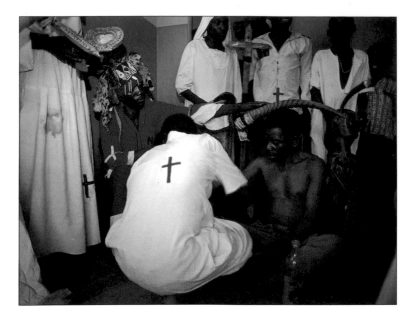

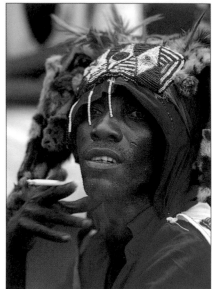

Baela's acolytes brusquely remove the victim's watch, then tear off his shirt and make a series of marks on his body. A curved horn with money tied to its base is placed on his head and a basket with a white cloth in it passed three times around him. Two young men – boys really – step forward, and with grubby razor blades make incisions on his neck and shoulders. Thin lines of blood ooze to the surface. He's questioned, but looks blankly back, and is then cut across the forehead. Some powder is rubbed into the wound which makes him start back. He is held still, his trousers are rolled up and cuts are made on the outside of his knees and toes. On the wall behind him is a text in a faded frame – 'True Love Never Ends'.

The bleeding victim is rubbed with polish and left in his corner whilst Baela and his gang disappear outside to be interviewed by the BBC.

Dr Baela's eyes freed from the goggles are red and watery, he smokes a very wide cigarette and his voice is a high-pitched sing-song. I ask him if he can tell if I have any evil spirits and he, through an interpreter, concludes that I have what is translated as an 'evil shadow'. It is the shadow of a woman.

In his curiously hypnotic monotone, Baela asks if the woman he is seeing is my wife. I ask him to describe her. His reply:

'Is not tall, fat a bit', lets Helen off the hook, but only adds to the confusion. Dr Baela goes on to say that my life could be in danger and things of mine will be stolen but that he can give me medicine which will 'drive out' any evil influence.

It all seems slightly laughable when written down, but Baela, who describes himself as a healer, not a witch doctor, has had some success in the village, and being surrounded by a couple of hundred people who believe every word he says is unsettling enough for me to take my shadow and his medicine more seriously than I'd expected. His prescription is a piece of tree bark which he gives me from a suitcase, with instructions to cut, pound up and wash with it, in a private place, saving some to place in each nostril.

First taste of Zambia: Dr Baela at work in Mpulungu, the interrogation, Baela relaxes with a big cigarette, me and my prescription.

Day 108: Zambia

In the evening, back at Denish's, Jake and his colleague Paul Murphy, a lean wiry English-born Zambian, cook us a splendid meal as a fierce thunderstorm breaks. I drink too much wine, but haven't come across any since Kenya, and feel the need to wind down after this extraordinary day.

As waves of rain lash through the trees I talk to Paul, it being election day in Zambia, about the problems of the country. In his opinion what the place needs is discipline. Liberalism, in the Western sense, cannot work in Africa. He quotes Malawi as an example of the way things should be done.

Also meet Chris and Jean Bigereaux, who employ 300 people in Mpulungu's biggest industry, fishing. The talk turns to malaria.

'The first time you have it, you never want to have it again. You just want to die,' says Chris.

Denish agrees, adding that he now expects to have malaria attacks about four times a year.

My head is muzzy by the time I reach the hut I'm sharing with Basil. Pushing open the door with infinite care so as not to wake him, I drop my torch, trip over Dr Baela's medicine and nearly bring down my mosquito net.

DAY 109 · MPULUNGU TO SHIWA

POLE
to
POLE

I can't help noticing that the lavatory on which I spend most of the night is called the Victory. A night of victory for myself and Mr Frederick Chiluba, the new President of Zambia. I only hope he feels better than I do. Acute stomach cramps and diarrhoea have kept me up since 2 a.m. I hear the sound of music from down in the town, the barking of Denish's dogs at the gates, persistent coughing from one of the overlander's tents and later, cocks crowing.

On the Victory at 5.30 a.m., my system seems on the verge of collapse. I'm not sure whether or not I've ever had cold sweats before, and maybe this is why the tingling in the hands, the shivering and the uncontrollable flood of perspiration is so alarming, even, to be honest, frightening. For five minutes I have no idea what is going to happen to me. My fingers are going numb, and I am shuddering and shaking and soaking in my own sweat. Isn't this what we were talking about last night? Isn't this how malaria begins? What happens to our journey if I've caught something bad? 'Pole to Mpulungu' doesn't have the same ring. It must be the evil shadow... I should never have had anything to do with Baela's world. We don't understand it and we should have left it alone.

This jumble of anxieties fills my mind until the attack passes. Basil fetches me a thick sweater and delves in his extensive pharmaceutical collection for some tablets. Breakfast is tea, Ryvita biscuit and honey and a faintly sickly solution of water and rehydration pills.

I look around the garden of the lodge. This morning it all looks different – the water drum at which I had waited patiently for much of the night to extract enough water to flush the Victory – the overlanders, blearily packing for another day of discomfort – the flies buzzing around the dogs.

Denish has done his best for us. His lodge, after all, was built for himself and a handful of occasional travellers, not for the 35 people who were sharing it last night. I'm sad to say goodbye to him but glad to leave Mpulungu behind.

On the road there is plenty of evidence of the euphoria following Chiluba's victory over Kaunda, which appears to have been a landslide. Men, women and children raise their hands in the finger and thumb salute of the MMD – the Movement for Multi-Party Democracy. I see a group of villagers clustered round a radio beneath a spreading mango tree, listening to Kaunda's resignation speech.

I remember Japhet on the boat telling me that whichever side won the election there would be 'no violence . . . Zambians are not like that'. Paul sees this as a negative quality. There are 8 million Zambians, anything can grow here he maintains, but the economy is in ruins because the people are too easy-going and acquiescent.

We pull in to the Modern Kwacha Relax Hotel in Kasama where much beer is going down in Chiluba's honour. His photo has been hoisted above the bar. 'This is the man we have waited seven years for!' they cry.

My hot and cold sweats have mercifully not been repeated but my system is very delicate and I excuse myself from the celebrations. But as soon as they realize we are from the BBC they are queuing up to be interviewed, and from being a stretcher-case I'm suddenly a news reporter. Their message is the same – tell the British people that this is a new dawn for Zambia, a dawn of open and incorrupt government. No one seems quite sure how practical change will accompany political change. The World Bank is vaguely mentioned, but this is not the point. The point is to tell the world that democracy has triumphed. When we tell them that we will tell the world but not for about a year, their enthusiasm turns to incredulity. BBC News and their deadline is a year ahead? I just don't feel strong enough to explain, and we move on, leaving them to their beer and their joy.

The drive down south toward Mpika is a further 130 miles of flat, Molumba woodland, much of it stripped and burnt for fuel and building materials. The road is metalled and quick, but darkness has fallen by the time we reach the extraordinary red-brick barns, Hardyesque cottages and gabled gatehouses of Shiwa – an English estate in the middle of Africa. John and Lorna Harvey and their son David receive us warmly, and David's dog Deeta takes my hat.

My system has survived the day without collapse, but after the bliss of a hot bath the stomach cramps return and I take to bed, unable to eat.

DAY 110 · SHIWA

Half-way through the night, as recurring twinges of cramp keep me padding off to the bathroom, I experience a quite irrational fear of being in the same room as a piece of tree-bark handled by Dr Baela. I see it lying on the table with my notebooks and maps and though I know I'm being ridiculous, I cannot help blaming it for this sudden reversal of fortunes. After all, Mercury isn't in retrograde until the end of the month so I can't blame that.

By the morning I feel stronger and better able to look the bark in the eye. Breakfast off toast and home-made marmalade at a huge table of mukwa wood designed by Lorna Harvey's father – Sir Stewart Gore-Brown, the man who created Shiwa.

Zambia – present and past: A voter shows the victory sign as Kaunda's 28 years are up, English country life endures at Shiwa Ngandu.

Sir Stewart came out to Africa early in the century as a member of the Boundary Commission, to, quite literally, draw the map of Africa, or at least that part of the continent bordering on the Belgian Congo and Rhodesia, and stayed on to construct Shiwa house, between 1928 and 1932, in an eclectic European style, with towers and pitched roofs and a formal English garden. In an article about the house, written in 1964, *Horizon* magazine summed up his achievement:

'Shiwa gradually became the showpiece of Northern Rhodesia, where a courteous squire, possessed of a taste for diplomacy, ruled his estate with benevolence and a hand of iron.'

On Sir Stewart's grave, set on a hill a mile away from the house, looking out over the forest-fringed lake of Shiwa Ngandu, is engraved the name Chipembele. I ask Lorna its meaning.

'It means rhinoceros, which was his African name . . . a rhino charges and then actually stops, and he was just like that . . . he would get very angry with you and then five minutes later he would be asking for a loan . . .'

John Harvey saw this as a positive advantage.

'As a politician he was a tremendous chap. He was a sort of Churchill, and he just rode over everybody and got his own way.'

He ran the estate feudally, as Lorna put it . . . 'as you would in Europe, the gardeners and people came through the back door, not the front door' but he had no time for the apartheid that existed in Northern Rhodesia, 'We were brought up that you respected a person for their age not their colour.'

John thinks Sir Stewart's influence helped avoid either a bush war of the kind that destroyed Southern Rhodesia or terrorism on the scale of the Mau-Mau in Kenya, though eventually he lost the political support of the Africans by championing a paternalist solution which fell short of the self-rule they wanted. He died in 1967 but Shiwa is full of his presence – not just in books and pictures and portraits and rhino motifs on beams and brickwork, but in spirit. The flag is still raised and lowered every day on the balcony outside the library, and the estate workers are still summoned, by drum, to a muster parade at 7 o'clock every morning.

At dinner with the Harveys tonight, the talk ranges from the long-distance lorry drivers' part in the spread of AIDS in Africa to the scandal of agricultural chemicals, banned in Europe, still being sold to Africa, and on to superstition and witchcraft. David Harvey, who farms in the south of the country and is as level-headed as you would expect from a graduate of agricultural college, respects witch doctors and has used them. He saw with his own eyes a witch doctor make his way down a line of farm workers, one of whom was thought to be guilty of stealing. He touched each man on the shoulder with his stick but as he applied it to one man the stick burned into his flesh and stuck fast. The man confessed.

Apparently many public figures believe in lucky charms and talismans. Even Kaunda, sober product of a mission school only a mile or two from here, was rarely seen without a certain white handkerchief. President Mobutu of Zaire never goes anywhere without his stick.

Back in my room I take the bark off the table and put it in my bag. At the bottom.

DAY 111 · SHIWA

Still alive. Cramps lessen but still disrupt the night. Patti is evidently quite poorly and displaying the symptoms of malaria despite taking the pills – 'fever, malaise, chills with sweating and headache'. Looking at Dawood I think I may have been quite lucky until I read that though the incubation period following a mosquito bite is a minimum of five days, '*as long as a year may elapse before symptoms appear, especially if antimalarial drugs have been used*'.

Today we see more of the estate, from its own model post-office complete with red letterbox – the postmaster says he's bored stiff there and can't wait to be transferred – to the school where the children are taught to build and thatch using local materials, but lack, according to John their teacher, such basics as 'books, desks and pens'.

David Harvey, meanwhile, is putting 2000 cattle through a dip. This must be done once a week to kill off ticks that can cause death. Africa seems to be constantly in the process of eating itself – from Strangler figs to cattle ticks to snakes and cheetahs and Anopheles mosquitoes, everything is munching away at everything else. Even as we speak white ants are chewing away at the wooden frames of the buildings. David reckons that any wood based dwelling, unless protected against the devouring ant, will have to be rebuilt after two years.

Even Shiwa, with all the care that has been taken and money that has been spent, is fighting for its survival. The Great Man has passed on and John and Lorna are struggling to discharge all the responsibilities required in maintaining an estate of 40 square miles in a country with 150 per cent inflation. They have tried timber, cattle-ranching, egg and poultry production, but none has survived for long. John is hopeful that the new government will improve matters, meanwhile he and Lorna have formed Shiwa Safaris, to exploit the tourist potential of the wildlife on their land.

At the end of the day John takes me down to the lake. It's a tranquil place, unmarked by human ambition and the inconstancy of fate. I feel he's happy here, released momentarily from the effort of keeping someone else's dream alive. I look around for the wildlife on which he is staking his latest hopes. A heron gracefully skims the water, a wattled plover screams overhead and a line of hippo tracks leads through the mud and into waters that reflect the ochre-red of another sunset.

DAY 112 · SHIWA TO KASANKA

Wake after another uncomfortable night. My digestive system still unruly. I would like to have felt fully recovered before venturing Polewards again. Patti is in a far worse state. Huge doses of chloroquin seem to have knocked out the fever but left her head and stomach aching. She leaves before the rest of us for a blood test at the Chilonga hospital.

Bid our farewells to the Harveys, who have been generous with their time and hospitality. On our way out we pass another testament to the Gore-Brown brand of colonialism. This is the estate hospital, opened in 1938. Now it has been downgraded to a clinic, and many of the buildings lie abandoned, pitched roofs open to the skies, discarded bed-frames rusting against the wall. But it is still useful, and up to date. 'Sex Thrills, AIDS Kills. Stick to One Sexual Partner', reads a poster on the office wall, from which one of the nurses is removing Kenneth Kaunda's portrait.

Today is immunization day and 200 women and children have arrived to be inoculated against whooping cough, polio, TB, tetanus and measles. They are dressed immaculately, the children in the fussiest knitted caps and coats and some women in tweed skirts and high heels despite the 90 degree heat. But the decay of the place, the smell of dust and dirt and the sweet sweat of humanity, is unavoidable. Africa is rewarding but demanding.

Uneventful ride south through trees and scrub. At a service station in Mpika I make my first acquaintance with the gloriously named 'Eet-Sum-Mor' brand of biscuits. Nigel manages to pick up commentary of the England–Australia Rugby World Cup Final as we bounce and weave through a forest. The more Australia score the weaker the signal becomes. This time no one complains when they break off for the news.

We fetch up for the night at another camp, this time in the small National Park of Kasanka, which is run, under a 10-year management contract, by a genial, enthusiastic and adventurous Englishman called David Lloyd, who once had an awful lot of money but lost most of it running up-market hunting holidays in Zaire. His lodge, situated beside a small, reedy lake, is clean, well-kept, and, thanks to the profusion of frogs, mosquito-free. I learn more about hippos here than in all my time beside the Mara River in Kenya. So thoroughly had this area been poached, says David, that when he took over the park in 1986, there were only two or three hippo.

'They didn't call at all for the first two years – dead scared.'

Now there are 15 altogether, seven or eight of whom are offspring of the original three. I ask him about the extraordinary noises of the hippo wind ensemble in Kenya. David tells me that every grunt means something. Hippos are 'highly intelligent', with over 100 separate sounds in their vocabulary.

Before supper I decide the time has come to do what I have put off for too long. Just in case. Not that it means anything, you understand. I take out Dr Baela's strip of bark from my bag, cut a slice off it with my Swiss army knife, grate it into powder, and, taking care to choose a private place, rub the powder all over my body before showering, keeping just enough aside to fill each nostril. The results are immediate. I sneeze uncontrollably for 25 minutes. No one, not Jake or David or any of their helpers seems to know which particular tree I have just inhaled, but for the first time since I left Mpulungu I feel well enough to really enjoy my dinner.

Turning in. Sounds of low voices round the remains of the fire and bullfrogs on the lake. Above a clear, intense, starlit sky. No reflections from anywhere. Pure sky. Pure night sky.

DAY 113 · KASANKA TO LUSAKA

 Sometime in the night I wake to hear a big wind blowing. It heaves and sighs around the hut with inexpressible mournfulness. I lie awake and think of the day ahead. If all goes well we should be in Lusaka by tonight, then Victoria Falls and from what I hear our troubles are over after that. Zimbabwe and South Africa are comfortable, efficient, Westernized. Akuna Matata. No Problem. Wild, uncomfortable, incomprehensible Africa will give way to tamed and tidied Africa – hot baths and iced beers, air conditioning and daily newspapers, French wines and credit cards. Lying here, listening to the aching wind in a hut by a lake in a forest, I feel a pain of sadness at the prospect of leaving behind all I have been through these past months and returning to a world where experience is sanitized – rationed out second hand by television and newspapers and magazines and marketing companies.

The next thing I hear is a knock on the door and a soft voice outside:

'Four and thirty minutes, sir.'

The dawn reveals a sky mottled grey from last night's storm, and a thin orange line cresting the trees across the lake. Another farewell, and along the stony track out of the Park and south towards Lusaka, capital of Zambia, over 300 miles away. We have moved and filmed for 17 out of the last 18 days, and there's some good old-fashioned exhaustion about. Patti's blood test could not indicate conclusively if she had malaria as the drug level was so high after the doses she'd been taking, but the hospital thought the symptoms fitted. She is too weak to work at the moment, but still has to travel, and squashed in the back of a bumpy minibus is not the best way to recuperate.

Our first experience of Zambian Railways, on the train from Kabwe to Lusaka, is not auspicious. The train is late and once arrived, so reluctant to move that a plaintive announcement has to be made over the PA:

'Would Express Two move from the platform to allow Express One to come in.'

This does the trick, but progress is still painfully slow. The interior of the Japanese-built coaches is in terrible shape. All the fans are broken and the upholstery torn and shabby. The track is badly maintained, so progress is not only uncomfortable but slow and uncomfortable. Not that any of the passengers seem worried. They sit reading newspapers and religious texts as the carriages lurch and swing. A kind gentleman, sensing my agitation, lends me his copy of the *Zambia Daily Mail*. It is full of sycophantic adverts taken out by public companies congratulating Mr Chiluba on his victory. 'The United Bus Company of Zambia says Bravo MMD. The Hour Is Now.' A leading article by one Leo J Daka, headed 'Zambia, Which Way Now', is less amenable:

'Zambia,' writes Mr Daka, 'is a hospital with the citizens as patients. When we were under colonialists we had no worry of major concern, now, with independence promoted by fellow blacks, I wonder. The point is something has gone mentally wrong with our leaders.'

The fact that such a piece is printed at all is one of the better things about Zambia. It is ironic that one of the achievements of Kaunda – the establishment of a two-party state and a free press, should be the instrument of his downfall.

DAY 114 · LUSAKA TO LIVINGSTONE

We are in and out of Lusaka without time to take much in. The hotel is bland and efficient. Patti is off her malaria-crunching course of drugs and perceptibly better. And the *Times of Zambia* carries barely believable evidence of the pace of the Soviet Union's Great Leap Backwards. The story, filed from St Petersburg (which was Leningrad to us, three months ago) reports that the Grand Duke Vladimir Romanov, heir to the throne of Russia has arrived in the Soviet Union for the first time.

We leave early, departing Lusaka via Saddam Hussein Boulevard, and swinging away again from our 30 degree line, to Livingstone, another 300 miles south-west on the Zambian side of the River Zambesi.

The main street of Livingstone is lined with low, run-down colonial-style buildings with verandahs. Money changers dart out as soon as they see a bus-load of tourists, miming their occupation suicidally and jumping out of the way only at the very last minute.

Our hotel is called 'Musi-o-Tunya', which is the local name for the Victoria Falls, and means 'The Smoke That Thunders'. It is modern but uncertainly run. A smell of drains wafts into my bathroom from a grille high on the wall. But I shouldn't complain, at least I have a bathroom. What I don't have are either of my bags. The staff at the Lusaka hotel failed to collect them from my room, and enquiries are under way. Apart from my clothes which are replaceable, my diaries and taped notes, laboriously assembled, are now unaccounted for, 300 miles away. But then, so is Dr Baela's bark.

DAY 115 · LIVINGSTONE

A half-mile walk through the well-watered gardens of the hotel takes me out onto the Upstream Trail which leads to the placid waters of the Zambesi as they flow gently, this being the dry season, toward a 250-foot precipice. In March and April the river floods and as the brochure describes it, 'the greatest known curtain of falling water', one mile wide, spills into this massive split in the basalt rock, formed by cooling volcanic lava.

I walk, unhampered by fences or warnings of any kind, across a river bed, sculpted by the action of stone and water into a weird and wonderful honeycomb of bore-holes and clefts and pipes and basins, to the very edge of the Falls, where what is left of the river makes its way innocently toward the void. Defying stomach-tightening vertigo, I stand as close as possible to the rim and peer over. Far, far below the falling streams accelerate into an inferno, smashing against the fissured black rock which streams with foam as the water is flung forwards, repulsed and hurled back again at the cliff. The spray that is the debris from this massive collision of rock and water is flung in all directions, blown by its own momentum skywards, way above the top of the gorge. In the flood season this cloud – The Smoke That Thunders – can be seen 20 miles away, and it was this that drew Livingstone to the falls in 1855, apparently the first white man to set eyes on them. As I turn back, reluctantly, to pick my way home across the riverbed, I, for once, appreciate the laid-back, shambolic, arbitrariness of Zambia, which has allowed me, with no fuss or bother, unhindered access to this gigantic, enthralling sight.

It even enables me to accept, without chewing the carpet, the news that my bags have been located, reached Lusaka airport, but have not been put on a plane.

I can't wear my T-shirt in this state for a third day, so I soak it, wash it and go down to dinner dressed in clothes Basil has lent me. It is fish night in the restaurant and all the waiters are dressed in straw hats.

Jake asks where the fish is from.

'America!' is the happy reply.

'America? How does it get *here*?'

'By sea . . .'

DAY 116 · LIVINGSTONE

POLE
to
POLE

The morning paper reports that President Chiluba has lifted Zambia's 27-year State of Emergency. The police have been ordered to remove all road-blocks (still common in countries like Sudan, Ethiopia and Kenya) and various powers of search and detention have been curtailed.

For myself and the crew another day of new experiences. If it's Saturday it must be white-water rafting, and we assemble by the swimming-pool to sign in, absolve the company taking us of any culpability and generally try to look cheerful. Basil is very silent. He has persuaded himself that the photo-opportunities outweigh the fact that he can't swim. But only just. Fraser has spent hours devising a waterproof method of recording my shouts, screams and cries. His solution is to encase tape-recorder, battery, microphone and all the wiring in a selection of condoms. 'I've never used so many in one day in my life,' he claims.

Nigel has a tiny waterproof camera on a huge harness, which sits on his shoulder like a parrot. Patti must be one of the very few who have been white-water rafting in the same week as having malaria.

The organizer of the expedition is a short, lean, bearded American called Conrad with an intense, some might say manic look in his eyes, softened by a ready smile. We are issued with lifebelts and then briefed by Heidi, another American who manages to put over dreadful information with a disarming, gung-ho jollity. Most of what she has to tell us has to do with what happens when, rather than if, we are flung off the boats and into the water.

'Just let yourself go. Don't try to swim . . . When you come up to the surface be sure to take a deep breath before you go under again.'

My legs are like jelly at the end of this and Basil is white. We select our life-jackets and head for the river.

What neither Conrad nor Heidi have prepared us for is the descent into the gorge, which involves a rough 30-minute scramble, in considerable heat, over smooth and slippery boulders. Bad enough at the best of times but with camera gear as well, it delivers us to the rafts in a state of terminal exhaustion.

257

We climb into the reassuringly solid, heavy-duty rubber rafts, made by Avon in England. Eight to a raft, with a driver mounted on a central crossboard. We pull out into the stream, dwarfed by sheer rock walls and pinnacles of basalt. The Zambesi, as it winds through the gorge, falls over a series of 20-odd rapids, of which we shall be tackling the first 10.

My companions are local people, some of whom, thankfully, know what to do. Our driver, Alex, a rangy black Zambian, rehearses us in the technique known as high-siding, which seems to mean flinging one's body as far forward in the raft as possible to keep the nose down, and stop us being turned over by the force of the water. Once rehearsed, we move across the deceptively tranquil, unruffled pool between Falls and rapid number one and wait for the camera crew's raft to go over first. Heidi, steadies them into position. Basil is tucked down at the back, almost on the floor of his raft, hanging on to everything it is possible to hang onto. Heidi guides them slowly to the lip of the rapid. Much depends on how she lines the raft up. Satisfied

she's hit the right spot, she allows the raft to glide forward and into the rapid. For a split second it accelerates like a rocket, twists, turns, carves into a reverse wave and momentarily disappears in a spectacular eruption of spray before bobbing away into safe water.

Seeing it happen to someone else merely increases the thud-rate of an already overworked heart, and only when we ourselves fly down the rapid, fling ourselves forwards on Alex's command 'Go!' and experience the exhilaration of total immersion do I begin to relax and even to suspect that I might enjoy myself.

Rapid five is the most spectacular, with a steep drop of more than 25 feet. Exhilaration and excitement makes up for fatigue as we progress into some longer, but less steep runs. I suppose the maximum time we spend on a rapid is no more than 45 seconds, but into that time is packed an enormous amount of action, and the outpouring of nervous energy can only be released by bawling one's lungs out.

The sheer relief at reaching the tenth and last rapid, with the day's filming done and soft evening light catching the walls of the canyon, leads me to do a Very Silly Thing.

The crew of my raft manage to persuade me that there is an even more wonderful experience than white-water rafting and that is to swim, or rather let your body be carried, down a rapid. I ask about the crocodiles we'd seen further up the gorge. No problem, they avoid moving water. I ask about the rocks. No problem, way below the surface. Such is their enthusiasm and my joy at having survived this far, that I surrender to a dangerous streak of natural impulsiveness, and jump, with them, off the raft and into the waters of rapid number ten.

As soon as I leave the boat I know I should have stayed in it. The current is fast and there is no way of controlling my progress. Within half a minute I'm swept and spun along before being tugged helplessly beneath the water by a reverse wave. I strike what is incontrovertibly a rock, and what's more a particularly sharp and unyielding rock.

The full force of the impact is taken on my lower back, protected, thank God, by my life-jacket, and probably Fraser's tape-recorder. My calf meanwhile cracks against another rock that wasn't supposed to be there either. Winded by the blow, I struggle up to the surface driven by a potent and uncontainable sense of indignation. This enables me to roar 'You bastards!' and take in a mouthful of Zambesi before disappearing again.

My companions are already ashore and gazing around with expressions of beatific happiness when at last I fight my way clear of the current and clamber up the rocky bank. I don't want to spoil the party so I keep smiling, and begin the slow ascent of the gorge, content in the knowledge that whatever I might have done to myself, Fraser's condoms are still intact.

At the hotel another bruise to add to the two already growing – one of my missing bags has arrived, the other has been lost by Zambian Airways and no one seems to hold out any hope of finding it.

Whatever baleful influence has been at work in Zambia, it has persisted to the end.

DAY 117 · LIVINGSTONE TO VICTORIA FALLS

Sleep for an hour with the help of two paracetamol tablets, then painfully and fitfully for two or three more hours fighting against sticky heat (the air-conditioning being completely ineffectual) and sharp pain from my ribcage whenever I try to turn over. At 3 o'clock I give up, manoeuvre myself awkwardly out of bed and begin to make some assessment of what was in my missing bag. Torches, my favourite boots, my favourite sweater, my personal diary (though not, thank God, my notebooks). What has vanished, to my great relief, is Dr Baela's bark. I feel a little better, almost immediately.

At 9 o'clock in the morning we clear Zambian customs and make our way across the Victoria Falls Bridge, which marks the border with Zimbabwe. Constructed nearly 90 years ago it is a road, rail and pedestrian bridge, and for today only, something more than that. A group of people are proposing to throw themselves off the bridge on lengths of elastic, in what the organizers, an outfit called Kiwi Extreme, believe to be the first ever Bungi jump in Africa. Bungi, I'm told by Byron, the leader of the team, who has a world record jump of over 800 feet to his credit, is an Indonesian word for the particular rubbery twine they use in their descents. Having nearly given my life to the Zambesi I am not at all tempted to fling myself upside-down into a gorge, but I recognize someone who is. It's Conrad, our organizer from yesterday. Slim and insubstantial beside the chunky white men in beer-brand T-shirts who seem to make up the bulk of the jumpers, he grins nervously as a red towel is wrapped around his ankles and the rope lashed carefully over it. Tied only by his feet, he climbs onto the parapet of the bridge, moistens his lips, murmurs something – I think it's 'goodbye' – and hurls himself out and away from the bridge. As he goes he flings his arms out, plummeting in a Christlike free-fall nearly 300 feet to the river below. Then, when he looks set for certain death, he freezes for a split-second, and begins to return rapidly back towards us.

We leave Conrad bouncing up and down in the Zambesi Gorge, and make our way across into Zimbabwe.

Zimbabwe is younger than Zambia by 18 years, and has just celebrated ten years of independence under the guiding hand of Robert Mugabe. On the wall of Immigration Shed A there is an old relief map of the country on which the word Rhodesia has been tippexed out and 'Zimbabwe' scribbled in. The old capital, Salisbury, has been recycled more ingeniously – a piece of tape with 'Harar' on it has been stuck over 'Salisbur', so it reads 'Harary'. Perhaps they weren't expecting independence to last this long.

Check in to the Victoria Falls Hotel, an immaculately clean white-painted complex with red roofs and shining green lawns. The gift shops on the Zambian side were pathetically empty, but here the shelves are full of all sorts of fluffy junk, though there is not a newspaper or book to be seen.

The room is comfortable and efficient. The carpets are soft and the curtains of flower-print pattern. The whole place feels like a very well-appointed Old Folks home.

The price for this soft-furnished cossetting is re-entry into the world of regulations. The 'I Presume' Bar has a sign warning that between '7.00

and 11.30', dress is 'Smart Casual. No Denims, No T-Shirts, No Takkies'.

A pleasant meal out in the open air, but surrounded by package tour faces. Roger and others leave early to hit the casino, but when I eventually hobble off to my bed I find them all gathered in the 'I Presume' Bar looking very cheesed off. Apparently all of them were banned from the casino for being improperly dressed. The doorman picked them off one by one – Roger, sandals; Paul the driver, trainers; Basil, canvas shoes and Nigel, denim jeans. It may hurt but at least I go to bed with a laugh.

DAY 118 · VICTORIA FALLS

I am taken to the local hospital for an X-ray. It's the sort of hospital you dream about when you nod off after a three-hour wait in a London casualty department. It has only been operational for a month, is spotlessly clean, well-equipped and almost empty. The lady in X-ray has so little to do that before attending to me she has to set down the book she's reading – a slim paperback by one Dr James Dobson entitled *Dare to Discipline – Permissiveness doesn't Work*. After four exposures she's satisfied and I take various studies

At the Victoria Falls: Bicycle and bungi on the Zambesi Bridge.

Day 118: Zimbabwe

of my ribcage along to the doctor who diagnoses a hairline crack and prescribes nothing more than paracodeine to help me sleep.

Nigel, who said all along that he thought it was a cracked rib, is sympathetic but realistic:

'There's nothing you can do. The pain wears off . . . in about six weeks.'

My biggest mistake was to do it off camera. Now I shall creak all the way to the Pole and everyone will think it's old age.

DAY 119 · VICTORIA FALLS TO BULAWAYO

A bombshell of a telex has arrived from Cape Town. There are no berths available on the *Agulhas* – the South African supply ship which was our only means of transport to Antarctica. The full complement has been taken up by scientists and survey staff.

We must go on to the Pole somehow. It is inconceivable to have come this far and not to reach our goal. Phone calls to the office in London to double-check the *Agulhas* and investigate any possible alternative.

Meanwhile, life must go on, and that means packing and moving on, yet again.

On the way through the hotel gardens to reception a group of tourists stands frozen beneath a low covering of mango trees through which a troop of baboons is rampaging, bombarding the red-tunicked porters below with sticks, branches and half-eaten mangoes. It's amazing how little it takes to cheer one up.

We assemble at Victoria Falls Station around 5 p.m. to take the overnight train to Bulawayo. Like everything else in the town the station is in immaculate condition. It's a low, elegant Greek revival gem with fresh-painted sky-blue doors and matching detail and on the platform an ornamental pond, palm trees, frangipani and striking red flamboyant trees.

The train rolls in an hour late but is worth the wait. The coaches are in a dignified, rather unfashionable livery of brown and cream and the interlinked initials 'R.R.' – Rhodesian Railways – can be found engraved on the windows and mirrors of the older coaches, whose dark, mahogany panelled compartments contain display photos of wildlife, the Falls and other Zimbabwean attractions. The past has been assiduously preserved here, in marked contrast to Zambia, where not even the present is well preserved.

The difference between the two countries is much on the mind of Elizabeth, a chatty Zimbabwean who quite unselfconsciously applies a squirt of underarm deodorant as she chats to myself and Angela and a very obliging Zambian.

'Zambians are . . . ,' she searches for the word, 'so humble. Maybe it is because of their poverty.'

The Zambian gentleman smiles benevolently, displaying patience rather than humility.

A few minutes after leaving a guard comes by to check I have everything I need.

'Where are you from, sir?' he asks.

'London.'

He points to his tie.

'Do you have a badge? I will put it on my tie.'

I apologize for not having a badge, whereupon he smiles broadly, crosses himself and leaves. No sooner do I have my map out to check the route than the door slides open once again and an attendant appears with a litter bag. This country has a most un-African obsession with tidiness. On my way down the corridor to the restaurant there is an instruction from Railways of Zambia, urging us, with graphic underlining, not to 'Expectorate in Corridors'.

Darkness has fallen by the time we reach Hwange, or Wankie as it used to be called. There is a large coalfield here, and perhaps because of this a number of steam locomotives – Beyer-Garratt compounds, burning seven tons of coal a day – are still working and the sight and sound of them under the night sky brings a lump to this old train-spotter's throat.

Zimbabwe time-warp: Rhodesian Railways rolling stock, Beyer Garrett compounds, trainee driver.

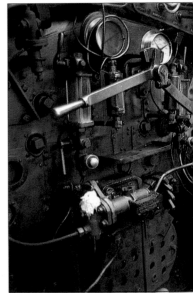

DAY 120 · BULAWAYO

POLE *to* POLE

From the moment our night train rolls at a leisurely pace through a cutting and past the lineside greeting 'Welcome to Friendly Bulawayo', the illusion of being in Surrey *circa* 1958 begins.

Steam engines are at work shunting goods-wagons and big yellow diesels bring in expresses from Plumtree and Mafeking, made up of varnished wood coaches with clerestory roofs.

We drive out to our hotel along wide streets – when they were laid out by the early settlers they had to be wide enough for a team of oxen to turn without backing up.

There *have* been changes – Selborne Avenue has become Leopold Takawira Avenue, Rhodes Street has become George Silikunda Street and Grey Street, Birchenough Road and Queen's Road have all been subsumed into Robert Mugabe Way – but this is still a city of boarding schools and bowling clubs, and when whites talk about it being multi-racial they mean it includes Scots, Irish, Germans and South Africans.

There are cricket pitches and even an Ascot Racecourse. The high street shops are British, of the pre-Tesco era, with names like Haddon and Sly, Townsend and Butcher, Stirling House, Forbes and Edgars, while some, like Kaufmanns and A. Radowsky, established 1907, reveal a Jewish influence among the early settlers.

The roads are full of Morris Minors, Hillman Minxes, Ford Anglias and solid old bicycles with delivery frames on the front, and at Mikles Store the 'Early Xmas Sale' begins today.

Not everything is comfortable and assured – an ominous sign in the centre of the city reads 'Save Water. Only 22 weeks water left in our dams' – but after Sudan, Ethiopia, Tanzania and Zambia, I have to pinch myself to make sure that I am awake and that Bulawayo is not some figment of my paracodeine-drugged mind.

This evening there is a four-hour thunderstorm and a downpour which should add a day or two more to the water supplies. After the rains, which broke a hot and humid day, the air is full of winged insects, committing mass hara-kiri against the windows. Paul says they're flying ants, out to find a mate, dig a hole somewhere and breed. They're eaten all over Africa, apparently, usually fried.

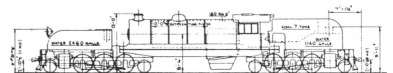

DAY 121 · BULAWAYO

Water is not the only scarce commodity in Zimbabwe. A report in this morning's *Bulawayo Chronicle* is headed: 'Shortage of Bibles':

'The sudden eruption of religious organizations during the past five years is said to be straining the supply of Bibles written in local languages. Religious leaders in Bulawayo said the influx of Pentecostal churches, breakaway groups from the mainstream Roman Catholic church, have led to a high demand.'

Demand is falling, however, at the Bulawayo Bowls Club. Pearle Sheppard, the secretary, blames independence. 'A lot of people have left the country . . . we used to have nearly 400 members . . . and now its gone right down to about 120.'

When we arrive to film Pearle is concerned that we don't get the wrong impression from a large sign which greets us at the clubhouse: 'BBC. Do Not Leave Things on the Verandah for the Thieves'.

'Oh dear no, BBC is for Bulawayo Bowls Club,' she explains apologetically.

Despite it being a dull, drizzly afternoon there are 20 bowlers out on the greens. The men are thin, erect and grey-haired. The women are generally, though by no means exclusively, buxom, and as you might expect, younger than the men.

'You get a very representative crowd, people from all walks of life and all ages and everything, all come and play bowls.'

I ask Pearle if the club has black African members.

'Er . . . we don't have any, no. Actually the Africans are not particularly interested in bowls. The only black bowlers we've got in Bulawayo belong to the Blind Bowlers Association . . . It's really quite fantastic to see some of them play, because they might not be able to see anything and yet they call out instructions to them, and they sometimes play incredible bowls.'

A Scots lady is the current Zimbabwean National Champion and she is on the green today, broad and tanned, her hat at a rakish angle, with a cigarette permanently on the go. She encourages her opponents vigorously:

'Beautiful weight, Doris . . . Oh, magic adjustment Ethel, well bowled!'

When her turn comes she delivers the bowl with one hand and retains her cigarette in the other. As the bowl describes the gentlest of arcs she straightens up, pulling slowly and thoughtfully on her cigarette as she encourages it across the green, 'Come on kiddo . . . come on little one.'

About 35 miles outside Bulawayo, in the modestly spectacular and historically fascinating region of the Matopos Mountains is buried the man whose

Bulawayo: Bowling champions, broad streets, banks.

foresight, determination and insatiable ambition created a country which bore his name for 57 years before becoming Zimbabwe in 1980. In a short life he had a massive influence over the whole of Southern Africa – opening up farming land, developing the gold and copper mines, and setting up communications. When he died in Cape Town in 1902 his own personal train, designed by the Pullman Company of America, brought his body to Bulawayo. He was a year short of 50, and had left precise instructions in his will: 'I admire the grandeur and loneliness of the Matopos in Rhodesia and therefore I desire to be buried . . . on the hill which I used to visit and which I called "The View Of The World" in a square to be cut in the rock on the top of the hill, covered with a plain brass plate with these words thereon, "Here Lie the Remains of Cecil John Rhodes".'

Ninety years later, and despite threats by Mugabe to dig up the body and send it back to London, this is exactly how and where Rhodes lies. The area is now National Park, a controversial move which involved the forced removal of local residents and accusations of desecration of holy places by the Ndebele people.

The grave lies on top of a great smooth pate of exposed granite, topped by a ring of massive boulders, some 20 feet high, frozen at a gravity-defying angle on the very tip of the slope.

This being Zimbabwe one cannot climb up to it without some official instruction.

'No one is allowed to take alcoholic stuff up to the grave. No radios. No noise. No domestic animals', reads the sign.

The view out across a rich and irregular landscape of rock-stacks, rounded hills and long smooth ridges shaded by woodland is very fine, and at sunset the dying light on the red and yellow lichen of the rocks creates a warm luminous glow.

In order to balance something against the pervasive influence of white culture I spend the evening in the Umtshitshimbo Beer Garden at the back of the Waverley Hotel where a band called Southern Freeway are playing live.

The Umtshitshimbo Beer Garden is not the sort of garden that Vita Sackville-West would recognize. The concrete tables and chairs are mounted on breeze blocks and the only greenery is on the wall in a series of ruggedly painted murals depicting scenes of African village life – cooking fires, drinking hooch, baboons scratching their bottoms. Around the front of the stage a crowd has already assembled. They sit right up close, beers lined up on the stage itself. Recorded music is blaring out and people are dancing.

Every now and then the music is interrupted for a long and explicit public service warning about the danger of AIDS, to which no one listens.

The beer – Black Label, drunk from the bottle, or Castle – is often augmented with spirits. Quarts of gin seem to be the popular choice. By the time Steve Dyer and his band mount the stage, the crowd are restless and beginning to stagger a little. Looking around the crowd I see no white faces apart from ourselves, one older man, a thin blond boy and Steve Dyer himself, who seems rather low key and apologetic for the occasion. Once the band gets going there is an infectious and generous response, especially when an impressive Diva by the name of Thandeka Ngoro takes the stage. She has a dramatic presence and a powerful voice which she may feel is more suited to La Scala in Milan than the Umtshitshimbo Beer Garden.

DAY 122 · BULAWAYO TO THE SOUTPANSBERG MOUNTAINS

POLE *to* **POLE** Up at 6 o'clock to pack and leave Bulawayo for our last African country. The next cities of any size on the line south will be Pretoria and Johannesburg in South Africa.

It all seems to be happening fast now. We can travel long distances on these straight, tarmacked roads and there are few diversions on the way. Today we are aiming to move another 400 miles closer to the Pole.

7.15: Bulawayo Bus station. For a republic founded and led by an avowed Marxist, Robert Mugabe's Zimbabwe displays a healthy respect for private enterprise. Among the innumerable bus companies are Sun-Shine Coaches, Hit-Man Buses, the Hwange Special Express and the magnificently titled Dubies Megedleni Omnibus Service. The buses are circled by salesmen with travel-aids of every description from Afro-combs to balls of string with which to tie up baggage.

Lunchtime: After a long and uneventful morning's drive by bus and minibus across monotonous miles of dry bush, we have reached Beitbridge, a nondescript frontier town whose most recent claim to fame was an appearance in the film *Cry Freedom*, for it was the crossing point where Donald Woods escaped South Africa dressed as a priest. (In Bible-booming Southern Africa I can see that this was the perfect disguise to choose.)

After a mixed grill at the Beitbridge Inn, on the Zimbabwean side, we drive across the Limpopo and into South Africa.

I wish I didn't have to dismiss the crossing of the Limpopo so lightly, for like the Ngorongoro Crater, Lake Tanganyika and the Zambesi, the Limpopo is one of those most mysterious and evocative of all African names. I wish I could say I bathed in it (as I did in Lake Tanganyika and the Zambesi) or at least paddled in it, or at least got a little closer to the hippos that wallow in its red and muddy water. But it has suffered the fate of all rivers that

become national boundaries – it is a security risk. Nowhere more so than on this border between the white-run economic giant of the south and black Africa to the north. Although apartheid is being rapidly dismantled, the thousands of yards of coiled razor wire, the two ten-foot-high steel mesh fences, the guard-posts and the searchlight towers at 20-yard intervals remain to guard the Republic of South Africa against the world, and the Limpopo from its fans.

The South African immigration office has a quarry-tiled floor, modern, efficient air-conditioning, computers and tinted glass. There are posters on the wall but they aren't displaying the beauties of the country. Instead, under the heading 'Look and Save a Life', they show you how to recognize an SBM limpet mine, a PMN (TMM) anti-personnel mine, a TM 57 land mine and grenades M75, F1 and RGD5.

Outside, the first white soldiers we've seen in Africa check the vehicles that go through. They seem an ill-disciplined, loutish lot, unhealthily red-faced and red-eyed. They deal mainly with commercial vehicles here, there are few private cars going through. Some African women are thumbing lifts on the big trucks belonging to Wheels of Africa or Truck Africa, as they grind through the checkpoint bringing cobalt and copper from Zambia and Zaire.

Clem has rented for me not only a BMW but a white BMW. Hardly the discreet way to enter the country, but when you've been on the road for four months and fourteen countries you seize whatever bonuses come your way. I check the map, slip Bob Seger's *The Fire Inside* – noisiest and liveliest of my tapes – into the cassette player, and flicking on the engine ease southwards into the Transvaal. The economic transformation from the wild, unruly and unavailable to the comfortable, expendable and the infinitely possible, which began at Victoria Falls and continued in Zimbabwe, is complete.

DAY 123 · THE SOUTPANSBERG MOUNTAINS TO JOHANNESBURG

POLE *to* **POLE** After a hot night at a motel in the Soutpansberg (Salt Pan Mountains), with my cracked rib giving me no relief unless I sleep sitting up, we are on the move, passing along a series of tunnels through the folded, faulted range that is part of the Drakensburg Mountains. If I'm not much mistaken the Verwoerd Tunnels (after Dr Hendrik Verwoerd, Prime Minister and staunch advocate of apartheid, assassinated in 1966) are the first tunnels we have been through in nearly 12,000 miles of travel. Forty miles further on I'm surprised to be reminded that part of South Africa is in the tropics, as we pass a tall, modern, chrome-tipped monument marking the Tropic of Capricorn.

How different my circumstances were when we crossed into the tropics nine weeks ago. From the Wadi Halfa ferry to a BMW.

We reach Pietersburg, to the passing eye clean, well-kept and affluent, and on through towns whose lumpy names, like Potgietersrus and Naboomspruit declare their origin in the years following the Great Trek of 1837 when 10,000 Boer settlers, unable to coexist with the British, left the Cape and moved north. Now they're proud communities announcing themselves with weighty concrete signs. Hotels and shopping malls are going up behind false brick façades and the car parks are full of BMW's like mine. Sanctions don't appear to have caused much pain up here.

We run on toward Pretoria, across another immense and spectacular African plain. This is the High Veld. The four-lane highways are in good condition and not busy. Puffy altocumulus clouds are stacking up in a wide blue sky.

We arrive at Pretoria, over 200 miles from last night's stop-over, in good time for the afternoon's big football match. Christopher, the black driver of the minibus into which we have transferred, is becoming increasingly agitated the nearer we get to the Atteridgeville Super Stadium. Atteridge is a black area, he says, and will not be safe for us. Looking around at the township, set on a hill, with a church and a lot of brick houses with pitched corrugated iron roofs, I can't see quite what he's worried about. The streets are unswept and there has been no attempt to plant a public tree or two, but no one is shaking their fist at us. The traffic begins to build up as we near the stadium and Christopher falls apart completely. This is not a safe place, they are all black people here, and do we not know what they do to white people in a place like this? They kill them.

Then suddenly his fear subsides. He has spotted several white faces queuing up for tickets for the game. All of them are alive and well.

The last country in Africa: The first tunnel on our journey, what a Tropic looks like, Atteridgeville Super Stadium — back row for weak bladders.

We follow an expensive red car into the ground. 'Soweto BMW' says the rear window sticker. Admission is five rand – about a pound, which is not bad value considering this is a cup semi-final between the local team, Sundowns, and the holders, Jomo Cosmos from Johannesburg.

The status of football being relatively humble here, Sundowns arrive squeezed into a minibus, bearing their motto which, with an unfortunate letter missing, comes out as – 'Sundowns. The Sky is the Limi'.

The Jomo Cosmos team is as far as I can tell the personal property of Jomo Sono, a Pele and a Charlton of South African football. It has been managed for the past nine years by a Scot from Arbroath called Ray Matthews. I am privileged to hear his warm-up chat in the dressing room. He exhorts his players in a broad Scots accent that gives no hint of 20 years spent in South Africa:

'Mothale, you feed Minkhalebe . . . Masinga overlap Singiapi . . .'

The players all nod as if they understand. I ask him how much difference he thinks his chat makes. He shrugs and shrinks even lower into his shoulders.

'It's like talking to children. You just don't know how they'll play on the big occasion.'

His team, nine blacks and two whites, run out onto a pitch respectably green considering the shortage of water. A concrete ramp surrounds the pitch. On it graffiti slogans like 'Viva Joe Slovo', 'ANC Lives', 'ANC Leads'. 'Smash Capitalists', co-exist with ads for Caltex, Shell and Philips. Under 'Socialism Never', someone has added 'failed'.

The first half is a bit of a plod. Half-time comes as a relief, in more ways than one. The top row of the cantilevered terracing becomes an impromptu urinal from which a gentle curtain of golden rain descends 40 feet to the ground.

There are few police in evidence and despite losing to a soft goal from Ray Matthews' team, the local crowd-behaviour is good. Everyone, including the players, seems quite free of the surly posturing that was once so common in English football.

Maize Power at Atteridgeville. Greater Horned football supporter.

Day 125: South Africa

Thirty-five miles away down swift, modern highways is Johannesburg – capital city of the Transvaal with 1.6 million souls. Tall, unblinking tower blocks of glass and steel climb up into the sky. As we wait in the muzak-sodden lobby of the Johannesburg Sun Hotel, Nigel looks helplessly round at the chrome and the preserved plants and the water-effects and asks: 'What happened to Africa?'

DAY 125 · JOHANNESBURG

POLE *to* **POLE**

'. . . Summer's here! Make it a good one with the Trimrite Trimmer. Only 179 Rand! . . . This is High Veld Stereo on 94.95 *Eff*-Em. . . . 22 to 23 degrees out there . . . real swimming-pool weather!'

A November Monday morning in Johannesburg. The silent skyscrapers are coming to life after the weekend and the traffic jams are growing on the freeways, like in any big city in the world. We are heading south-west, out of town, to visit somewhere quite unlike any other city in the world.

Soweto, 12 miles south-west of Johannesburg, comprises 33 townships with a population of 3.5 million people. The first buildings went up in 1933 and a competition was held to decide on a name. Verwoerdville was one of the unlikely contenders but Soweto – South Western Township – was chosen. It's a cold and functional name for a cold and functional purpose – to house a cheap disenfranchized work-force with which to exploit the mineral wealth of the area. That wealth, needless to say, went back into Johannesburg and not Soweto, which is why, nearly 60 years on, the contrast between the two is such a shock. The skyline of Soweto is unbroken by cover of any kind. Row upon row of basic single-storey houses sprawl across bare, unlandscaped hillsides. The streets are full of uncollected rubbish, some of which has just been set on fire where it lies. The rest blows and swirls in the wind. The stations from which hundreds of thousands of workers leave for the city each morning are currently patrolled by guards with Armalite rifles, following a spate of violent attacks on passengers. As many people as can afford it have taken to using the ubiquitous minibuses, privately owned, which cover the city. The stories of Inkatha violence are sickening. They have added to the fear in the city. As someone told me, 'When Mandela was released everyone was wearing ANC T-shirts, now you don't see any.'

This is the grim first impression of Soweto, but as soon as you look beyond the physical differences, beyond the outrageous disparity between the quality of surroundings in two cities so close to each other, and so dependent on each other, there are plenty of signs of life and hope. I am here to visit a family from Soweto who were once our neighbours in London, and who

Faces of Soweto: Mandela Village, Mandela's house, Prestige Park.

Day 125: South Africa

have recently been allowed back into their own country. We are accompanied by a Sowetan called Jimmy, who has made a good living from guided tours of the area. Jimmy, full of wisecracks – he tells me in Soweto BMW means 'Break My Windows' – is by turns charming, congenial, garrulous, curt and businesslike. He is a professional and a survivor. He offers breakfast at his house, which is a long way from the traditional image of the tin-roof shack.

It is approached through wrought-iron gates and past newly-planted jacaranda trees. Inside is a fitted kitchen with all mod cons hung with pictures and paintings. He is particularly proud of a personally signed copy of a Robert Carrier cook book.

Whilst we eat breakfast he is constantly on the phone doing deals of some kind. He breaks off just long enough to give a public wigging to Roy, the gardener, who has arrived half-an-hour late this morning.

'Blue Monday', nods Jimmy, as Roy retires chastened, 'the people here they just drink all weekend long.'

I ask him if there are any whites in Soweto.

'Oh sure . . . 20 per cent of the taxi businesses here are white-owned . . . there's a lot of whites work at the power station . . . there's an area there called Power Park which has a lot of white residents . . .'

As we leave Jimmy's house, Roy is scooping dog-shit off the lawns.

In Jimmy's neighbourhood – the Diep Kloof extension, or Prestige Park as it is known – there are streets full of architect-designed, venetian-blinded villas with double-garages, clipped lawns and herbaceous borders. Mercedes back lazily out of radio-controlled garages and one mansion boasts the ultimate in Soweto chic – a white security guard. These houses went up in the last five years and were bought by businessmen, doctors and lawyers. One was for a man who makes a 150,000 rand a year profit from the butchery business, another cost the Reverend Chikane 800,000 rand (£150,000).

'Money makers in the name of the Lord,' muses Jimmy as we drive by.

At our insistence and with, I detect, a slight weariness, he shows us another side of Soweto, a shanty town known as Mandela Village. Looming in the distance, beyond the tin roofs and the undrained streets are the long straight lines of the gold mine dumps.

A baby is born in Soweto every five minutes, says Jimmy. 50 per cent of the population is under 16. Many thousands of them live in conditions like these, makeshift cabins which can be put up overnight, made of anything their occupants can lay their hands on. There are frequent fires and no sanitation other than a few plastic lavatories provided by the council. The shacks consist usually of one room, with maybe the added luxury of a scavenged gas-ring or an old car-seat. Very often the inside walls are papered with pages from sales catalogues or fashion magazines. Three-piece suites,

televisions, showers, refrigerators and all the other things the occupants can't afford form a constant backdrop to their lives.

The 'Blue Monday' effect can be seen in a number of sad characters who lurch along the dirt track between the huts, but the children are wide-eyed and curious, quick to smile, easy to make laugh. It is fairly unbearable to dwell on their prospects in life – taken away from the simple, hard but traditional way of life in a mud hut in the bush to a life equally hard, but suddenly not as simple.

Having seen the unreal best and the depressing worst of Soweto I'm ready for a little normality – a dose of straightforward friendship uncluttered by projections and statistics. I repair to the Orlando district to see the Gwangwas. Outlawed from South Africa for belonging to the ANC, Jonas, a musician and co-composer of the music for *Cry Freedom*, his wife Violet and their two children took refuge in many cities including London. I never imagined I would ever see them in their own home, and the pleasure of the reunion is tremendous. Violet welcomes me with such a hug that I fear another rib will crack, and on the yard of their house is what I am assured is a traditional African greeting – 'Welcome Michael, To Gwangwa Family' – marked out in dried cow-dung.

Violet apologizes for Jonas' absence. 'He's at a meeting with Nelson Mandela.' Now there's an excuse.

We go to lunch at a shebeen, originally the name for an illicit liquor shop, but now applied to a rather decorous front room in a nearby street where, over a licit can of Castle lager Violet talks about being back home.

After eight years away she finds the surroundings worse – 'seventy-five per cent of people can't afford the new houses they're building' – a growing middle class and a growing violence and uncertainty, but she recognizes the danger of the returned exile coming back to tell those who live here how to run their lives. Her travels round the world echo my own feelings:

'Most countries you go to, you find that people want to be hospitable, they're proud of their country, you know, whatever, whether they're rich or poor, they want to make you feel welcome and they want to sort of show you how they live, and I think that's the same here too.'

Later I meet Jonas – another short, sharp shock for the rib-cage – back from his meeting. I ask how Mandela was.

Jonas smiles, 'He still has a powerful handshake.'

Jonas has been away for 30 years and is still dazed by the reaction, 'people I haven't seen since the sixties coming up and shaking my hand.'

When I ask him if he detects a difference in the people he nods very firmly.

'They're broad-shouldered now you know . . . before they walk looking down, they were cowed so easily.'

On which optimistic note we leave Soweto.

The last thing I hear from High Veld Stereo, '94.95 *Eff*-Em', is that Terry Waite has been released.

DAY 126 · JOHANNESBURG

First good night's sleep – five unbroken hours – since my dip in the Zambesi. Probably just as well for today promises no respite for the body. We are to go down one of the gold mines on which the wealth of Johannesburg and indeed the whole of South Africa is based. One third of the country's export earnings come from gold and the proceeds from coal, platinum, uranium and other minerals found in these rich seams, raise this to almost two thirds. A new mine can cost 20 billion rand (£3.8 billion) to develop. It isn't surprising therefore that mining is a tight, white-run operation.

The Western Deep Mines, developed by Anglo-American, one of the six private companies that control 95 per cent of gold production, is kept almost pathologically clean and tidy. Despite the water-shortage, sprinklers gently douse the lawns on the approach to the offices, and men with pointed sticks are at work removing curbside litter.

We are briskly and efficiently processed, like patients at an expensive private hospital, into a reception-room where coffee and pastries are served under the clean-cut, clear-eyed gaze of the directors of Anglo-American whose framed photos are the only decoration. Then we are shown into a changing-room where every single item of our clothing has to be exchanged for a company outfit, and minutes later, we re-emerge, in white boiler suits, safety helmets and rubber boots, as Western Deep Visitors.

Western Deep – above and below: At the gold face,
in the car park – Fraser, Mirabel, Roger, Paul Murphy, MP,
Patti and Nigel, the entrails of the mine – 2½ miles down.

Martin de Beers, solidly-built, moustachioed in the style of a Southern Hemisphere cricketer, begins a long and doubtless ritualized public relations spiel as we are fitted out with headlamps and batteries.

Western Deep Mine is in *The Guinness Book Of Records* for the deepest penetration of man into the Earth's crust – 3773 metres, that's nearly two and a half miles. Within the next year that will be surpassed by a new shaft which will be sunk beyond the 4000-metre mark. It has been honoured on a 30-cent postage stamp as one of the three best achievers in technology in South Africa since 1961, along with Christian Barnard's heart transplants and a machine for harnessing wave power. At any one time there are 7000 men working beneath the surface, and it takes four hours to get them all down. The work force is 72 per cent migratory labour, the majority coming from the Siskei and Transkei (two 'homelands' set up in the spirit of apartheid, to encourage Bantus to develop separately), but also from Mozambique – 'very placid, they are the only people who mix freely with all the other tribes'. Martin prefers to talk rather than be asked questions. I sense that there is anger in there, probably a lot nearer the surface than anything else at Western Deep.

Have seen no black faces yet, apart from the gardeners. I presume they're all underground. We pile into a lift to join them. It rattles and clangs towards the earth's core at 70 metres a second. Another form of transport to add to the list. Two kilometres down we are released into a world, almost as spotless as the one we've just left. It smells of fresh cement – like a newly constructed underground car park.

I ask Martin if this is a model mine, the showpiece of the company.

'This is Anglo-American standard, the model mine's the South Mine. They all drive around in Land Rovers down there.'

Temperatures at this depth are around 50 Centigrade, and so Anglo-American have had to air-condition the earth's crust to a maximum of 28.5 degrees . . . 'the limit set by the human sciences laboratory.'

So far the experience has been curiously undramatic, the surroundings clean and spacious. Then quite suddenly there comes a point where underground car-parking becomes pot-holing and all of Anglo-American's environmental cosmetics cannot disguise the realities of mining.

The shaft narrows to a slippery rock passage, full of water. The only light is from my helmet, and footholds are not easy to find. A scramble up spilled rock-fall leads through to a narrower chamber. The noise of the drills makes it difficult to hear instructions and it is no longer possible to stand upright. Away from the air-conditioning the heat quickly rises and the sweat begins to run. We edge carefully through into a man-made cave with little more than three foot clearance where crouching miners are at work on the rock-face. There is great heat and terrific noise when the drills are in action.

Three-men gangs work at the face in temperatures approaching 90 Fahrenheit for 6 hours per shift. One operates the drill, another checks the equipment and a third directs water into the hole keeping the dust down. A fourth man, and the only white in the team, is the mining engineer who has to check the face and mark in red paint the bands to be drilled. I am close enough now to the gold seam to reach out and touch it. It doesn't glitter. The gold here is in carbon form, in fact the gold-bearing strip only inches wide, studded with white quartzite pebbles against a dark background of limestone and lava looks more like black pudding.

Before we leave Western Deep we're allowed limited access to the Holy of Holies – Number 2 Gold Plant – where at temperatures of 1600 Centigrade one of history's most ancient, magical and mysterious processes comes to its conclusion as black pudding is turned into gold. Security is tight, a steel mesh doorway is locked behind us. Every camera angle is checked by armed security men, and Nigel is given strict instructions:

'You must shoot nothing west or your camera will be confiscated.'

Tension builds as the crucible is slowly upturned and the molten material begins to flow.

'Is that gold? . . . Is that gold?' we first-timers keep asking, but the experts peering through the green visors that enable them to look at the quality of the smelt shake their heads. For the first minute only slag appears. I should have remembered from the rivers of Lapland that gold is always at the bottom. Then a lighter, whiter stream comes through and every one breathes a sigh of relief as each ingot tray is filled with gold worth £150,000.

I'm told that if I can lift an ingot I can have it. But they've only ever lost one like this.

On the way back from Western Deep through a landscape scarred by flat grey spoil heaps 50 feet high and yellow and white plateaux of rubble hundreds of yards long I keep trying to find the answer as to why gold should still be so sought-after, so valued as to create monster technological feats like Western Deep Mines. No one seems to have a satisfactory answer.

Back at the hotel I ring my son whose 21st birthday it is today and realize after I put the phone down that I'm a very long way away from home, and still have a lot further to go.

Our future progress is still uncertain. The *Agulhas* remains adamant that there are no places, and the only alternative would be to approach Antarctica from a quite different direction, such as Australia, New Zealand or the tip of South America. But we are booked on the Blue Train to Cape Town, and as reservations on this exclusive express are almost as valuable as the ingots I tried to lift earlier, there seems no point in not completing our crossing of Africa, even if we don't know what on earth it's leading to.

DAY 127 · JOHANNESBURG TO CAPE TOWN

Discomfort in my back at night is still acute. Time will heal, people keep reassuring me, but I wouldn't mind a bit of help. A cheerful and obliging Johannesburg chemist recommends arnica, a homoeopathic remedy, and bonemeal tablets. They join the growing stash of pain-relieving drugs which have just about made up in weight for the bag lost in Lusaka.

Johannesburg station is deserted at 10.15 a.m. apart from a straggle of passengers and their porters booking in beside the sign 'Bloutrein Hoflikheids Diens'. The Blue Train porters must be the smartest in the world, in their blue blazers, grey trousers with knife-edge creases and leather shoes polished to a mirror-like sheen. Sadly, they wear rather sour expressions as if they all might have toothache, but as our man leads us into a lift he makes it pretty clear what he's surly about.

'Sorry about the smell,' he turns to pull the gate across, 'it's the coons. They piss all over the place.'

A group of fellow-travellers is squashed onto a piece of carpet at a specially erected check-in area, in the middle of an otherwise long and empty platform. They look a little nervous and exposed, as if the ability to take the Blue Train marks you out as one of the world's most muggable prospects. Some are scanning the information board which gives details of unashamed luxuries that await us.

'Dress is smart casual for lunch and elegant for dinner.'

Rack my brains to think of anything in my depleted wardrobe that could by any stretch of the imagination be described as elegant. Fail.

Two azure-blue diesel locomotives, bringing the 17 coaches of colour co-ordinated stock down from Pretoria, ease into the curve of the platform and quietly glide to a halt, whereupon stewards move smartly forward to lay out matching carpets, monogrammed with the letter 'B', before each door.

And so it goes on. My compartment has a wall of a window – big and double glazed – air-conditioning, carpet, individual radio and temperature controls, half a bottle of champagne, a newspaper and an electronically operated Venetian blind.

Just before 11.30 a husky female voice breathes over the intercom, 'The Blue Train is ready to depart,' and barely noticeably, we begin to pull out of Johannesburg, due to cover the 900 miles to Cape Town in 22 hours. For the first time since Tromsø we are moving *west* of our 30 degree meridian and may not meet it again until, God willing, I reach the South Pole.

A travel-worn maroon and white local from Soweto passes us, heading into the city. We gather speed through grubby stations like Braamfontein and Mayfair, whose platforms are crowded with blacks in headscarves and

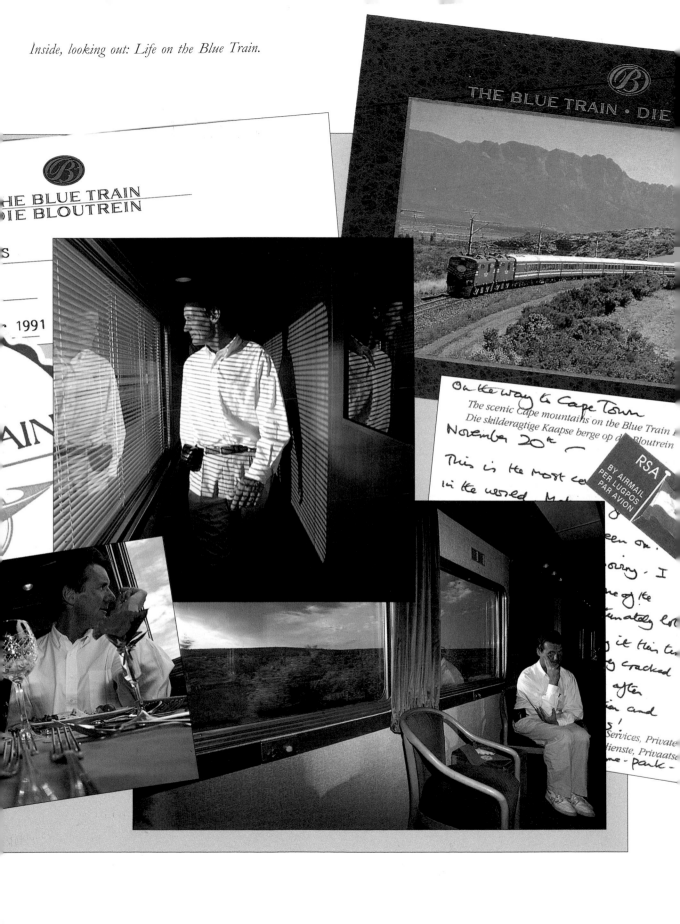

Inside, looking out: Life on the Blue Train.

THE BLUE TRAIN
DIE BLOUTREIN

1991

THE BLUE TRAIN · DIE

The scenic Cape mountains on the Blue Train
Die skilderagtige Kaapse berge op die Bloutrein

On the way to Cape Town

November 20th

This is the most

in the world

RSA
BY AIRMAIL
PER LUGPOS
PAR AVION

Services, Private
ienste, Privaatse
me - park

sweaters, accelerating into the smarter suburbs with names like Unified and Florida. It is the most comfortable train ride I've ever experienced, and combined with the air-con and the thick glazing and the wall to wall carpets it is like being in an hermetically sealed capsule, enabling the passenger to observe the outside world whilst remaining completely detached from it – an unconscious paradigm, perhaps, of the apartheid system, officially abolished only five months ago.

There are 92 people in 17 coaches – as opposed to 4000 in 18 on the Nile Valley Express. No one is allowed to travel on the roof. On Zambian Railways the restaurant car was out of food altogether, on the Blue Train I count 13 pieces of cutlery in front of me at lunchtime. Terrine of kingclip (a local fish) and Cape salmon are served as we move across the wide, flat expanse of the High Veldt. Grain and gold country. Far in the distance the mountains are temporarily obscured by a thunderstorm.

The *Johannesburg Star* carries more evidence of the rapid emergence of the country from the years of isolation. South Africa is to be allowed to take part in the Olympics for the first time in 30 years. There is an advert for the resumption of South African Airways services to New York and a report that Richard Branson hopes to bring Virgin Airlines into Johannesburg by 1993. Meanwhile uniformed attendants move discreetly along the carpeted corridors collecting clothes to be pressed. Muzak lightly dusts the tranquil atmosphere, occasionally interrupted by train announcements:

'You can look out for some rhinos now on the compartment side.'

We search unsuccessfully for rhinos. All I can see is telegraph poles.

'Well, we don't seem to be in luck today.' Fade up Strauss waltzes.

But they don't give up easily. Fade down the Strauss waltzes.

'Ladies and Gentlemen you can now look out for flamingoes on the corridor side.'

Have a shower before dinner, and taking my all-purpose tie out to add that indefinable touch of elegance, saunter down to the bar. The windows are of such a size, with minimum partitions giving maximum view, that one has this strange sensation of floating, unsupported, over the countryside. Fraser says he saw a car coming towards him on a road running alongside and instinctively moved to one side. Poor old sod.

The barman Matt is put to work by Basil to make the perfect martini, but after three attempts Basil drinks it anyway. Matt comes up with the surprising information that the noisiest tourists he deals with are the Swiss.

'Swiss people are noisy?'

He relents a little: '. . . Well, not noisy, but they're happy drinkers.'

A glorious sunset over the town of Kimberley which boasts of being the home of the World's Largest Man-Made Hole. At one time there were

30,000 frantic diamond prospectors digging in the hole at once. When it was closed in August 1914 it was three and a half thousand feet deep with a perimeter of a mile.

Meet one or two of my fellow travellers. A couple from Yorkshire whose daughter manages a vineyard on the Cape, a Swiss tour-guide (Swiss and Germans are the most numerous tourists), a lady from the Irish Tourist Board who thinks that they have similar problems to South Africa in attracting visitors – beautiful countries but political problems – and an exotic couple, she Colombian, he German, who are working in Gabon. We get back to the hoary old subject of malaria. Their view is that the pills are as bad for you as the disease, quite seriously affecting digestion and eyesight.

Fortunately my digestion is, for once, settled, as I move through to the restaurant and the mountain of cut-glass that awaits me.

DAY 128 · JOHANNESBURG TO CAPE TOWN

5.30: Woken with piping-hot tea in a white china pot. For the first time since Victoria Falls I was able to sleep without a pain-killer, and for the first time in Africa I was able to sleep well on a train. I now regret that I gave such enthusiatic instructions to be woken at sunrise.

We are travelling across the Karoo, a wide landscape of bare mountains and scrubby plain, deriving its name from the Hottentot word meaning 'thirstland'. Stimulated by this information I make my way down to the restaurant car, past train staff already polishing the door handles.

We are close now to the end of Africa. Beyond a succession of tightly folded mountain ranges lies Cape Town, the richest corner of a rich province. God's Own Country. Sit and watch the sun warming the mountains and allow myself a nostalgic drift back to a sunrise in August as we drew in from the Mediterranean and saw the lights of Africa for the first time. It's now late November and high summer has turned to early spring. I don't exactly know what lies ahead but I have a sudden surge of optimism that everything is going to turn out right. We have been tried and tested by Africa in every possible way and, bruised and battered maybe, we have survived. My children call these moments of mine 'Dad's happy attacks', and, as we glide out of an 11-mile tunnel into a dramatic, sweeping bowl of land filled with vineyards I know that this one may last some time.

The magnificent landscapes of Africa build to a tremendous climax. Towering haze-blue mountain ranges – the Matroosberg, the Swarzbergen and the Hex – part like stage curtains to reveal the final epic image of Table Mountain and the wide Atlantic. It is a breathtaking display of natural beauty and one which raises all our tired spirits.

The end of Africa: Looking for inspiration at the Cape of Good Hope. Table Mountain, Cape Town: View from the cable car, traveller and two oceans – Indian left, Atlantic right.

DAY 130 · CAPE TOWN

POLE
to
POLE

Yesterday I stood on the Cape of Good Hope, a low stack of rocks pounded by the ocean and strewn with giant seaweed, and this morning I sit on top of Table Mountain, a sheer cliff rising 3500 feet above the city of Cape Town. It's a warm spring morning and the rock hyraxes start mating wherever we point the camera and the magnificent view extends towards Cape Point where the warm waters of the Indian Ocean meet the cold waters of the Atlantic. Everything about this coastline is on the grand scale. The rolling breakers steaming in from thousands of miles of open sea, the long white beaches and the tall craggy walls of exposed rock that circle the city to the east – Signal Hill, the Lion's Head, the Twelve Apostles and Table Mountain itself. A brisk wind blows in off the sea, combining with the sun and the scenery to cleanse and reinvigorate an over-travelled system.

Looking down at the massive natural harbour it is ironic to think that

this most prosperous corner of Africa was dealt a serious blow by one of the poorest when de Lesseps chose to build a canal through the Egyptian desert 130 years ago. All at once the trading ships from India and the East had a shorter, more convenient and more sheltered route to Europe and Cape Town's 200-year monopoly as a supply and maintenance base for East–West shipping came to an end. There isn't much activity in port today, with the poignant exception of a sturdy red-hulled survey vessel making final preparations for an eight-day journey to the Antarctic. With a pair of strong binoculars I can just about make out the name on the hull – MV *S.A. Agulhas*.

Though there could be worse places to be marooned than Cape Town the good news is that after some feverish international telephonic activity we have secured an alternative passage to the Antarctic via the town of Punta Arenas in Southern Chile. The bad news is that we must abandon any hope of clinging to the 30 degree meridian and any further surface travel. We have only two options left open to us, to fly into the Antarctic or to fail altogether.

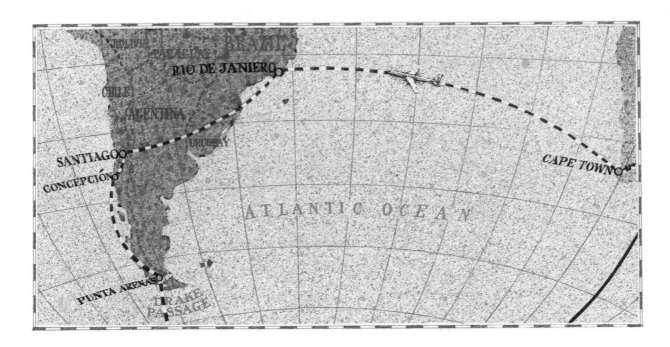

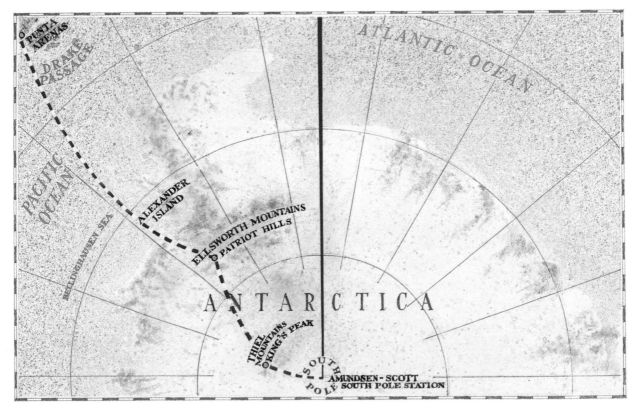

DAY 133 · SANTIAGO, CHILE

Santiago. Tuesday morning. It took us nearly three months to travel 6800 miles down the length of Africa, and only 48 hours to travel 6200 miles from South Africa to Chile.

Nor, after all this, are we any nearer our final destination. Santiago and Cape Town are both, at 33 degrees South, some 4200 miles from the South Pole. There are other similarities. Both cities have a temperate climate and a distinctly European feel, reflecting the style and taste of the early settlers – Spanish in Chile and British in the Cape. Both produce good wine. Both have a recent political history of violence, oppression and varying degrees of international ostracism. The father and two brothers of Patricio, our guide and fixer in Santiago, were arrested and imprisoned in 1973 for supporting President Allende, General Pinochet's socialist predecessor, and Patricio himself was expelled from the university for his political views. He is not angry any more, nor does he regard himself as particularly unfortunate. Pinochet's police arrested 250,000 suspected Allende supporters and held them in national sports stadiums for up to three months – 2000 are still missing without trace. Though Chile now has a reformist, liberal President, Patricio Aylwyn, they are still missing and Pinochet is still Commander in Chief of the Army.

This morning it's sunny at the foot of the Andes, with temperatures rising into the 70s, and the army band is parading outside the Moneda, the elaborate colonial-style Presidential palace whose name means 'the Mint', which is what it was designed as in 1805. It was here that President Allende committed suicide 19 years ago after the building had been rocket-attacked by Hawker Hunter fighters ordered in by Pinochet and his rebellious armed forces.

A well-drilled changing of the guard takes place and then, with much preparation and flourish the 60-piece military band breaks into the unmistakable tones of 'Happy Birthday To You'. Not just one chorus, but a long symphonic variation which keeps a small crowd mystified for some five minutes. It's presumed that this is for the President, but no one seems at all sure.

We eat lunch in the glorious covered market, a classical façade outside and an elaborate and elegant cast-iron construction within. The produce looks plentiful and fresh – asparagus, strawberries, avocados, cherries and pineapples and a rich and exotic selection of sea fare, especially conger eel and some things called picorocos, strange sightless rubbery creatures living in rocks. In order to eat them you have to buy the rock as well and drop it in boiling water for a couple of minutes. Piures, an even less attractive

The Trooping of the Microphone in Santiago: Fraser wearing ceremonial stripes. The Presidential Palace, with musical accompaniment.

Day 133: Chile

delicacy, resemble marine cowpats and contain some evil-looking orange parasites which Patricio recommends highly.

'Pure iodine . . .'

'Iodine?'

He nods enthusiastically:

'Very good for sex.'

Having restaurants in a food market seems such a sensible idea, and my meal with Patricio at the Marisqueria Donde Augusto is one of the best. Good food, good wine and an introduction to the Pisco Sour.

Pisco is an eau-de-vie served with a third of lemon juice, some white of egg and a lot of ice. It's fresh and quite fierce. Whilst we're drinking some musicians come by, playing traditional instruments like the quena – a set of pipes, preferably bamboo, now plastic, and a charrango, a 10-stringed instrument, preferably of armadillo shell, now, for ecological reasons, made of wood. The sound is haunting and according to Patricio, so old and traditional that Pinochet tried to ban the instruments for being too representative 'of the left'.

For a panoramic view of the city we take a funicular railway up beyond the zoo, onto a hill crowned by a 40-foot statue of the Immaculate Conception. Following a bent metal sign reading 'A La Virgen' we toil up paths and steps only to find that the Virgin is closed. Peering inside I can see a small chapel. The wall outside is extensively decorated with sentiments of a non-religious nature – 'Norma! Te Amo!', 'Mejay 2000', 'Depeche Mode' and, intriguingly, 'Gladys y Dario 1/08/91'.

Above me the steel Virgin, cast in France in 1908, and brought here 'To celebrate the 50th anniversary of the dogma of the Immaculate Conception' stands, arms outstretched, head slightly raised and eyes gazing into the middle distance, which is I presume how you are when that form of conception occurs.

DAY 134 · SANTIAGO TO PUNTA ARENAS

6.30 a.m. It's 9 degrees Centigrade as I leave the hotel, wearing thick shirt and a sweater for the first time since Northern Norway. We carry with us bulky bags of Antarctic clothes hastily flown out from London. Santiago Airport is packed, and, with 41 pieces of baggage to check-in amongst the six of us we have few friends in the queue for LanChile's flight to Concepcion and Punta Arenas.

Punta Arenas, at the tip of South America, only a mile or two across the water from Tierra del Fuego, is somewhere none of us in this well-travelled crew has ever been before. Because of the rapid change of plan at

Cape Town even Clem, who reconnoitred as much of our route as possible, is a stranger to the next 4000 miles.

As we wait to board we can only talk in rumour and speculation about what lies ahead. There are so few facts to go on. A company called Adventure Network does exist – well, at least they answer telephones, take bookings and have headed notepaper – and they do claim to have direct flights from Punta Arenas to an Antarctic base at the Patriot Hills, and to be able to provide further air transport from there to the South Pole. The fact that none of us can find the Patriot Hills on any map of the Antarctic only adds to the confusion. Some gloom-monger remembers our visit to Patric Walker in Lindos.

'When was Mercury going to be in retrograde again?'

'Late November . . . early December, wasn't it . . .'

The public address system bursts into life again. 'LanChile Flight 085 for Concepcion and Punta Arenas is ready for boarding.'

I take a last look at the destination board. It's 27 November.

The first, moderately disconcerting, thing about the flight is that the plane is a Boeing 707, a perfectly fine aircraft but not in service on any airline I've travelled with for a while.

As we take off, a Walt Disney cartoon plays on the cabin video.

It's a short hop to the city of Concepcion, but already the landscape is changing. The hills are steep and pitted, the narrow valleys running down to the sea are green and forested. The cabin announcement as we taxi to the terminal advises us to remain on board. 'Our staying at this airport will be approximately 20 minutes.'

Seven and a half hours later we are still at Concepcion. We have played cards, read books, drunk beers and coffees and have even been bussed into a city centre hotel for a gloomy set lunch. Patti and Fraser have managed some time for shopping, or retail therapy as they call it. I've met a scientist who is off to do coastal research in the Antarctic. He has stood on the South

Pole. It had been 50 below . . . 'and your breath just gets swept away. It's so short anyway. You're at 10,000 feet.'

It had never occurred to me that besides being bleak and inhospitable and pitch dark half the year the South Pole was as high as an Alpine peak.

The reason for our delay, Mercury apart, is all to do with the 707, which I have a feeling was a last-minute replacement. When the time came to re-start the engines there was no generator at Concepcion Airport powerful enough to provide the necessary charge. The engines are eventually restarted and we take off again in late afternoon. This time the air-conditioning has failed and as we begin to see icy peaks and glaciers below, the temperature on board verges on the Sudanese.

Somewhere below us the Trans-America Highway runs out and with it all road connection to Punta Arenas. The long Chilean coastline fragments into a breathtakingly spectacular array of mountainous islands, straits and fiords, of which the thickening cloud cover offers only tantalizing glimpses.

At half-past seven, 10 hours into what should have been a two and a half-hour flight, we turn and bank over the Straits of Magellan and down across sparsely-covered grassland into Carlos Ibanez Airport, Punta Arenas. We have reached latitude 53 degrees South. I should feel at home, I was brought up on 53 degrees – North of course.

This realization does bring home to me the scale of the travelling that still lies ahead of us. Punta Arenas may be the last stop before Antarctica, but it is still as far from the South Pole as Sheffield is from the North Pole.

DAY 136 · PUNTA ARENAS

 Woken by the sound of a car alarm, which makes me think for a happy moment that I'm back in London. Conscious-ness slowly clarifies my surroundings into the narrow, unadorned walls of a room in the Hotel Cabo do Hornos, Punta Arenas, Chile. The Cape Horn Hotel is a romantic name for an unromantic eight-storey slab of a building, whose pale yellow brick walls and low gabled roof stand on the brow of a hill dominating downtown Punta.

I sent off a postcard to my daughter yesterday and wanted desperately to lie to her and say that my room looked out over Tierra del Fuego. Basil's room looks out over Tierra del Fuego, but on my side of the corridor we look down on the main square, with it's labelled trees, as neat and proudly kept as those of any French provincial town, protectively clustered around a flamboyant bronze statue of Ferdinand Magellan. The great man stands, one foot on a cannon, atop a plinth on which striving mermaids hold aloft the shields of Spain and Chile. Patagonia is marked on one side and Tierra del Fuego on the other, together with a bronze relief of Magellan's plucky little boat fighting it's way between the two, as he became, in 1520, the first Westerner to sail from the Atlantic into the Pacific. Whoever designed the statue wouldn't let it lie and added two subjugated Indians beneath Magellan's feet. To kiss the toe of one of these Indians is supposed to ensure safe passage back from Antarctica. Since Dr Baela's bark I've been rattled by all superstitions, so I give the toe a quick peck.

Some last-minute shopping in Punta. Short on underpants, I make my way to a promising emporium only to find that this is not Africa and people do not speak English. I have to mime. It isn't very good and the assistant brings me a pair of trousers. My next mime is shamelessly graphic. She colours a little and brings me a belt. By now I'm desperate and reach into the top of my trousers to show her the actual garment itself and find out that she can speak English after all, even if it is only to shriek, 'No! . . . not here!'.

On to the nearby Navigantes Hotel to meet our fellow polar travellers for a briefing ahead of tomorrow's planned departure.

Some are dauntingly well qualified. Graeme Joy, a keen, humorous New Zealander has skiied to the North Pole. It had taken him 56 days and they had seen polar bear tracks regularly.

'That kept us together,' he grinned, '. . . no one wanted to be last.'

He leads a party of seven Australians and New Zealanders who are aiming to climb Mount Vinson – at 16,000 feet, the highest point on the continent of Antarctica. For some of them it will be the last in a series of expeditions to climb the highest peak of every continent. Graeme's co-leader is Peter Hillary, son of Sir Edmund, the first man known to have climbed Mount Everest.

A woman in the party, an Australian doctor, has flown a light plane from California to Sydney, across the USA and Europe. There is much talk of self-reliance, of testing themselves. An Australian lawyer and company director quotes Peter Hillary as his inspiration.

'It's the challenge of knowing what the limits are within which you can go, and pushing it right up to that limit.'

I'm quite relieved to meet Rudolph – 'Rudy, please' – W. Driscoll, a quiet, somewhat lugubrious American, who was already booked to fly to the Pole when we arrived. Rudy has not climbed mountains or flown light planes but since his divorce ten years ago he has been to the North Pole on a Russian ice-breaker (with 89 others) and on the Trans-Siberian Railway.

'My son said, "Go on Dad, have a go". And I did.'

The rest of the party are Japanese – three neatly and identically attired mountaineers and the rest aiding and abetting a genial, shaggy-haired character called Shinji Kazama. Kazama-San, as his team refer to him, is attempting to make the first motor-bike journey to the Pole. He's already driven a bike 15,000 feet up Everest. He has an assistant, Antonio, and an immaculately dressed film crew of three.

In England many people thought I was mad to attempt to go from Pole to Pole overland. Here, in the lounge of the Hotel Navigantes in Punta Arenas, I reckon I'm about the sanest in the room. Excepting, that is, the local head of Adventure Network, who is not a wild man in a beard or a lean and weathered six and a half footer, but a slight, delicately attractive, soft-spoken Scot called Anne.

She conducts the briefing, telling us that Adventure Network, and an outfit splendidly named Antarctic Airways, were founded in 1983, by two Canadian mountaineers and 'a seasoned Antarctic pilot, Giles Kershaw'. This last she said without flinching, which cannot have been easy as Kershaw, by all accounts a brave man and an extraordinary character, died in an accident out there a year ago. She had been married to him for eighteen months.

Two years later Adventure Network set up a permanent base camp at the Patriot Hills, 78 degrees South.

The main dangers in Antarctica, she warns us, are the cold and the wind and the snow. Exposed areas will get quickly frostbitten, and snow-blindness is painful and easily acquired. A snowstorm can come down at any time so 'always move in a party of people'. When we leave the hotel tomorrow morning we must be wearing and personally carrying everything we need; 'You must be a self-contained unit, and able to operate should the aircraft put down anywhere in Antarctica.'

We're assured there is a permanent doctor on the base. His name is Scott, 'and', as some wag shouts from the back of the room, 'his rates for open heart surgery are very reasonable'.

'His success rate isn't quite as reasonable,' comes the reply.

I'm surprised, talking to Anne afterwards, to find how few people have ever been to the South Pole. Higher, colder, less accessible than the North, it remained unvisited for 44 years after Scott left in January 1912. The US Navy landed there in 1956 and scientists have worked at the Pole ever since, but few outsiders have visited. Anne estimates that in six years of operation Adventure Network have taken no more than 25 or 26 people all the way to the Pole.

Which makes me feel even more special, and even more apprehensive when, later, I look out over the multi-coloured roofs of this compact, characterful town, and go through my check-list for the last time.

DAY 137 · PUNTA ARENAS

At the airport, but the news is not good. Bruce Allcorn, our pilot, a white-haired, white-bearded, broad-shouldered Canadian with 25 years flying experience in the Arctic, and three years down here, is bent over the computer in the meteorological office. He beckons me over and points out four low pressure systems between here and the Patriot Hills. A few days back there had been nine frontal systems in the area. He shakes his head.

'This doesn't happen anywhere else in the world. If you saw a weather map like that in Europe you'd all move.'

He's worried that there is a lot of wet weather around, and the combination of wet weather and height leads to icing. Also it's important to have 'good visual' on the mountains. What this actually means is that he won't believe they're there unless he can see them. There's no guided navigation down here. In fact below about 60 degrees South there is not even satellite coverage. All of which is why Bruce likes to see where he's going.

He introduces me to his co-pilot, Louie:

'He's a fully qualified stuntman, you know.'

A youngish, angular, handsome face. Eyes that look back impassively. These two, like everyone else on the edge of the Antarctic, are straight out of Central Casting.

'So . . . we're not going in today?' I ask Bruce.

'We're definitely not going today.'

'Tomorrow?'

Bruce shrugs: 'I'll come over here at about 7.15 tomorrow morning . . . we'll make a decision by 7.30.'

I must be looking at him like a dog waiting for its dinner. He doesn't want to disappoint me but he can't bear me looking at him like that.

'It's very common to have five to ten day delays . . . with the weather . . . not to put you off.'

Back to the Cabo do Hornos with its plaintive sign in the elevator: 'Please Push Only One Time the Button'. I'm in limbo-land. All dressed up and no Pole to go to. We visit a nearby penguin colony but a fierce storm hits us and Nigel is unable to film.

An early night after a bad paella. Lie awake worrying about footling things. What happens if we're stranded there until Christmas? Did I buy enough underpants? Is Mercury still in retrograde?

Anne Kershaw

DAY 138 · PUNTA ARENAS TO PATRIOT HILLS

 December already. Christmas cards. Present lists. Parties. A telephone rings. My bleary eye catches the clock as my hand reaches for the receiver. It's 7.15, and a voice is telling me that we leave for Antarctica at midday. Into my thermal vest and long-johns, Gap denim shirt, faithful moleskin trousers, thick knitted sweater, two pairs of socks, Asolo boots and down jacket made by RAB of Sheffield. Ring home to tell them I am leaving for the South Pole. There's no one in. Leave a message on the answering machine.

'Going the South Pole. Byee!'

Hopefully for the last time I push 'only one time the button', and say farewells once more to the helpful staff at the Cabo do Hornos. They seem to be quite used to being used as a jumping off point for Antarctic explorers, and will keep our rooms free tonight, just in case.

Collecting various hung-over Australians on our way we drive out of Punta Arenas past Unisex Pamela and Unisex Splendid Hair Salons and the Club Hipico – 'Horse Racing once a Week'. Someone mentions the oft-quoted statistic that Punta Arenas has more brothels per head of population than any town in South America, and a local Chilean is surprised that I haven't visited the Red Zone . . . 'the cathouses', as they call them. They were a notable omission from the list Adventure Network issued us with on arrival: '101 Things to do While in Punta Arenas'.

The classic outline of a Douglas DC-6, blue and red streak along it's white and silver fuselage, stands in a corner of the airstrip. Beside it, instead of Bogart and Bacall, are Bruce Allcorn and his wife Pat, supervising the loading and refuelling. Yesterday Anne Kershaw told me the plane was built in 1948. Bruce shakes his head as if to reassure me:

'No . . . no . . . no. 1953.'

I'm about to reply 'before my time', when I realize that this was the aeroplane of my childhood. This was what I drew when I drew an aeroplane.

We board by a perilously slim extending ladder, with a piece of rope for support. Inside there is none of the squash and squeeze of a conventional airliner. Basically it is an empty shell into which whatever is required for the flight has been fitted. There are 28 of us going to Patriot Hills, so there are some 30 seats set out in readiness. A bulkhead separates the passengers from the cargo hold, where Kazama-San's motorbike occupies pride of place. Pristine white, it stands on its frame like a knight on a tomb. Bruce, in his captain's overalls with four stripes on the epaulette, and Louie the qualified stuntman insert themselves into the cramped cockpit and make their final checks.

Onto the last continent: Bruce's DC-6 — ten years younger than me, Bruce on the DC-6 — riding Motorbike Class. First sights of Antarctica: Iceberg production line, nunataks pierce the ice-cap.

There is a general air of nervous excitement. Bruce's dry drawl comes over the speakers:

'It's going to be a little bit rough to start off . . . a bit of turbulence over the mountains . . . We'll be landing on a blue-ice runway . . . the ice is a little rough and the aeroplane wiggles around a bit . . . Lots of engine noise . . . It's all normal . . . You're welcome to come to the cockpit, but if you use a flash camera, please warn me . . . Kinda startles the hell out of me.'

Louie adds a reminder that the aircraft is not pressurised, and there is no air-conditioning and asks us to observe the no-smoking sign. This raises a cheer and a shout of approval from the Australians:

'There are human beings on board!'

I see Basil, who would like nothing more than a relaxing puff or two before heading into what the old maps used to write off as Terra Australis Incognita, sink further into his seat.

At 12.10 the first engine is started, and as all four come on stream and the frame of the aircraft rocks and shakes, everyone is filming everyone else, and Anne is waving a relieved goodbye as we taxi out for take-off.

At 12.30, after final weather clearance, the DC-6 rumbles down the runway, rises confidently into the sky, then turns and heads south down the Strait of Magellan away from the oil refineries and the brightly coloured roofs of Punta Arenas and the wide treeless plateau of Tierra del Fuego.

As we climb to our cruising height of 10,000 feet the first wisps of cloud drift by the windows and we catch a last glimpse of the majestic, snow-capped Andes mountains running 4500 miles north from here to the shores of the Caribbean.

Using a *National Geographic* map of Antarctica pinned to the partition, Rob, a tall, slim young Canadian from Adventure Network runs down the eight and a half hour journey for us. 1700 nautical miles at 220-knot cruising speed, estimated time of arrival 8.30 this evening. First four hours over the Drake Passage. Nearer to the continent the first sight of icebergs and the ice-shelf as we cross the Bellingshausen Sea. Landfall over Alexander Island, at 70 degrees South, and in over the Ellsworth Mountain range.

Unlike the Arctic — a moving ocean covered with ice several feet thick — Antarctica is a landmass, covered with an ice-sheet 12,000 feet thick in places. It is larger in area than the USA and yet there are probably fewer than 4000 people on the entire continent. (By my rough calculation, this means that if and when we land our film crew will make up one six hundred and sixtieth of the total population of Antarctica.)

About three hours flying time from Punta Arenas, as we're all walking about finishing a serve-yourself picnic lunch, the plane appears to make a very quick jump, dipping and almost instantly regaining height. As we struggle to regain our balance Bruce's laconic tone can be heard over the intercom.

'We just went over the Antarctic Circle.'

The first ice-floes are sighted. Huge white floating platforms tinged a piercing jade-green at the base, some of them as much as three-quarters of a mile across and 800 feet high (though only 200 feet may be above water). The pack-ice, which begins by looking like curdled milk on a cup of dark coffee, then fractured eggshell, coalesces into a continuous band of ice which makes it difficult to distinguish where the ice-shelf ends and the continent begins. Fierce winds are blowing, turning the sea white and whipping snow trails high off the cliffs. They call these katabatic winds, caused by a mass of intensely cold air sinking onto the polar plateau and flowing downhill, accelerating as it hits the coast, sometimes at speeds of 180 miles an hour. It may look beautiful and serene from an aircraft, crisp and cool as Hockney's Los Angeles, but the land below is the most inhospitable on earth.

Below us the flat white waste is broken by nunataks – peaks that are tall enough to break through the ice-sheet – and eventually by the longer ranges of crumbly black rock that make up the Ellsworth mountains.

Much of Antarctica is still unmapped and a race to name new mountains, plateaux, bays and glaciers is underway. To prevent complete confusion there is an international committee that vets names and claims. From the latest map it would seem they've run sadly short of inspiration – one set of mountains is called the 'Executive Committee Range'. If they can get away with that, surely I can find a 'Palin Peak'.

One of the Canadians is enthusing about what Antarctica does for her.

'I go through a sort of cleansing process out here . . . I don't drink coffee, I don't smoke.'

I could certainly do with a bit of cleansing. Beneath my nose I feel a spot about to break through – my own personal nunatak – my throat is dry and sore and my rib aches. What sort of awful germs will I be unloading on this purest of continents?

We are getting close to landing. Bruce likens putting down on a blue-ice runway to landing on a cobbled street. The sun has melted pockets in the ice, called 'suncups', which makes it trickily uneven. The ice is so slippery that he cannot risk using brakes and must control the aircraft with engine throttle only. But a big wheeled aircraft like this could never put down on snow.

At 7.45, turning one last time in the lee of a low rocky range, Bruce lowers the DC-6 onto the translucent, glassy, blue-green surface of the Antarctic ice-cap. There is much noise as the tone of the engines rears higher and we are bumped and swung. Snow swirls past the window as we create a temporary blizzard. After a moment or two of sound and fury, everything settles down and Bruce eases the aircraft round and taxis toward a cluster of oil drums and a converging group of Ski-Doo-hauled wooden sleds.

The dangers of Antarctic life begin as soon as you set foot on the ground. It is an extremely slippery continent, and all of us shuffle about trying not to fall over and generally getting in everyone's way. There is not much time for a welcome. It is probably the busiest day of the season at Patriot Hills. Twenty-eight people and their gear have to be unloaded and dragged across the ice to the camp, a half-mile away. The plane must be refuelled and on its way back again to Punta Arenas within two hours, otherwise the engines will freeze up.

I decide to walk to the camp.

Ahead of me, a crusty surface of wind-blown ice and snow ridges called sastrugis, stretches to the horizon.

The sky is clear, and we are back in the land of the Midnight Sun.

The wind is mercifully light and my thermometer reads 22 Fahrenheit. Minus 6 Centigrade. Nothing serious.

I think of where I am, now only 600 miles from the South Pole. On my globe at home I would be on that dark, unseen area at the base which never gets dusted. How ironic that the reality should be quite the opposite. Clean, clear, dazzling brightness. And silence except for the crunch and squeak of snow under my boot.

The Patriot Hills base is a collection of modern lightweight tents of varying sizes and colours – mostly red and white – made from Coldura, a reinforced nylon fabric. Patti has one to herself but five of us and Rudy will share. There is one tent which operates as kitchen, dining-room, drying room, radio room, office, library and general meeting place. As far as I can see there is no such thing as a washing or bathing tent and the lavatory is a wooden frame over a plastic bag, with a low snow wall on three sides offering a degree of protection from the wind and the public gaze. It is easy to tell when it is occupied, and by whom, from the head above the wall.

I'm laying out my sleeping bag when I hear the low roar of an aircraft, and get my head out of the tent just in time to see the DC-6 swoop less than 30 feet above the camp and away towards the mountains. Bruce is on his way back home and with him our only practical means of escape.

In the mess tent Scott, the doctor, and Sue from New Zealand have cooked up a hot, thick and nourishing meat and veg soup for everyone, after which the climbers – Japanese, Australian and New Zealanders – are ferried by single-engined Otter aircraft to the Mount Vinson Massif, one and a half hours away. Every bit of good, settled weather must be taken advantage of.

Peter Hillary is in the second wave of climbers to leave. He and his party will not be back for two weeks. I ask him if, as the son of Sir Edmund, he could ever have been anything other than a mountaineer.

Life on the ice: Sastrugis and Single Otter, a man at the end of a long journey,
Sue in the kitchen. An afternoon walk in the Patriot Hills, Kazama-San rehearsing
for polar arrival, Mike Sharp talks to the world, Dan the Pilot.

May the world stay in peace
May Antarctica be used for peaceful purposes only
May high-tech propel pollution-free motorization
With my gratitude to my family and friends for their support

January 1st. 1992
Shinji Kazama, at the south pole

'Well, I think if anything Dad really almost discouraged us from going to the mountains . . . he really didn't particularly want any of his children to get into mountaineering.'

Whatever went wrong Peter seems to have become the best sort of enthusiast – resourceful, adventurous and well aware of taking it all too seriously.

With Bruce and the Vinson party gone a certain tranquillity returns to the base. Kazama-San's team are putting up their own tents. His motorcycle stands, like a council sculpture, in the middle of the camp. Fraser is taking photographs of a shovel – 'through' a shovel, he insists. Nigel is sipping Scotch in the sunshine outside our tent. It's two hours after midnight but none of us can take our eyes off this shiny, white landscape.

DAY 139 · PATRIOT HILLS

POLE
to
POLE

Away from the coast, there is no life, and therefore no bacteria; no disease, no pests, no beasts of prey, no human interference. It is a clinical environment . . . It can only be compared with life under the ocean or in space.

I read this description of Antarctica, from Roland Huntford's book *The Last Place on Earth*, over an early morning cup of tea in the mess tent. Outside the air is barely moving. The silence is almost indescribable. It is as if everything you know that makes noise, that gives life has been suddenly switched off. Bruce's wife had described it as a deafening silence, which is exactly what it is.

I slept fitfully, still troubled by a rumbling, discontented stomach, which has a knack of knowing when I'm furthest from a lavatory. It isn't just a question of getting out of bed and going next door. It is a question of getting out of bed without waking five other people, putting on trousers, a sweater, a jacket, two huge boots, a neck band, a head band, a balaclava, sunglasses and a pair of gloves, walking a hundred yards across the ice, remembering you've forgotten your roll of toilet paper, coming back, treading on someone's head, and then finding a Japanese motorcyclist has got there before you.

Still, once enthroned in solitary splendour, one does experience an acute feeling of accomplishment at having got there at all. The view from the loo is immense and empty. There is no one out there, for thousands of miles.

No waste of any kind is allowed to be left in Antarctica. Any effluent, human or otherwise, will make an epic journey, not via some dark drain and sewer, but by Bruce's Douglas DC-6, 1700 miles back to South America to be finally disposed of. Later I notice one of the staff replacing the lavatory bag. It has 'Felices Fiestas' and pictures of Father Christmas all over it. Mike

Sharp and his staff of five are, quite rightly, concerned to limit any pollution of this still pristine continent. Men are allowed to pee on the ice but only at a certain spot, marked by a red flag, which gives vital wind direction information as well. Anyone who thinks they can get away with a quick one outside the tent is in for a shock, as urine turns the snow bright orange.

There is a chance that we could go to the Pole tomorrow. Weather is being checked with the Amundsen-Scott Base there. What little human activity there is in Antarctica is centred around a number of scientific research stations. (An international treaty bans, for the next 50 years, any exploration or exploitation of mineral rights, so the big money boys are not here, yet.) These stations or bases rely on each other for information and they chat at various times of the day, like fellow members of an exclusive club, often without ever meeting.

Adventure Network is the only tourist operation on the continent. There would be more if Mike Sharp had his way.

'You get so many different people through here . . . sixty or so in a season . . . beforehand it was always closed up, and the governments had control over Antarctica. I mean, someone like the BBC, for instance, would have to follow the British government's line on Antarctica, whereas now they can just be free to look at the place . . . and it's made a difference. Government organizations are clearing up their fuel drums and getting their garbage out of here, whereas in the past they just dumped it.'

At the end of the season the camp is packed away in a snow cave, four feet underground, which is reopened a year later. Even aircraft can be buried and retrieved. A Cessna 185 was buried with its tailplane sticking out so they could find it again, but in the fierce winter gales the tailplane was broken by an overturned oil drum. Today it's being replaced by Bill Aleekuk, an Eskimo engineer in his first season with the company. There are no polar bears in the Antarctic and until Bill arrived last November, there were no Eskimos either.

Gradually the mess tent fills up. Tea and coffee is made from snow melted in a metal tank which is attached to a kerosene-powered heating unit. Beside the tank is a plastic container of fresh-cut blocks of snow — the Antarctic equivalent of a coal scuttle or a basket of logs.

Kazama-San is preoccupied with the testing of his bike. It is a Yamaha, powered by a specially-designed engine, low on noise and fuel pollution and with a thick tyre at the back, studded like a punk's belt for better grip in the snow. Kazama-San is a charismatic, infectiously jolly character. He has been by motorbike to Everest, the North Pole, and now, with luck the South Pole. I ask him where next.

'Moon!' he shouts with a manic grin. I believe him.

2.45 p.m.: Kazama-San and his team leave after due Japanese ceremony.

He ties a yellow ribbon bearing good-luck messages around his waist and heads his white Yamaha out of the camp. It's so light and silent and insubstantial that he looks like a samurai on a poodle. He is followed by Rob, driving a Ski-Doo and pulling two sledges, one containing a solar-powered radio. It's all very environmentally conscious but the environment isn't appreciative. The sledge sticks on the very first rise and has to be pushed.

Later, in the distance, Kazama's bike leads the procession across the snowy wilderness like a pied piper. They hope to be at the Pole in 28 days.

Less than two hours later Rob returns with the news that because of the unusually warm weather (only minus 1 Centigrade today) Kazama's environmentally friendly bike has become embedded in the snow. He plans to continue, travelling only at night.

In the evening I manage to make radio contact with my wife, via Anne Kershaw in Punta Arenas. To be speaking to my little house in London from the wastes of Antarctica is perhaps as much as I can hope for, the fact that due to excessive distortion, Helen's voice sounds like a strangled gannet, is evidence that we are not in the mainstream of international communication. But apparently she can hear me and one of her gurglings is translated as wishing me luck and a warm hug.

Sue has cooked us pasta, which we polish off with Chilean red wine. Later Basil and Nigel disappear into the sun-drenched night with a Ski-Doo and an ice pick, reappearing triumphantly with a chunk of ice from beside the nearby hills which is as old as the rock itself.

Basil looks very pleased with himself as he drops a chunk into a glass.

'There we are. Ten-year-old whisky. Two-million-year-old ice!'

In this limbo-land of 24-hour daylight I lose track of time. All I know is that when I leave the mess tent, Billie Holliday's voice follows me from the cassette-player and Basil is drinking in earnest with a stubbly-bearded, red-eyed old-timer from Canada called Dan who, weather willing, is flying us to the South Pole tomorrow.

DAY 140 · PATRIOT HILLS TO THE THIEL MOUNTAINS

Wake from utterly warm, comfortable, womb-like night, curled up half-dressed inside my RAB sleeping-bag, to the desolate sound of a polar wind, sighing, hissing, slapping at the sides of the tent like some irascible neighbour. As if pleased with itself for having at last woken me it seems to grow in intensity. Look around the tent. Fraser is invisible – somewhere in his sleeping-bag I presume, Clem snores reassuringly, as I feel he might do if the battle of Waterloo were being fought outside, Basil, his face masked against the daylight, looks like a cross between a bank robber and someone halfway through cosmetic surgery. Nigel lies awake, probably wondering, like me, if this change in the weather means a further delay. Rudy is already up and about.

Ablutions in the Antarctic are perfunctory, to say the least. We may be living on top of 70 per cent of the world's fresh water, but it is not easy to get at and unless some thoughtful soul has been up, cut some snow and slipped a block of it into the tank you might as well be in the middle of a desert.

The only washing point is in the kitchen, and shaving into the sink is discouraged. Even in the tent the temperature is only 42 Fahrenheit, so taking clothes off is not comfortable. How on earth anyone has a proper wash in Antarctica I can't imagine, though Patti claims to have managed it.

When I catch sight of myself in the mirror I see disturbingly gaunt features. The cold has tightened my skin. My eyes have sunk and my nose seems to have grown an inch or two. A dark beard-line adds to the impression of a man at the end of his tether, if not at the end of the world.

Make a cup of tea and join Rudy who is deep into an account of Shackleton's expedition to the Antarctic. Shackleton made it to within 97 miles of the Pole, three years before Amundsen.

We still have 600 miles to go. There is no sign of Dan the pilot or anyone else for that matter. The wind rises and falls. Through the window I can see trails of snow scurrying across the ice.

The door is pulled open with difficulty and a round, wrapped bundle is silhouetted against the bright sky before the door slams shut. This bundle stands for a moment, apparently frozen, arms stretched out in front like a penguin, before heaving a deep sigh and beginning to unwrap. Only after several layers of headgear have been shed can you be absolutely sure who has come in.

Scott cooks sourdough pancakes for breakfast. We eat them with 'Lumberjack' syrup. Mike calls the South Pole for a weather check. Visibility is a little hazy, otherwise good. Temperature minus 26 Centigrade. Wind 14 knots. There is no reason for us to stay here. The go-ahead is given to start loading the plane.

Dan, who looks like a plump Lee Marvin, learnt his flying in the USAF and later in Alaska. As we assemble our gear I catch him looking thoughtfully at the plane. I ask him if he knows the Pole well.

He scratches at a white-haired chin: 'Never been there.'

He must enjoy seeing my jaw move up and down, soundlessly, for his eyes have a twinkle as he adds:

'I'm from the north, I've come down south here for the winter . . . to enjoy the nice weather.'

I try to make the best of it, tapping the side of the plane.

'Still, I'll bet this aircraft must have seen plenty of polar action . . .'

'Nope. This'll be the first trip for a single engine turbine Otter to the Pole.'

It transpires that neither pilot nor aircraft, nor even Scott, our Adventure Network escort, has ever been to the Pole. We're all first-timers.

Now I know what Mike Sharp was talking about when he told me yesterday that Adventure Network's success was 'based on enthusiasm . . . really . . . We're an ex-company of adventurers that . . . still want the adventure.'

At 3.45 p.m. we say our farewells, not just to Patriot Hills, but to Basil and Patti, who have to stay behind. Though they have known this all along, it doesn't make it any easier to leave them so close to our final destination.

We squeeze into tiny seats, made smaller by the bulkiness of our clothing. It is rather like sitting at nursery school desks. We share the cabin with a drum of kerosene as well as camera, camping and catering equipment, pumps and ice shovels. The only empty space is the gangway, and that is soon filled with an aluminium ladder.

At 3.50 this tightly-packed collection of people and their props taxis out across the ribbed and rutted ice, turns, and begins the longest and most unconvincing take-off I've ever experienced. It's nothing to do with the pilot, who is completely unconcerned, it's just that the relentless bumping and buffeting of the aeroplane's skis over the sastrugis doesn't seem to be allowing us to gain momentum. The fragmented rock face of the Patriot Hills is approaching fast and my grip tightens on the seat in front. Then with two or three gazelle-like bounces we are airborne, and within seconds the waving group below become specks against the snow.

We are flying into what the locals call 'the interior' – a flat plateau with few distinguishing features, rising from 4000 feet at Patriot Hills to an official 9348 feet at the Pole, though local atmospheric conditions there give a pressure altitude of 10,600 feet.

On the way we have to put down at the Thiel Mountains for a refuelling stop, and to give Dan time to drop some fuel for Kazama-San's expedition, which will pass nearby.

After two or three approaches as Dan and Scott search for the oil drums, we put down on the ice, at a spot called King's Peak. After two and a half hours sitting in the plane, unable to change position, it is a relief to clamber down onto the ice, even if it is into the teeth of a strong, bitingly cold wind.

Scott puts Rudy and myself to work, assembling a tent. It is, I'm sure, quite simple to those familiar with these matters, but I have never been a happy camper and the cluster of fibreglass rods spells nothing to me but confusion. Scott's patience is wholly commendable.

'They're all colour coded,' he points out, a little tersely. This is no help as my sunglasses distort most colours completely.

After much grunting and groaning and wrestling hopelessly to combine precision assembly with thick polar gloves, we have the tent up and crawl inside to drink tea and coffee and nibble chocolate whilst we wait for Dan to return from dropping Kazama's fuel, some 50 miles away.

Of course, in the dim recesses of one's mind the awareness that we are in sub-zero temperatures 300 miles from the South Pole with no means of transport does cause a flickering of doubt. Not often can one's survival be said to depend on one man, but the prospect of Dan not coming back doesn't really bear thinking about.

The wind-driven snow licks around us. It must be infinitely worse out in the open, away from the protective barrier of King's Peak. All of us are more relieved than we care to show when the scarlet flash of the Otter comes around the mountain again.

Dan takes a last weather check with the Amundsen-Scott Base. As with Russ at the North Pole a great deal of responsibility rests on the pilot at times like this. Dan knows that there is no safe place, no fuel cache at which to land between here and the Pole. It's entirely up to him to evaluate the information and make the final decision. He decides we should go in.

11.30 p.m. We have seen the last of the rock-strewn slopes of the escarpment, now there is nothing but whiteness below in every direction. In front of me Clem settles to sleep. Dan has changed his sealskin hat for a baseball cap, held in place by his headset. Scott is concerned to know if any of us are feeling the effects of altitude – for we are the equivalent of 20,000 feet above sea-level, in an unpressurized plane. I sense that I am taking shorter breaths, but apart from that I feel good, bumped by the excitement of my situation from the tired, almost melancholy heaviness I felt as we sat at King's Peak an hour ago.

DAY 141 · TO THE SOUTH POLE

12.30 a.m. Over the noise of the engine Dan shouts back that we are 47 minutes from the Pole.

1.00 a.m. Radio communication from air traffic control at the South Pole base.

'There is no designated runway and the US Government cannot authorize you to land. How do you copy?'

Dan: 'OK.'

'OK. Have a good landing.'

Scott gives Rudy a shot of oxygen. The effects of the height can now be clearly felt. Shortage of breath, every movement requiring twice the effort.

1.10 a.m. We can see the South Pole ahead. It is somewhere in the middle of a complex of buildings dominated by a 150-foot wide geodesic dome. Vehicles and building materials are scattered about the site. It is the busiest place we've seen in Antarctica.

1.20 a.m. We land at the Amundsen-Scott South Pole Station, scudding to a halt on a wide, cleared snow runway.

Two well-wrapped figures from the base wait for us to emerge from the plane, and shake our hands in welcome, but the senior of them, an American called Gary, advises us that it is not the policy of the National Science Foundation, who run the base, to offer assistance of a material kind to NGA's – Non-Government Agencies – such as ourselves. Scott confirms that our expedition is self-sufficient and that Adventure Network has a cache of fuel and accommodation located nearby.

Gary, having officially informed us that we are not welcome, brightens up considerably and invites us in for a coffee.

It's as we walk towards the dome, past Portakabins and stacks of wood, insulation equipment, all the flotsam and jetsam of a builders yard, that I become aware of how much effort is required just to keep going. It's as if I'm in a dream. However hard I try the dome doesn't seem to get any nearer.

After what seems like a lifetime we descend between walls carved from the ice to a wide underground entrance, above which a sign informs us that 'The United States of America welcomes you to the Amundsen-Scott South Pole Station.'

No pretence of neutrality here. After travelling 23,000 miles we have found the end of the earth, and it is America.

Pulling open a door as heavy as that on a butcher's deep-freeze we enter a warm, brightly-lit canteen. Music plays. 'If You Leave Me Now', by Chicago. Fresh orange juice and coffee on tap. T-shirts read 'Ski South Pole – 2 miles of base, 12 inches of powder'. A man in Bermuda shorts is piling a tray with chilli dogs, turkey soup, potato chips and lemon poppyseed cake. One of the chefs even *recognizes* me:

'Hey . . . wow! Michael Palin . . . !' He rubs lemon poppyseed cake off on his overalls and proffers a hand.

'Welcome to the Pole!'

The South Pole is on New Zealand Time. Everyone is eating, not because it's 2 o'clock in the morning and they can't sleep, but because we have leapt forward 16 hours, a time-shift of record-breaking proportions. These people are coming in for their evening meal.

Gaze longingly at the hamburgers and French fries, wondering if consumption of either or both would contravene the rules of the National Science Foundation but after a coffee, we trudge back outside. Scott, Fraser, Nigel and Clem go off to dig up the tent which was left here last year, so that we can eat and sleep. Rudy goes back to the plane. I'm about to join them when I realize that in the midst of all these rules, regulations, coffees and poppyseed handshakes I have completely forgotten why we are here.

The temperature, with wind chill, is a cutting, almost paralyzing minus 50 Centigrade, and it's 3.15 in the morning at 10,000 feet when I set out on the final lap of this extraordinary journey.

A few hundred yards from the dome, out on the snow, is a semi-circle of flags of all the nations working in Antarctica, in the middle of which is a reflecting globe on a plinth. This is the 'Ceremonial South Pole' at which visiting dignitaries are pictured.

Crunching slowly past it, numb-faced and short of breath, I come at last to a small bronze post sticking three feet above the ground. It looks like an unplumbed lavatory outlet but it exactly marks 90 degrees South. From this spot all directions point north. At this spot I can walk around the world in 8 seconds. At this point with one bound I am back, on 30 degrees East . . . and 30 degrees West, and 72 degrees East and 23 degrees West. I am on the same longitude as Tokyo, Cairo, New York and Sheffield. I am standing at the South Pole.

In the distance I can see a group of anoraked figures pacing the snow, stopping occasionally, forming a circle, pointing then striking at the earth with a shovel. They seem to be repeating this strange ritual over a wide area. Eventually Clem and Nigel and Fraser and Rudy give up looking for the tent and we all stand together at the bottom of the world. Or the top. It depends which way you look at it.

AFTERWORD

The first newspaper headline I saw on my return home last December ran 'USSR Will End On New Year's Eve'. Months earlier such a thought would have been laughable. Now, so much has happened that some of our experiences on *Pole to Pole* seem, within less than a year, to belong to another era. Not only has the Soviet Union disappeared, other countries have sprouted in its place. The same journey done today would go through 20 countries instead of 17 – Estonia, Belorussia and Ukraine adding to our tally and the atlas compiler's nightmare. Leningrad is now St Petersburg and the Hammer and Sickle nothing more than a good name for a pub. On a more serious note: Greenland has laid claim to Santa Claus, 'Greenland's PM Accuses Finland of Stealing Santa', was another recent headline; and the Novgorod plate, amazingly, reached London in one piece, only to be broken on the 10-mile journey from there to Watford.

The crew has proved there *is* life after *Pole to Pole* – Fraser was back at the Ngorongoro Crater within a few months of our return. Patti's malaria has, at the time of writing, made no reappearance, my rib healed in the predicted six weeks, and I have suffered no other side effects apart from a recurrent fear of waking to find my body tattooed with a Tanzanian Railways serial number.

The saddest news was of the deaths of Lorna and John Harvey of Shiwa, six months after we stayed with them. They, and many others, provided us with the patient, considerate, generous hospitality without which our journey from Pole to Pole would never have been possible.